AF661907

INDIAN
FAIRS & FESTIVALS

INDIAN FAIRS & FESTIVALS

Religious & Sociocultural

By

G.D. Gururani

AKANSHA PUBLISHING HOUSE

NEW DELHI - 110 002 (INDIA)

AKANSHA PUBLISHING HOUSE
4649/21-B, Ansari Road
Daryaganj, New Delhi - 110 002
Phones: 23263193, 9811582579
E-mail: ektabooks@yahoo.com

Indian Fairs and Festivals

© Reserved

First Published, 2007

ISBN 81-8370-077-2

[All rights reserved. No part of this publication may be reproduced, stored in a retrieval system or transmitted, in any form or by any means, mechanical, photocopying, recording or otherwise, without prior written permission of the publisher.]

PRINTED IN INDIA

Published by M.P. Misra for Akansha Publishing House, New Delhi - 110 002 and Printed at Capital Offset Press, Delhi

To

Saraswati

the Goddess of all knowledge & learning

this book is humbly dedicated

Contents

Preface

Enjoyment and merry-making are innate with human nature and psyche. Even when he was a cave-dweller, he used to find many occasions of expressing joy on trivial issues like hunting an animal, finding new shelter, victory over opponent groups, raining, or any other change in favourable climatic conditions. With the growth and development of civilization, it became part and parcel and life. Man started celebrating fairs and festivals in routine way.

Festival is considered to be a day or period set aside for celebration or feasting, especially with religious fervour or significance; celebration, especially one which commemorates an anniversary or any other significant event; or an organised series of special events and performances, usually in one place. It is a time of revelry and merry-making. Fairs are a travelling entertainment with sideshows, rides especially one that visits places at the same time each year. May be a gathering of producers of and dealers in a given class of products to facilitate business.

India is vast land of various colours and creeds—multiracial, multireligious and multilingual with varied cultural diversity, no doubt with unity at the core. Besides primordial religions, Hinduism, Buddhism, Jainism and Sikhism are the major religions of Indian origin, whereas Islam and Christianity have a large number of followers in India. Thus, India represents a unique blend of socio-religious and cultural synthesis.

It is remarkable to note that most of the festivals celebrated in India, have religious ethos at the core. Hindus are considered the 'nature worshipper'. They believe that there is presence of god behind every object of the nature. On the other hand, some festivals have socio-cultural links while some others are celebrated to commemorate great national events and personalities. Many festivals have association with ensuing new seasons. Primarily, Indian society is agrarian in nature. As such harvesting and sowing new crops is celebrated in all regions in different manner.

A unique characteristics of Indian fairs and festivals is its 'regional ethos'. If we celebrate Bihu in Assam in the north east we also celebrate Baishakhi in Punjab and Onam and Pongal in the South.

Religious festivals are celebrated at various sacred places of pilgrimage. We have four Dhams, i.e. Badrinath in the north, Rameshwaram in the South, Puri in the east and Dwarka in the West. Kedarnath, Gangotri, Yamunotri, Haridwar, Prayag, Benaras, Gaya, Guwahati, Ujjain, Vaishno Devi, Amarnath, Amritsar, Pushkar, Ajmer, Mathura, Vrindavan, Amarkantak, Nasik, Panchavati, Tirupati, Shirdi, Madurai, Gangasagar and many other places are of great sanctity and religious importance.

India is the land of saints, sages, seers and mystics who played prominent role at different times from the remote past for the good of mankind. By preaching Truth,. Goodness and virtues they have tried to bring about the 'religion of humanity. Many saints and seers took birth in India. Many festivals are celebrated to commemorate their jayanti (anniversary) like Mahavir Jayanti, Buddha Purnima, Guru Nanak Dev Jayanti, Ravidas Jayanti, Valmiki Jayanti, Ram Navami, Shrikrishna Janmashthami, etc. Mahakumbha Mela is celebrated at four places—Haridwar, Prayag (Allahabad), Ujjain and Nashik at different times after interval of twelve years. Gandhi Jayanti, Independence Day and Republic Day are our national festivals.

Fairs are also held at many places with different motives—socioreligious and commercial. Some fairs have attracted attention of people from far and wide.

A good quantity of literature is available on Indian fairs and festivals. This modest attempt aims at presenting kaleidoscopic view of Indian fairs and festivals. We have grouped the information in three parts. Part first presents religious festivals wherein prominent festivals are presented in alphabetical order of names. The second part highlights prominent sociocultural festivals while the last part deals with major fairs of India. Glossary of religious terms is an added feature.

Each festivals is given probable elaborate treatment. Main reasons behind the origin, myths and legends thereabout, manners and methods of celebration etc. are also given. Help is taken from writings of various scholars, as such no claim of originality.

We express our gratitude to all those who have assisted, helped and inspired us while working on this project. Our publishers deserve all appreciation to transform our crude efforts in a superb publication. It is hoped, this attempt will prove inspiring and informative to all inquisitive readers.

—GDG

1

Baisakhi

> A greater poverty than that caused by lack of money is the poverty of unawareness. Men and women go about the world unaware of the beauty, the goodness, the glories in it. Their souls are poor. It is better to have a poor pocketbook than to suffer from a poor soul.
>
> —*Thomas Dreir*

Baisakhi is one of the major festivals of Sikhs and is celebrated with lot of enthusiasm and gaiety in the state of Punjab and all throughout the world where there is a significant Sikh population. For the large farming community of Punjab, Baisakhi Festival marks the time for harvest of rabi crops and they celebrate the day by performing joyful bhangra and gidda dance. For the Sikh community, Baisakhi Festival has tremendous religious significance as it was on a Baisakhi Day in 1699, that Guru Gobind Singh, the tenth Sikh Guru laid the foundation of Panth Khalsa—the Order of the Pure Ones. Date of Baisakhi Festival falls on the first day of Vaisakh month (April-May) according to Nanakshahi or Sikh Calendar. For this reason, Baisakhi is also popularly known as Vaisakhi. According to English calendar, the date of Baisakhi corresponds to April 13 every year and April 14 once in every 36 years. This difference in Baisakhi dates is due to the fact that day of Baisakhi is reckoned according to solar calendar and not the lunar calendar. The auspicious date of Baisakhi is celebrated all over India under different names and different set of rituals and celebrations. People of Punjab celebrate the festival of Baisakhi with exuberance and devotion. As the festival has tremendous importance in Sikh religion, major activities of the day are organized in Gurdwaras. People wake up early to prepare for the day. Many also take bath in the holy river to mark the auspicious occasion. After getting ready people pay a visit to their neighbourdood gurdwara and take part in the special prayer meeting organized for the day. At the end of the Baisakhi ardas, congregates receive specially prepared Kara prasad or sweetened semolina. This is followed by a guru ka langar or community lunch. Later, during the day people of Sikh faith take out a Baisakhi procession under the leadership of Panj piaras. The procession moves through the major localities of the city amidst the rendition of devotional songs by the participating men, women and children. Mock duels, bhangra and gidda performances make the procession joyous and colourful. Celebrations by Farmers. For the large farming community of Punjab and Haryana, Baisakhi marks a New Year's time as it is time to harvest rabi crop.

On Baisakhi, farmers thank god for the bountiful crop and pray for good times ahead. People buy new clothes and make merry by singing, dancing and enjoying the best of festive food. Cries of "Jatta aai Baisakhi", rent the skies as gaily men and women break into the bhangra and gidda dance to express their joy. Everyday farming scenes of sowing, harvesting, winnowing and gathering of crops are expressed through zestful movements of the body to the accompaniment of ballads and dhol music.

In several villages of Punjab Baisakhi Fairs are organized where besides other recreational activities, wrestling bouts are also held.

There are various legends associated with the colourful and vibrant festival of Baisakhi. A study of these interesting legends of Baisakhi reveal that the day of Baisakhi is significant not just for Sikhs but also for Hindus and Buddhists alike.

Besides, it is joyous to note that as a harvest festival, people of all communities in Punjab celebrate Baisakhi in a harmonious manner. Baisakhi Festival marks the time for the harvest of Rabi crops and is therefore celebrated with utmost joy and enthusiasm in the state of Punjab where agriculture is the predominant occupation of the people. To celebrate the occasion, people dress themselves gaily and perform the joyful bhangra and giddha dance on the tune of the dhol. Farmers in Punjab celebrate Baisakhi Festival to hilt by feasting and merrymaking before they hit on tiring but joyful task of harvesting from the next day. As a harvest festival, Baisakhi is also celebrated by different names and with different rituals in several regions of India. Regional celebrations of Baisakhi are marked as Rongali Bihu in Assam, Naba Barsha in Bengal, Puthandu in Tamil Nadu, Vishu in Kerala and Vaishakha in Bihar. The day of Baisakhi marks the birth of Khalsa Panth and therefore holds tremendous significance for the Sikhs. It was on the *Baisakhi Day* meeting organized at Anandpur Sahib, in 1699, that the tenth Guru of Sikhs, Guru Gobind Sigh laid the foundation of Khalsa Panth and called on the Sikhs to sacrifice themselves for their community. Besides, it was on the Baisakhi Day that Guru Gobind Singh administered amrit (nectar) to his first batch of five disciples, the *Panj Piaras* making them Singhs, a martial community. After the Baisakhi Day in 1699 the tradition of gurus was discontinued, and the Granth Sahib - the Holy book of the Sikhs was declared the eternal guide of the Sikhs. According to a popular legend in Sikhism, it was on the day of Baisakhi in 1567 that Guru Amar Das had first institutionalized Baisakhi as one of the special days when all Sikhs would gather to receive the guru's blessings at Goindwal. Martyrdom *of Guru Arjan Dev Yet* another legend related to Baisakhi, says that on the day of Baisakhi Guru Arjan Dev was martyred by the Muslim rulers. It is said that in an act of barbaric cruelty Muslim rulers threw the Guru alive into a cauldron of boiling oil. The day of Baisakhi Festival is also important for the Hindus as it on this day in 1875 that Swami Dayanand Saraswati founded the Arya Samaj - a reformed sect of Hindus who are devoted to the Vedas for spiritual guidance and have discarded idol worship. For the Buddhist, the day of Baisakhi Festival is significant, as according to a popular legend it was on this auspicious day that Gautam Buddha attained enlightenment or Nirvana under the Mahabodhi tree in the town of Gaya. For this reason, the day of Baisakhi is celebrated as *Buddha Purnima* is several parts of the country.

Baisakhi Day or Vaisakhi Day of March 30th, 1699 is of significant importance for the Sikhs. It was on this day that Guru Gobind Singh - the Tenth Guru of the Sikhs founded the Akal Khalsa (Community of the Pure) at a ceremony organized at Keshgarh Sahib near Anandpur. The Akal Khalsa played a significant role in resistance against Mughal rule. Every year on April 13 Sikhs celebrate with pomp and gusto the birth of the Khalsa Panth. In the year 1667 Aurungzeb, the Mughal Emperor installed himself as the Emperor of India after annihilating almost all his family opposition. Immediately after gaining power, Aurungzeb embarked on a policy of religious persecution and started the process of Islamization of India. Brahmins became the prime targets of Aurungzeb in this regard as his clerics made him convinced that once the Brahmins accepted Islam the others would follow. Pursuing his agenda, Aurungzeb levied unethical religious taxes against Hindus and shut their temples and places of learning. The Brahmins, particularly those of Kashmir, desperately felt the need for a dynamic leadership to fight this subversion by the Mughal Emperor. They approached Guru Tegh Bahadur (1621-1675), the ninth in the line of Sikh Gurus, who was on the throne of the Sikh religion and asked him for guidance on the issue. During this meeting, Guru Tegh Bahadur's nine-year-old son, Gobind Rai, was sitting beside him. Finding Guru Tegh Bahadur under deep contemplation, the young son asked the reason of his repose.

The Guru explained the situation to the child and said the world is aggrieved by oppression and no brave man had yet come forward to willingly sacrifice his life to free the earth from the burden of Aurangzeb's persecution of Hindus. To this young Gobind Rai replied, *"For that purpose who is more worthy than thou who art at once generous and brave."* Pleased with his son's reply, Guru Tegh Bahadur entrusted the Guruship to Gobind Rai and proceeded towards Delhi, the seat of the Mughal Empire. Just as they reached Delhi, the mighty Aurangzeb imprisoned the Guru and his loyal attendants. Foreseeing his ecclesiastic journey during imprisonment, Guru Tegh Bahadur thought of testing his son's courage and capability to carry on the Guru's mission. In a letter to Gobind Rai, the Guru wrote, *"My strength is exhausted, I am in chains and I can make not any efforts. Says Nanak, God alone is now my refuge. He will help me as He did his Saints."* In his reply young Guru Gobind Rai wrote, *"I have regained my Power, my bonds are broken and all options are open unto me. Nanak, everything is in Thine hands. It is only Thou who can assist Thyself."* Later, Guru Tegh Bahadur was martyred in Delhi in the presence of hundreds of people. The executioner abandoned the Guru's body in the open. But no one dared to come forward to claim the body to perform religious rites. Even the ardent disciples withdrew unrecognized. It was only when the stormy weather occurred, that two persons took advantage of the situation and covertly took the body of Guru Tegh Bahadur for cremation. This cowardice of Sikhs incited in Gobind Rai an urge to endow his Sikhs with a distinct identity. With the desire to instill courage and strength to sacrifice among his fellow men, Gobind Rai became the tenth Sikh Guru. At the age of 33, Guru Gobind had Divine inspiration to actuate his designs. The Guru found the occasion of Baisakhi could serve his purpose, as every year thousands of devotees would come to Anandpur at the time of Baisakhi (springtime) to pay their obeisance and seek the Guru's blessings. Early in the year 1699, months before Baisakhi Day, Guru Gobind Rai sent special edicts to congregates far and wide that that year the Baisakhi was going to be a unique affair. He asked them not to cut any of their hair and to come with unshorn hair under their turbans and chunis. Besides, men were asked to come with full beards.

The Baisakhi Day of March 30, 1699 at the call of the Guru, thousands of people gathered at the Anandpur Sahib, the famous Golden Temple of Amritsar, India on the Vaisakhi Day, March 30, 1699. To instill courage in the fellow men, Guru Gobind made a powerful oration and revealed to them his divine mission of restoring amongst Sikhs and preserving the Sikh religion. At the end of his speech, the Guru flashed his unsheathed sword and said that every great deed was preceded by equally great sacrifice and demanded one head for oblation. To the Guru's call, Daya Ram, a Khatri of Lahore offered himself. The Guru took him inside a tent. A little later he reappeared with his sword dripping with blood, and asked for another head. One by one four more earnest devotees - Daram Das - a Jat of Delhi, Mohkam Chand - a washerman of Dwarka (Gujarat), Himmat - a cook of Jagannath (Orissa) and Sahib Chand - a barber of Bidar (Karnataka) offered their heads. Every time the Guru took a person inside the tent, he came out with a bloodied sword in his hand. Astonished with their Guru's behavior and believing him to have gone berserk, people started to disperse. Shortly after, Guru Gobind emerged with all five men dressed piously in white. He baptized the five in a new and unique ceremony called *'Khande di Pahul'* (the double-edged Sword Amrit), what Sikhs today call *Amrit.* After this, the Guru asked the five baptized Sikhs to baptize him as well. They were then knighted as *Singhs,* as the Five beloved ones, the first members of the new community of equals, to be called the Khalsa, meaning "pure". Guru Gobind proclaimed that the *Panj Pyare or the Five Beloved Ones* would be the embodiment of the Guru himself, "Where there are Panj Pyare, there am I. When the Five meet, they are the holiest of the holy." These "saint soldiers" were to dedicate their lives to the service of others and the pursuit of justice for people of all faiths. The Guru also said whenever and wherever the five baptized or *Amritdhari Sikhs* comes together, the Guru would be present. All those who receive Amrit from five baptized Sikhs will be infused with the spirit of courage and strength to sacrifice. Thus with these principles, Guru Gobind established Panth Khalsa, the Order of the Pure Ones. The Guru also gave his new Khalsa a unique, indisputable, and distinct identity. The Guru gave the gift of *bana,* the distinctive Sikh clothing and headwear. He also offered five emblems of purity and courage.

Apart from fighting the political tyranny, Guru Gobind also sought to eliminate social discriminations in the name of caste with the establishment of Khalsa Panth. The Panj Piyaras set by the Guru amalgamated people of low and high caste into one as it consisted of people of different strata of the society. To further do away with the system of caste discrimination and to give to all Sikhs an opportunity to live lives of courage, sacrifice, and equality, the Guru gave the surname of Singh (Lion) to every Sikh and also took the name for himself. From Guru Gobind Rai, he became Guru Gobind Singh. He also pronounced that all Sikh women embody royalty, and gave them the surname *Kaur* (Princess).

Joyful festival of Baisakhi is celebrated with lot of charm and gusto in the vibrant state of Punjab. People perform set Baisakhi customs and traditions for the day with sincerity and devotion. Since Baisakhi is celebrated as the birth of Guru Gobind Singh—the Tenth Sikh Guru and the foundation day of Khalsa Panth, major activities for the festival are centred on gurdwaras - the Sikh place of worship. As a harvest festival Baisakhi is celebrated in open fields with energetic bhangra and gidda dance by gaily dressed men and women of Punjab. People following Sikh faith wake up early in the morning on a Baisakhi day and pay visit to gurdwaras to attend special prayer meetings. While most Sikhs strive to visit the revered Golden Temple or Anandpur Sahib, where the Khalsa was pronounced, those who are unable to do so visit their neighborhood gurdwara.At a gurdwara, the *Guru Granth Sahib*, the holy book of Sikhs is ceremonially taken out and is given a symbolical bath with milk and water. After these simple rituals, *Guru Granth Sahib* is placed on its throne with care. The book is then read out to the followers gathered in the gurdwara.

Just as on a *Baisakhi Day* ceremony held in 1699 under the guidance of Guru Gobind Singh where Panch Pyaras or the Five beloved ones chanted verses, five priests going by that name chant verses recited by the five originals. Similarly, just as Guru Gobind Singh Ji had used amrita prepared in an iron vessel to bless the panch pyare, even to this date amrit or holy nectar is prepared in an iron vessel and is distributed amongst all gathered after the chanting of sacred verses. As a tradition, devotees sip amrita five times and take a vow to work for the brotherhood, the Khalsa Panth. Religious songs (kirtans) are sung after the amrit is drunk for the spiritual upliftment of those gathered. At noon, after the Baisakhi ardas, the Karah Prasad or sweetened semolina is offered to the guru for his blessings. It is then distributed to the congregation.

The ceremony culminates with a special guru-ka-langar or the community lunch. People sit in rows with their heads covered as volunteers serve them with vegetarian meal. Later, during the Baisakhi day, sacred Guru Granth Sahib is taken out in a procession. At the head of the procession are the Panj Piaras, symbolizing the journey made by the five fearless devotees from their homes to Anandpur, to be baptised by Guru Gobind Singh. *Baisakhi processions* are attended by men, women and children alike with faith and enthusiasm. The procession moves through major localities of the city and is welcomed by citizens and members of social and cultural societies. Colourful bhangra and gidda dance apart from mock duels are performed during Baisakhi processions. Another fascinating part of Baisakhi celebrations is the accompaniment of drummers, bands playing religious times, devotees singing religious songs and men swinging swords. Loud Sikh chants of 'Bole so nihal', 'Deg teg fateh' and rhythmic chants of *'Sat nam'* and *'Wahe guru'* ring out from the middle of the singing and drumming. Some men may wear the headgear (bana) of Guru Nanak, others that of Guru Gobind Singh.In their discourse at the end of the ceremony, Sikh religious leaders strive to promote the feeling of charity amongst people, especially children in honor of Guru Gobind Singh. In some places, especially Punjab, such processions are taken out even before Baisakhi.

Since Baisakhi is also celebrated as a harvest festival, farmers in Punjab celebrate Baisakhi with energetic performance of bhangra and gidda dance. Men and women clad themselves in their traditional Bhangra dress and dance to the beat of dhol in a joyful festive atmosphere. Vibrant Festival of Baisakhi is considered to be an extremely important festival in India for number of reasons. Apart from being important for the farmers as a harvest festival, the festival is of prime importance in Sikhism as a foundation day of Khalsa Panth.

The festival of Baisakhi falls on April 13 every year and April 14 once in every 36 years. Change in date is because of the fact that date of Baisakhi is reckoned according to the solar calendar. Astrologically, the date of Baisakhi is significant as marks sun's entry into Mesh Rashi. For this very reason, many people also know Baisakhi as Mesha Sankranti.

The auspicious date of Baisakhi is celebrated all over India under different names and rituals. It is celebrated as 'Rongali Bihu' in Assam, 'Naba Barsha' in Bengal, 'Puthandu' in Tamil Nadu, 'Pooram Vishu' in Kerala and 'Vaishakha' in the state of Bihar. Significance of Baisakhi for Farmers For the agriculturally rich state of Punjab and Haryana, Baisakhi marks the time for harvest of Rabi (winter) crops and is therefore extremely significant for the farmers. Baisakhi Festival is also celebrated as a Thanksgiving Day festival in these states. After waking up early and dressing themselves in new clothes, farmers visit temples and gurdwaras to express gratitude to God for the good harvest and seek blessing for ensuing agriculture season. Farmers also celebrate Baisakhi by performing energetic bhangra and gidda dance and participating in Baisakhi Fairs. Significance of Baisakhi in SikhismBaisakhi is of major importance for the people following Sikh faith. As it was on a Baisakhi Day, in the year 1699 that the Tenth Guru of Sikhs, Guru Gobind Singh founded Khalsa Panth or the Order of Pure Ones and gave a unique identity to Sikhs. On the same day the guru administered Amrit (nectar) to his first batch of five disciples making them Singhs, a martial community. By doing so, he eliminated the differences of high and low and established that all human beings were equal.Sikhs celebrate Baisakhi by participating in special prayer meetings organized at gurdwaras. They also carry out joyful Baisakhi processions to mark the day.

Baisakhi marks the arrival of the harvesting season. The festival always falls on April 14 and marks the beginning of the solar year. Just before the festival the farmer returns home with his bumper crop, the fruit of his whole year's hard labour.

This festival is in celebration to thank God for good harvest for the year and coming year also. Early morning of Baiskhai, people take dip in holy rivers. Cries of "Jatta aai Baisakhi" rent the skies as the people of Punjab attired in their best clothes break into the Bhangra dance to express their joy.

The dancers and drummers challenge each other to continue the dance. The scenes of sowing, harvesting, winnowing and gathering of crops are expressed through zestful movements of the body to the accompaniment of ballads. Both men and women, celebrate the day with Bhangra and Gidda.

Fairs are organized at various places in Punjab, where besides other recreational activities, wrestling bouts are also held. The occasion is celebrated with great gusto at Talwandi Sabo, where Guru Gobind Singh stayed for nine months and completed the recompilation of the Guru Granth Sahib. The Sikhs celebrate this day by visiting gurudwaras and distributing kada prasad. Processions led by the Panj Piaras or the five religious men are taken out. Kirtans and recital of passages from the Granth Sahib are also organized in gurdwaras, where people line up to receive the delicious prasad and perform kar sewa-that is, offering help in the daily chores of the gurdwara. The most sacred pilgrimage centres is Amritsar, where Golden Temple is situated. Relatives and friends are welcomed and offered lassi and sweets. This festival brings bright hopes for the future.

India's rich and glorious civilization is mirrored in its innumerable festivals. These festivals mark the seasons which signal to man the time for work and the time for relaxation, the commencement of the agricultural cycle with sowing in spring, and its culmination with the harvesting of the golden grain. And then, of course, we have, in endless variations of legend and myth, the hallowed perceptions that there is an ever-renewed war of light and darkness, of the divine and the demoniac in the unceasing evolution of the world.

Generally, the sites of these festivities are on the banks of the rivers which have their sacred import with myths and legends woven around their origin and names.

Baisakhi, marks the beginning of New Year, particularly in the northern part of India. It is among the few Indian festivals that has a fixed date. Baisakhi is always on April 13th. In Kerala, Baisakhi is called as "*Vishu*" and in Tamil Nadu, it is celebrated as "*Puthandu*".

Considered a holy day, the devout celebrate the Baisakhi with a dip in the holy rivers just around the break of dawn. It is on this day that Sun enters Aries, the first sign of Zodiac. This signifies ushering of the new year.

The celebrations of Baisakhi are similar to the three-day schedule of the the celebrations of other Gurpurabs. It is generally celebrated on 13th April every year.

This also marks the beginning of a month long *Vaisakha* bathing. The pilgrimage to the holy shrine of Badrinath, in the Himalayas, also commences from this day. The charities done during Vaisakha month are believed to earn great religious merits and so people generously give money, grains and other things to the poor and needy and the *Brahmins*, and observe fast, chant the glories of the lord and practice such other pious activities.

The holy book of the Sikhs, 'Granth Sahib' is taken in a procession, led by the 'Panj Pyaras' (five senior Sikhs) who are symbolic of the original leaders. It was on this day that Guru Gobind Singh organised his first batch of five disciples making them Singhs, a martial community. Kirtans and recital of passages from the 'Granth Sahib' are also organized in gurdwaras, where people line up to receive the delicious Kada prasad (sweetened semolina) and perform kar sewa-that is, offering help in the daily chores of the gurdwara. The occasion is celebrated with great gusto at Talwandi Sabo, where Guru Gobind Singh stayed for nine months and completed the recompilation of the Guru Granth Sahib and in the Golden temple in Amritsar. .

2

Bihu

> Nature never hurries: atom by atom, little by little, she achieves her work. The lesson one learns in fishing, yachting, or planting, is the manners of Nature; patience with the delays of wind and sun, delays of the seasons, bad weather, excess or lack of water.
>
> —*Ralph Waldo Emerson*

Assam, a major northeastern state of India, is bestowed fabulously with natural resources by the Nature. Might rivers, hills, forests, riverine plain, large tea gardens and other plantations petroleum, rich crops etc. make Assam a prominent state.

The population consists of different ethnic groups, living fun, fair and gaity. The breathtaking hills and valleys of Assam come alive with the sound of Bihu thrice a year. A festival that marks the change of season, Bihu is accompanied both by prayer and great rejoicing. One of the seven northeastern states of India, Assam is renowned for its picturesque landscape, exotic fauna and fun-loving people.

Originating in the pre-Aryan days around 3500 B.C., the festival of Bihu used to last for a whole month, though nowadays work pressure has reduced it to a week. A no holds barred dancing session is the most intriguing part of the festival and symbolises the fertility rites of the original inhabitants of the hilly regions of the northeast in India.

The farmers fancied that the erotic content of the songs would sexually arouse the earth's body, leading to an abundant harvest. Bihag Bihu or Rangoli Bihu, the first of the three Bihus, is celebrated in the month of April on the dates coinciding with the *sankranti, chait* or *baisak* (13, 14 and 15 April).

According to the solar calendar that the Assamese follow, the New Year usually falls on 14th April. Brilliantly-coloured flowers and luxuriant foliage dress the whole of Assam in all the hues of the rainbow during the month of April. An abundance of *kopoful* (orchids), mostly purple in colour, in unusual shapes and sizes dot the trees, and the *bhebel* creepers are in full bloom creating an enchanting kaleidoscope of colours.

No one can fault the Assamese his choice of seasons for the Bihu festivals. The vivid attire of the Assamese youth and the colourful accessories like kopoful adorning the hair of the young lasses blend with the hues of nature, spreading joy and good cheer. The day is marked with dancing, though restricted exclusively to men, who participate with unbridled enthusiasm and energy. But the winds of change have blown through this remote state also. Surrendering to contemporary trends, youngsters gather in the town centre and learn the steps from an old hand much in demand on this day.

Assamese women are well-versed at weaving the *gomacha*, a towel with intricately woven designs, ceremonially presented as *any bihu* (bihu presents) to the men of the family. A young girl too may gift these beautiful souvenirs to her beau as a token of love. Young lads love to flaunt their prizes by tying them around their waist or as headbands while dancing. But things start warming up as the approach.

Coming to the bihu dals, they are wandering minstrels who come visiting through the week, dancing and singing devotional songs (hosari) in praise of Lord Krishna (the black god of the Hindus), invoking his blessings for health, wealth and happiness. They sing to the accompaniment of an eclectic collection of musical instruments like the dhol (drum), pepa (made of buffalo horn), gogona (made from bamboo and held between the teeth) and small cymbals. Bihu dals along with other groups gather in open grounds called bihu tolis where dancing competitions and beauty pageants are held, and the winners get to see their names in print in the local newspapers.

Garur Bihu

The first day or garur bihu also called uraka falls on the day of sankranti and is devoted to the cow that is considered to be a sacred animal in India. The rationale behind the worshipping of cows is very simple. They are the greatest assets of a farmer because not only do they produce milk but also help plough fields, transport men, crop and so on. A lot of tender, loving care is showered on cows on this day, starting with bathing them in the pond. The horns and hooves are brushed with whisks made from deegloti or makheatr (lilsoca salocrfolea). A mixture of twigs, turmeric and moong dal (pulses) acts as a disinfectant, and is applied as a paste. A hearty meal of gourd and brinjal is fed to the cows after which their foreheads are marked with vermilion. As the night falls, the tired but satiated cows are led back to their sheds and thoroughly cleansed. Only then does the household sit down for a sumptuous meal of assorted preparations of chirwa (flat rice) and a mind-boggling array of sweets. The following day is welcomed as manuhor bihu or the bihu of human beings. The Assamese celebrate their New Year on this day. A lavish feast called bihu kabo loi is laid out for the day and married daughters along with other relatives are invited to partake of the meal. On this day, delicacies such as pitha (made from rice and coconut), laddoo (made from shredded coconut) and til laddoo (made from sesame seed) are prepared. of course, no festival in India is complete without buying new clothes and Bihu is no exception. Everyone receives gomachas as presents from the ladies of the house. Women look very graceful in their new mekhele chadar, woven with the golden-coloured muga silk that is indigenous to Assam. The chic look is completed with the accessories like gumkham bracelets made from an alloy of silver and gold nuggets found in the rivers.

Gabhori Bihu

Gabhori bihu falls on the third day of the festival and is earmarked as the day for young ladies. The fair maidens of Assam look gorgeous in their muga silk wear and ornate gumkham bracelets. The orchids adorning the hair of the ladies add a whimsical touch to the formality of the outfit. Swaying to the beat of the toka (drum) and gogona (made from bamboo held between the teeth), the women dance the night away under the gentle breeze of banyan trees. Couplets are created spontaneously. Starting with a slow tempo, the rhythm builds up to a crescendo.

Once the merrymaking is over, it is customary to present fermented betel leaves over a gomacha to the dancers. On the final day, the festivities end on a religious note wherein families inscribe a mantra (religious hymn of the Hindus) on the leaves of *nahar pat* (Indian ironwood tree). Through this mantra, Lord Shiva (the Destroyer in the Holy Hindu Trinity of Creator-Preserver-Destroyer) is invoked to protect everyone against disease, storms and rain, and to bring peace and prosperity in the forthcoming year.

Kati Bihu

The second bihu named kati bihu or kangali bihu is held in the month of *kartik* (September or October). But there is a world of difference in the celebration of this bihu from the former. Slowly but surely, winter is approaching, heralding the season for sowing seeds.

This is a solemn occasion as people worship the deities

for a rich harvest. The young learn to value hard work so that they do not squander money away. Predictably enough, this bihu is dedicated to the worship of none other than Goddess Lakshmi who is the dispenser of wealth to mortals. As night falls, lamps are lit in the paddy fields where farmers have toiled through the day.

At the end of a hard day's work, all the members of a family pray to the benign Goddess for the well-being of their crop and cattle. Sacred to the Hindus, the *tulsi* (basil) tree is planted or pruned in the courtyard of each household. Water is poured over the plant with great reverence after puja is performed every day. The medicinal properties of tulsi are well known the world over; the age-old recipe of tulsi leaves mixed with a few grains of black pepper and *misri* (sugar in the form of crystals) is a surefire way to stay in good health.

Magh Bihu

The Magh bihu that generally falls on 14th January on the sankranti of the month, is the third bihu that calls for a grand celebration in Assamese homes. This is again a joyous occasion as the granaries are stocked with the recently harvested crop. Seven days of non-stop fun and frolic mark this festival. But the best thing about this bihu is the elaborate and sumptious cuisine that is prepared. This grand feast known as *bhog* is held on the night of the first day of the festival that is also called *uruka*.

Everyone indulges in *khel dhemali* (fun and games). Each village holds its share of fights between various creatures, big and small including cockfights and buffalo fights, for the entertainment of the locals. An inexpensive way to have fun, though the poor animals might beg to differ. The chilly winters offer the best excuse to light bonfires in the great outdoors and dance around them with gay abandon. All this is reminiscent of the festivals of Lohri in Punjab, *Pongal* in Tamil Nadu and Goopi in Andhra Pradesh, which is not surprising as sankranti is a time for festivals all over India.

Thus, Bihu of Assam is an inportant event the national calender of festivals. Many tourists visit Assam during Bihu to share the gaity of the festival.

3

Buddha Purnima

Brotherhood is the very price and condition of man's survival.

—*Carlos P. Romulo*

Buddha Purnima, which falls on the full moon night in the month of Vaisakha (either in April or May), commemorates the birth anniversary of Lord Buddha, founder of Buddhism, one of the oldest religions in the world. Notwithstanding the summer heat, pilgrims come from all over the world to Bodh Gaya to attend the Buddha Purnima celebrations. The day is marked with prayer meets, sermons on the life of Gautam Buddha, religious discourses, continuous recitation of Buddhist scriptures, group meditation, processions, worship of the statue of Buddha and symposia. The Mahabodhi Temple wears a festive look and is decorated with colourful flags and flowers. The Chinese scholar, Fa-Hien, has also recorded celebration of this festival.

It is an important to give a summarized description on the Buddhist festivals in India, especially in the main places of worship. The principal annual ceremony for all the Buddhist is the Vaisaka Purnima known in Sri Lanka as Wesak festival and in India as Buddha Jayanti. Vaisaka Purnima day is fixed by the full-moon day of the month Vaisaka, which falls in May. Like all other Buddhist festivals it falls according to the Lunar year. It was of this day of the year, according to the year. He attained Supreme Enlighten, or Buddha hood, beneath the Bodhi-tree at Boddha Gaya. Forty-five years later at the age of eighty, he finally passed away in Parinivana on the same day of the year at Kushinagar. Vaisaka Purnima is celebrated especially in Boddha Gaya, Lumbini and in Kushinara as they are the holy places that were connected with the blessed ones birth, enlighten and the Parinirvana. Buddhists in Sri Lanka, Myanmar, Thailand, Tibet, China, Korea, Laos, Vietnam, Mongolia, Bhutan, Cambodia, Nepal, Japan and quite a number of western Buddhists participate Vaisaka Purnima Day religious activities in a festive mood. Sarnath the capital of Buddhism too celebrates Vaisaka Purnima day in a grand way. The great Buddhist festival, Vaisaka, although is an occasion for rejoicing doesn't encourage hectic gaiety and abandon. The happiness that the Buddhists feel, when they are celebrating it is a tranquil, peaceful joy. The festival has its gay side as well. In most of the Buddhist countries the villages, roads, streets, temples and houses are brightly illuminated with color lanterns, electric lights and colorful, tasteful decorations.

The decision to agree to celebrate Vesak as the Buddha's birthday was formalized at the first Conference of the World Fellowship of Buddhists (W.F.B.) held in Sri Lanka in 1950, although festivals at this time in the Buddhist world are a centuries-old tradition. The Resolution that was adopted at the World Conference reads as follows, "That this Conference of the World Fellowship of Buddhists, while recording its appreciation of the gracious act of His Majesty, the Maharaja of Nepal in making the full-moon day of Vesak a Public Holiday in Nepal, earnestly requests the Heads of Governments of all countries in which large or small number of Buddhists are to be found, to take steps to make the full-moon day in the month of May a Public Holiday in honour of the Buddha, who is universally acclaimed as one of the greatest benefactors of Humanity."

Hence on Vesak Day, Buddhists all over the world commemorate three great events: The birth, enlightenment and the passing away of Gautama Buddha. As Buddhism spread from India to all parts of the world, the teachings were readily assimilated with the cultures of the people who accepted the teachings. As a result, Buddhist art and culture took on a rich variety of forms with profound gentleness and kindness as the Buddha expressly forbade the use of force. The practice of Buddhism was adapted in many ways to suit the nature of the various cultures that accepted it. As a result of this, Vesak is celebrated in many different ways all over the world. But in essence many practices have become universal. This sacred day is purely a religious festival, and not a festive occasion. On this day all Buddhists are expected to reaffirm their faith in the Buddha Dhamma and to lead a noble religious life. It is a day for meditation and for radiating Loving-Kindness.

Buddha Jayanti or Buddha Purnima is marked as the most important day, commomerating the three most significant events in the life of Gautama Buddha that occurred on the same day. His birth, enlightenment and death (nirvana), all happened in the month of Vaishak, on a full moon night in April/May. Thus, this makes the day—called Buddha Purnima Festival or Buddha Jayanti Festival-all the more sacred for Buddhists.

The Bodhi tree in Bodhgaya has stood for centuries as a reminder of the Buddha's attainment of enlightenment. Gaya is a sacred place of pilgrimage for Buddhists. Each year, the tree is venerated and the viharas nearby resound to the chants of Buddhist monks. The great celebration of the month of Vaishakh falls on the full moon day on which Gautama, the Buddha, was born. To Buddhists the world over, all full moon days are festive and important. However, the full moon of Vaishakh is the most auspicious of all. Gautama, the Buddha was born in 544 BC in Lumbini,

Nepal. Unlike most other religious teachers, he was born into a roval family and surrounded by wealth and material ease. According to Buddhist lore, Mahamaya his mother, often dreamt of white elephants at the time of her pregnancy and thus knew that a divine child of miraculous charisma and destiny would Then as a young adult Siddharth, the prince born to King Suddhodhana and Queen Mahamaya, undertook a short journey in the course of which he observed the futility of human life. He saw the way a man grew into adulthood passed into old age and then became helpless, sick and feeble before death. Saddened by the realization that life was a meaningless and hollow passage from one state of being to the next, the prince went into deep meditation under a Bodhi tree near Gaya, until he finally attained enlightenment, once again on the full moon day of Vaishakh. He was then 35 years of age and thereafter became known as Gautama, the Buddha. He gave his first sermon in Sarnath, near the holy city of Varanasi, to his followers who formed a Sangha, also on the Vaishakh Purnima. A tableux shows the Buddha delivering his first sermon at the deer park in Sarnath, near the holy city of Varanasi. A golden idol of the Buddha seated in repose, at Bodhgaya.

Vesakha or Buddha Purnima, is a festival of lights in many Buddhist countries. In Sri Lanka it is particularly beautiful and picturesque. The Buddha, who is considered the ninth avatar of Vishnu, reached Nirvana or the extinction of self and freedom from the cycle of rebirth, also on the full moon day of Vaishakh. Therefore Buddha Purnima marks the three major events in the life of this great apostle of peace. Buddhist countries like Japan, Burma and Sri Lanka celebrate this festival with special fervour. In Sri Lanka it is celebrated like Diwaliwith paper and bamboo stick lanterns twinkling under the night sky. Kheeris shared by families and distributed to the poor. Buddhists free birds from their cages and refrain from eating meat on this day.

Buddha was a real historical character at the same time he was a mythical man of legend. Buddhist mythology is replete with legends relating to his birth. It is believed that Buddha had come into being after through a series of birth and death. In some he was reborn as human and in some, as an animal. And that Buddha is the final phase in which he achieved the ultimate Nirvana, the parinirvana. According to a Tibetan belief, that he would be reborn, had been prophesied many years before Gautam Buddha was born.

Like all prophets his birth was legendary. According to one story, Queen Mayadevi was strolling in the garden at Lumbini. Feeling tired, she sat under a tree and fell asleep. She dreamt that a six-tusked white elephant had entered her body. Following this the queen gave birth to a child through the right side of her ribcage. After the birth of the child, named Siddhartha, his horoscope was made.

The horoscope predicted that he would become either a world monarch or a great ascetic.Since Suddodhana did not want his son to become a hermit, he raised him in great luxury. Nothing sad or painful was allowed to touchthe life of Siddhartha.Shielding him from the harsh realities of life, the King created a paradise on earth for his beloved son.

So, Siddhartha lived his early life as a prince. And the prince was a man of exceptional physical appearance. In fact, there are numerous references to the perfection of his physical body.And the charming young Prince was married to Princess Yashodhara at a tender age. So as to get him more involved in worldly affair. Soon Siddhartha became father. But things soon turned out to be altogether different.

Legend says, it was a matter of four passing sights that brought in to light the ascetic in him and drove him out in quest of Truth. This is how the Prince saw them.

While the prince was traveling in his royal chariot, he chanced upon an old man, a sick person, a dead body and an ascetic. This was the first time he was exposed to the sufferings in the world. The decrepit old man made him aware of the old age, the final phase of life cycle. The sick man made him aware of the pangs of an ailing uncared man. The corpse made him aware of the Death, that terminates human life. He was deeply distressed.

Now restless and dissatisfied with his opulent lifestyle, Siddhartha decided to renounce his kingdom, even his wife and son. He was just 29 then. And he longed for finding out some answers to the questions of life. The quest for eternal truth.

Siddhartha renounced his kingdom in search of 'truth'. But 'truth' was not easy to be found. He took to the life of an ascetic, like the one he saw as the last of the Four Passing Sights. The ascetic, with a peaceful face, inspired him most.

During his search, he traveled to distant lands. And for six years he lived as a solitary forest-dweller, at first as the disciple of two renowned Hindu masters. Then, after deciding he had learned all that they could teach him—which he felt was not enough - he joined a band of ascetics and with them he practiced such extreme austerities and ate so little that he was about to die.

Study with the Hindus had not brought him the enlightenment he was seeking, nor had his experiment with asceticism. Rejecting self-indulgence as well as self-mortification, he determined to follow what he called the Middle Path and to devote himself to a course of mental cultivation and mystical concentration. In the town of Bodhgaya in Northeast India, Siddhartha sat down beneath a tree to embark on an extended period of meditation. And he determined not to rise until he had found the truth. For 49 days he meditated, formulating a body of wisdom which was to bring mankind a new religion. When he arose he was enlightened, he was the Buddha, ready to go forth and teach others how to become enlightened.

The tree under which he meditated came to be known as the 'Bodhi Tree', the tree of wisdom.

And the place where this happened is still known as Bodh Gaya, now in north eastern part of India. It is believed that he attained nirvana on the day of the full moon in the month of Vaishakha, or Vesakha. It became a great Holy Day for the Buddhists. It was also on this day Buddha gave his first sermon at Sarnath, also in the North Eastern India.

This is why the Buddhists rotate the prayer wheels in the belief the prayers written on the wheels get dispersed on this day. The day when Prince Siddhartha became Gautam Buddha and again the day when he gave his first sermon at Sarnath.

Soon after his enlightenment the Buddha preached to a small group of the curious and those who heard his words became his disciples. From then on the Buddha devoted the rest of his life to teaching those who sought his advice, his compassion, his wisdom. The growth in the number of his disciples led to his establishment of the Sangha, the Buddhist monastic order. It was his disciples who passed along his teachings, by word of mouth, from generation to generation. Not until some considerable time after his death, were the words of the Buddha recorded in written form.

Finally Buddha liberated himself from the cycle of rebirth and achieved mahaparinirvana, also on the auspices of Vesak. Buddhism is one of the most ancient and highly philosophical Indian tradition. "Buddha" means "Awakened One", someone who has awakened from the sleep of ignorance and sees things as they actually are. Buddhism, is Buddha's teachings and the inner experiences or realizations of these teachings. Buddha have eighty-four thousand teachings. All these teachings and the inner realizations of them constitute Buddhism.

The day falls in the Vaishaka month of the Indian

calendar. Prayers, sermons and non-stop recitations of Buddhist scriptures resonate in monasteries, religious halls and homes. In monasteries in Sikkim, monks hold day-long readings of the scriptures before the Buddha's statue. The lay people listen to these recitals, and also give gifts to the monks and the statue.

The statue of Buddha, in fact, receives special attention everywhere, with people offering it incense, flowers, candles and fruits. The Banyan tree—called the Bodhi tree for its part in Buddha's enlightenment—also receives a fair share of garlands and coloured flags adorn it. People also sprinkle milk and scented waters on its roots and light rows of lamps around it.

On Vesak day, devout Buddhists are expected to assemble in various temples before dawn for the ceremonial hoisting of the Buddhist flag and the singing of hymns in praise of the holy triple gem: The Buddha, The Dharma (his teachings), and The Sangha (his disciples). Devotees may bring simple offerings of flowers, candles and joss-sticks to lay at the feet of their teacher. These symbolic offerings are to remind followers that just as the beautiful flowers would wither away after a short while and the candles and joss-sticks would soon burn out, so too is life subject to decay and destruction. Devotees are enjoined to make a special effort to refrain from killing of any kind.

Devout Buddhists understand how to lead a noble life according to the teaching by making a daily affirmation to observe the eight Precepts. However, on special days, notably new moon and full moon days, they observe additional disciplines to train themselves to practice morality, simplicity and humility.

The Eight Precepts are:

1. Not to kill
2. Not to steal

3. Not to engage in improper sexual activity
4. Not to indulge in wrong speech
5. Not to take intoxicating drinks and drugs
6. To abstain from taking food at unreasonable time
7. To refrain from sensual pleasures such as dancing, singing and self-adornment
8. To refrain from using high and luxurious seats in order to practice humility.

Buddhist are expected to listen to talks given by monks. On this day monks will recite verses uttered by the Buddha twenty-five centuries ago, to invoke peace and happiness for the Government and the people. Buddhists are reminded to live in harmony with people of other faiths and to respect the beliefs of other people as the Buddha had taught.

Celebrating Vesak also means making special efforts to bring happiness to the unfortunate like the aged, the handicapped and the sick. To this end, Buddhists will distribute gifts in cash and kind to various charitable homes throughout the country. Vesak is also a time for great joy and happiness. But this joy is expressed not by pandering to one's appetites but by concentrating on useful activities such as decorating and illuminating temples, painting and creating exquisite scenes from the life of the Buddha for public dissemination. Devout Buddhists also vie with one another to provide refreshments and vegetarian food to devotees who visit the temple to pay homage to the Blessed One.

The Buddha himself has given invaluable advice on how to pay homage to him. Just before he died, he saw his faithful attendant Ananda, weeping. The Buddha advised him not to weep, but to understand the universal law that all compounded things (including even his own body) must disintegrate. He advised everyone not to cry over the disintegration of the physical body but to regard his teachings

(The Dhamma) as their teacher from then on, because only the Dhamma truth is eternal and not subject to the law of change. He also stressed that the way to pay homage to him was not merely by offering flowers, incense, and lights, but by truly and sincerely striving to follow his teachings. This is how devotees are expected to celebrated Vesak: to use the opportunity to reiterate their determination to lead noble lives, to develop their minds, to practise loving-kindness and to bring peace and harmony to humanity.

4

Chhath

> Humor is the most philosophic of all the emotions. It is a recognition in our instinctive nature of what our minds in their purest contemplation can inform us, that pleasure and pain are, except for the incidental purpose of preserving us, indifferent—that failure is just as interesting as success.
>
> —*Max Eastman*

Chhath festival is gaining popularity day by year afte3r year these days. Once confined to Bihar and adjacent areas, it is bet being celebrated in many parts of the country. The Chhath festival of sunworship is celebrated mainly in Bihar, Eastern UP and other parts of India where large of Bhojpuri speaking populace is present. It is a festival in which mothers pray for long and healthy life of their children. The Mothers observes fast for the full day and in the evening when moon rises she gives worships moon. Again in the morning mother worships Rising SUN by standing in the river water or pond.

Chhath Puja is an Indian thanksgiving festival dedicated to the Sun God. During the celebrations of Chhath Puja, people gather on the banks of the River Ganges to bathe in its sacred water, pray and make ritual offerings to the Sun God. Chhath Puja is a highly elaborate festival noted for its impressive display of colorful costumes, music, singing and extravagant rituals. When *Chhath* Puja takes place, sometime during the months of October and November, immediately following the six-day festival of lights known as Diwali. Chhath Puja lasts for one night and one day.

Chhath Puja is celebrated mainly in the northern regions of the Indian state of Bihar. The festival takes place, on the banks of the River Ganges, in people's homes and at the Sun Temple of Baragaon, two kilometers outside Nalanda, in Bihar. Chhath Puja is also celebrated in Varanasi in the state of Uttar Pradesh.

- — On the day before the festival of Chhath Puja, it is customary for participants to gather on the riverbanks and cleanse themselves, briefly, in the water of the River Ganges.
- — Before Chhath Puja, people fast throughout the day and into the early evening.
- — After cleansing, a token amount of sacred water is retained for use as offerings during the festival of Chhath Puja.
- — The fast is followed by worship in the home. Festive fare consisting of freshly harvested rice, puris (a local bread type delicacy), and fruit such as bananas, coconuts and grapefruit are then served to the family.
- — On the second day of Chhath Puja a strict 24-hour fast is observed; not even water is consumed.
- — Cooking utensils are purified by the senior women of the household, as part of the ritual preparation of offerings for the main part of the celebration of Chhath Puja.
- — At sunset, worshippers proceed to the riverbank bearing their offerings in baskets held high to avoid the impure touch of human hands.
- — The participants then pay homage to the Sun God, at the precise moment of the setting sun.
- — Further celebrations take place at nightfall under temporary canopies made from sugar cane stalks

where offerings are laid out as a tribute to the god of fire.

— Well before sunrise, when the sky is pitch black, worshippers return to the riverbank to pray to the rising sun; this ritual is considered the focal point of the ceremony of Chhath Puja.

Useful Terms

— Surya: The sun (the Sun God is worshipped during the festival of Chhath Puja).

— Chhath: In the context of Chhath Puja, Chhath refers to the number six and the importance of this date on the Indian festival calendar

— Puja: Various interpretations exist of the word "puja," including worship with offerings, especially of flowers, and ritual anointment with sandalwood paste. Puja is the combination of the Sanskrit words for sin and birth.

— Prasad: Ritual offerings.

— Puris: This deep-fried bread, made from wheat flour, is traditionally offered at the festival of Chhath Puja.

— Thekuwa: This is a wheat-based cake served during the festival of Chhath Puja.

5

Christmas

> It wasn't until 440 A.D. that the fathers of the Church got around to selecting a date upon which to celebrate the birth of Christ—the day of the winter solstice, and even then the exact day and year have never been satisfactorily settled.
>
> Christmas customs have descended from seasonal, pagan and religious ceremonies with legend and tradition woven heavily into the pattern. Association of the customs with pagan feasts of the winter solstice couple them to the beginning of time and link them very closely to the birth of Christ.
>
> Church fathers exercised considerable wisdom in selecting the day of the solstice since it was the time of their most important festival. Flexibility in man-made calendars have caused the time of the solstice and the date of Christmas to vary by a few days.

As Christians form a good portion of India's population, CHristian festivals are also celebrated with pump and show in all parts of India. Chruches are the main attraction.

In fact, under the sway of modernization of westernization, people from other religions also take keen interest in Christmas. It is more popular among the school children.

Jesus "Christ" is known as the founder or central figure of "Christianity." Christmas is a Christian holiday on

December 25 that commemorates the birth of Jesus. Ancient Romans also commemorated Jesus' birth by marking a division of the calendar still in use today. The years before Jesus' birth are marked as B.C. (Before Christ), and the years after Jesus' birth are marked A.D. (Anno Domini, which means, in the year of our Lord).

Christmas literally means the Mass (celebration) of Christ. "Christ" is a Greek word and title, meaning "anointed" or one set apart by God for a special purpose. "Christ" is equivalent to the Hebrew word "Messiah." Based on the words of ancient prophets, the first century Jewish people expected the arrival of the Messiah promised by God as a great deliver of the people. The word *Christmas* is derived from Middle English *Christemasse* and from Old English *Cristes masse*. It is a contraction meaning "Christ's mass". The name of the holiday is often shortened to Xmas because Roman letter "X" resembles the Greek letter *x* (chi), an abbreviation for Christ.

In Jesus' adult years, Jesus claimed to be this King, the Jewish Messiah Ultimately, Jesus' claim to be Christ caused controversy and the religious trial leading to his execution. Christians commemorate Jesus' execution and believed return from the dead (resurrection) during "Easter."

Jesus also described His birth on earth as the most important "Good News," signifying that God Himself chose to come from heaven to earth to help make earth more like heaven Many people throughout the world have been prompted to ask questions about the life, death, and message of Jesus. Here's some of what you can investigate further at Jesus Institute, an educational resource about the person of Jesus: Christmas is a Christian holiday held on December 25 which celebrates the birth of Jesus. Eastern Orthodox Churches, which use the Julian Calendar to determine feast days, celebrate on January 7 by the Gregorian Calendar. Both dates are merely traditional and neither is thought to be the actual birthdate of Jesus. Christ's birth, or nativity, is said to fulfill Old Testament prophecies concerning the coming of a messiah, or savior.

In Western countries, Christmas has become the most economically significant holiday of the year. The popularity of Christmas can be traced in part to its status as a winter festival. Many cultures have their most important holiday in winter because there is less agricultural work to do at this time. Examples of winter festivals that are believed by some to have influenced Christmas include the pre-Christian festivals of Yule and Saturnalia.

In Western culture, the holiday is characterized by the exchange of gifts among friends and family members, some of the gifts being attributed to Santa Claus (also known as Father Christmas, Saint Nicholas, and Father Frost). However, various local and regional Christmas traditions are still practiced, despite the widespread influence of American, British and Australian Christmas motifs disseminated by film, popular literature, television, and the nativity narratives in the Gospel of Luke and the Gospel of Matthew focus on different aspects of the event. The Gospel of Mark, considered the earliest and most historical gospel according to the doctrine of Markan priority, does not include a nativity narrative.

In Luke, Mary learns from an angel that the Holy Spirit has caused her to be with child. Mary points out that she is a virgin and the angel responds that "with God nothing shall be impossible." Shortly thereafter, she and her husband Joseph leave their home in Nazareth to travel about 150 kilometres (90 miles) to Joseph's ancestral home, Bethlehem, in order to register for a census ordered by Emperor Augustus. Finding no room at the inns, they lodge in a stable. There Mary gives birth to Jesus. An angel of the lord goes to the fields and tells the shepherds the "tidings of joy." A heavenly host proclaims, "Glory to God in the highest, and on earth peace to men on whom his favour rests." The shepherds come to the manger to adore the infant Jesus (Luke 1:5-2:20).

In Matthew, magi arrive at the court of King Herod in Jerusalem and ask, "Where is the child who has been born king of the Jews? We have observed the rising of his star, and we have come to pay him homage." (Compare to Numbers 24:17.) The word *magi* is traditionally translated as "wise men." The word connects them to the magi of Babylon who select Daniel their chief in the Book of Daniel. Daniel's magi interpret dreams and other portents. The book was well-known in ancient times for its prophecy concerning the messiah (Daniel 9:24-27), a man who will be sent by God to lead the Jewish people.

Neither the names of the magi nor their number are specified in the *Bible*, but tradition tells us there were three: Balthassar, Melchior, and Caspar. Balthassar is a Greek version of the Babylonian name Belshazzar. This is the name of a king in Daniel. Melchior means "The king is my light" in Aramaic. Caspar is a Latinized version of Gondophares, a Parthian (i.e. Persian) name. The magi are sometimes called kings because of prophecies that kings will do homage to the messiah (Isaiah 60:3, Psalms 72:11).

Herod is disturbed by the magi's words and questions them closely, attempting to determine when the star first appeared and when the child was born. The king asks his advisors where the messiah will be born. They answer Bethlehem, birthplace of King David, and quote Micah 5:2-4. "When you have found him, bring me word so that I may also go and pay him homage," a deceitful Herod tells the magi.

As they travel to Bethleham, the magi follow a star that leads them to a house where they find Jesus. Jesus is no longer in the manger described by Luke. He is a child (*paidion*), not an infant (*brephos*). The magi present Jesus with gold, frankincense, and myrrh. (If these gifts were chosen in view of Isaiah 60:1-7, it may explain the magi's earlier trip to Jerusalem.) In a dream, the magi received a divine warning of Herod's intent to kill the child, who he sees as a rival. Consequently, they return to their own country without telling Herod the result of their mission. An angel tells Joseph to flee with his family to Egypt. Meanwhile, Herod orders that all male children of Bethlehem under the age of 2 be killed. After Herod's death, the family settles in Nazareth (Matthew 2:1-23).

Although no one knows what date Jesus was born on, there were several reasons for early Christians to favor December 25. The date is nine months after the Festival of Annunciation (March 25), and hence the Incarnation. It is also the date on which the Romans marked the winter solstice.

Around 220, the theologian Tertullian declared that Jesus died on March 25, AD 29. Although this is not a plausible date for the crucifixion, it does suggest that March 25 had significance for church even before it was used as a basis to calculate Christmas. Modern scholars favor a crucifixion date of April 3, AD 33 (also the date of a partial lunar eclipse).

By 240, a list of significant events was being assigned to March 25, partly because it was believed to be the date of the vernal equinox. These events include creation, the fall of Adam, and, most relevantly, the Incarnation. The view that the Incarnation occurred on the same date as crucifixion is consistent with a Jewish belief that prophets died at an "integral age," either an anniversary of their birth or of their conception.

Aside from being nine months later than Annunciation, December 25 is also the date the Romans marked the winter solstice, which they referred to as *bruma*. For this reason, some have suggested the opposite of the theory outlined above, i.e. that the date of Christmas was chosen to be the same as that of the solstice and that the date of Annunciation was calculated on this basis. (The Julian calendar was originally only one day off, with the solstice falling on December 24 in 45 BC. Due to calendar slippage, the date of the astronomical solstice has moved back so that it now falls on either December 21 or December 22).

The idea that December 25 is Christ's birthday was popularized by Sextus Julius Africanus in *Chronographiai* (AD 221), an early reference book for Christians. This identification did not at first inspire feasting or celebration. In 245, the theologian Origen denounced the idea of celebrating the birthday of Jesus "as if he were a king pharaoh." Only sinners, not saints, celebrate their birthdays, Origin contended.

In 274, Emperor Aurelian designated December 25 as the festival of Sol Invictus (the "unconquered sun"). Aurelian may have chosen this date because the solstice was considered the birthday of Mithras, a syncretic god of Persian origin. Mithras is often identified with Sol Invictus, although Sol was originally a separate Syrian god.

Christmas soon outgrew the Christological controversy that created it and came to dominate the medieval calendar. The forty days before Christmas became the "forty days of St. Martin," now Advent. The fortieth day after Christmas was Candlemas. The Egyptian Christmas celebration on January 6 was adopted as Epiphany, one of the most prominent holidays of the year during Early Middle Ages. Christmas Day itself was a relatively minor holiday, although its prominence gradually increased after Charlemagne was crowned on Christmas Day, 800.

Although the nativity narrative is among the most compelling stories in the Bible, other Christian holidays such as Easter are more significant from a strictly religious point of view. The popularity of Christmas can be better understood if it is viewed as a form of winter celebration. Agricultural societies typically hold their most important festival in winter since there is less need of farm work at this time.

The Romans had a winter celebration known as Saturnalia. This festival was originally held on December 17 and honored Saturn, a god of agriculture. It recalled the "golden age" when Saturn ruled. In imperial times, Saturnalia was extended to seven days (December 17-23). Combined with festivals both before and after, the result was an extended winter holiday season. Business was postponed and even slaves feasted. There was drinking, gambling and singing naked. It was the "best of days," according to the poet Catallus. With the coming of Christianity, Italy's Saturnalian traditions were attached to Advent (the forty days before Christmas). Around the 12th century, these traditions transferred again to the "twelve days of Christmas" (i.e. Christmas to Epiphany).

Northern Europe was the last part to Christianize, and its pagan celebrations had a major influence on Christmas. Scandinavians still call Christmas *Jul* (Yule), originally the name of a twelve-day pre-Christian winter festival. Logs were lit to honor Thor, the god of thunder, hence the "Yule log." In Germany, the equivalent holiday is called *Mitwinternacht* (mid-winter night). There are also twelve *Rauhnächte* (harsh or wild nights).

Santa Claus hands out gifts to Union soldiers during the US Civil War in Thomas Nast's first Santa Claus cartoon, *Harper's Weekly*, 1863. During the Reformation, Protestants condemned Christmas celebration as "trappings of popery" and the "rags of the Beast". The Catholic Church responded by promoting the festival in a more religiously oriented form. When a Puritan parliament triumphed over the King Charles I of England, Christmas was officially banned (1647). Pro-Christmas rioting broke out in several cities. For several weeks, Canterbury was controlled by the rioters, who decorated doorways with holly and shouted royalist slogans. The Restoration (1660) ended the ban, but Christmas celebration was still disapproved of by the Anglican clergy (and, therefore, more thoroughly enjoyed by Catholics and Dissenters).

The phrase "Christmas tree" is first recorded in 1835 and represents the importation of a tradition from Germany, where such trees became popular in the late 18th century. Queen Victoria and her German-born husband Prince Albert enthusiastically promoted Christmas trees, as well as the idea of placing gifts under them. The royal family's tree of 1848 was widely publicized and imitated. Christmas cards were first designed in 1843 and became popular in the 1860s. The commercial calendar, created to answer children's questions concerning when Christmas would come, dates from 1851.

The Puritans of New England disapproved of Christmas and celebration was outlawed in Boston (1659-81). Virginia and New York, meanwhile, celebrated freely. Christmas fell out of favor after the American Revolution, when it was considered an "English custom". Interest was revived by Washington Irving's stories, by German immigrants, and by the homecomings of the Civil War years. It was declared a federal holiday in 1870.

Santa Claus is derived from Saint Nicholas, or *Sinterklaas,* who gave candy to the Dutch children on December 6. Dutch settlers in New York brought this tradition with them. Irving writes of Saint Nicholas "riding over the tops of the trees, in that selfsame wagon wherein he brings his yearly presents to children." The connection between Santa Claus and Christmas was popularized by the poem "A Visit from Saint Nicholas" (1822) by Clement Clarke Moore, which depicts Santa driving a sleigh pulled by reindeer and distributing gifts to children. His image was created by

German-American cartoonist Thomas Nast (1840-1902), who drew a new image annually beginning in 1863. By the 1880s, Nast's Santa had evolved into the form we now recognize. The image was standardized by advertisers in the 1920s.[14] Father Christmas is first recorded in the 15th century, but was associated with holiday merrymaking and drunkenness until Victorian Britain remade his image to match that of Santa.

In the midst of World War I, there was a Christmas truce between German and British troops in France (1914). Soldiers on both sides spontaneously began to sing Christmas carols and stopped fighting. The truce began on Christmas Day and continued for some time afterward. There was even a soccer game between the trench lines in which Germany's 133rd Royal Saxon Regiment is said to have bested Britain's Seaforth Highlanders 3-2.

Although Christmas may be celebrated on December 25 in historically Catholic and Protestant nations, in eastern Europe it is often celebrated on January 7. This is because the Orthodox church continues to use the Julian calendar for determining feast days.

The Orthodox churches fast during the forty days before Christmas. Christmas is dubbed the "Feast of the Nativity of our Lord, God, and Saviour Jesus Christ." Armenian Christians celebrate Christmas on January 6.

Dates for the secular aspects of the Christmas celebration also vary. In the United Kingdom, the Christmas season traditionally runs for twelve days beginning on Christmas Day. These twelve days of Christmas, a period of feasting and merrymaking, end on Twelfth Night, the eve of the Feast of the Epiphany. In medieval times, Swedish law provided for a Christmas peace (*julefrid*) of twenty days during which fines for robbery and manslaughter were doubled. On Knut's Day, the twentieth day after Christmas (January 13), Swedish children celebrate and throw out the family Christmas tree (*julgransplundring*).

The Christmas festive period has grown longer in some countries. In the U.S., the pre-Christmas shopping season begins on the day after Thanksgiving. In the Philippines, radio stations usually start playing Christmas music during what is called the "-ber months" (September, October, etc.).

Countries that celebrate Christmas on December 25 recognize the previous day as Christmas Eve and have various names for the day after Christmas. In the Netherlands, Germany, Scandinavia, Lithuania and Poland, Christmas Day and the following day are called First and Second Christmas Day. In many European and Commonwealth countries, December 26 is referred to as Boxing Day. In Finland, Ireland, Italy, Romania, Austria, and Catalonia (Spain), the day is known as St. Stephen's Day. In Quebec, the December 26 holiday is referred to as *Lendemain de Noël* ("the day after Christmas").

One belief in the United Kingdom, United States, and other countries passed down through the generations is the idea of lists of good children and bad children. Throughout the year, Santa supposedly adds names of children to either the good or bad list depending on their behaviour. When it gets closer to Christmas time, parents use the belief to encourage children to behave well. Those who are on the bad list receive a booby prize, such as a piece of coal or a switch with which their parents beat them, rather than presents.

The French equivalent of Santa, Père Noël, evolved along similar lines, eventually adopting the Santa image. In some cultures Santa Claus is accompanied by Knecht Ruprecht, or Black Peter. In other versions, elves make the holiday toys. His wife is referred to as Mrs. Claus. Many shopping malls in North America, the United Kingdom, and Australia have a Santa Claus children can visit to ask for presents.

In many countries, children leave empty containers for Santa to fill with small gifts such as toys, candy, or fruit. In the United Kingdom, the United States, and Canada children hang a Christmas stocking by the fireplace on Christmas Eve because Santa is said to come down the chimney the night before Christmas to fill them. In other countries, children put their empty shoes out for Santa to fill on the night before Christmas, or for Saint Nicholas to fill on December 5, the eve of his saint's day. Family members and friends also bestow gifts on each other.

In the Netherlands, Saint Nicholas's Day remains the principal day for gift giving while Christmas Day is a more religious holiday. In much of Germany, children put shoes out on window sills on the night of December 5, and find them filled with candy and small gifts the next morning. The main day for gift giving in Germany is December 24, when gifts are brought by Santa Claus or are placed under the Christmas tree. It is the same in Hungary, except that the Christmas gifts are usually brought by Jesus, not by Santa Claus. In Spain, gifts are brought by the magi on Epiphany (January 6). In Poland, Santa Claus gives gifts on two occasions: on the night of December 5 (so that children find them on the morning of December 6) and on Christmas Eve, December 24, (so that children find gifts that same day). In Finland, *Joulupukki* personally meets children and gives gifts on December 24. In Russia, *Grandfather Frost* brings presents on New Year's Eve, and these are opened on the same night.

The song "Twelve Days of Christmas", celebrates an old British tradition of gifts each day from Christmas to Epiphany. In most of the world, Christmas gifts are given at night on Christmas Eve or in the morning of Christmas Day. Until recently, the British gave gifts to non-family members on Boxing Day.

The Declaration of Christmas Peace has been a tradition in Finland from the Middle Ages every year, except in 1939 due to the war. The declaration takes place on the Old Great Square of Turku, Finland's official Christmas City and former capital, at noon on Christmas Eve. It is broadcast on Finnish radio and television.

In the United States and Europe, rolls of paper with secular or religious Christmas motifs are manufactured for the purpose of wrapping gifts. Common motifs include Christmas trees, wreaths, Santa Claus, the Nativity, angels, Christmas tree ornaments, candies, stars, snowflakes, snowmen, and penguins.

Christmas trees may be decorated with lights and ornaments. The interior of a home may be decorated with garlands and evergreen foliage, particularly holly and mistletoe. In Australia, North and South America and to a lesser extent Europe, it is traditional to decorate the outside of houses with lights and sometimes with illuminated sleighs, snowmen, and other Christmas figures.

Since the 19th century, the poinsettia has been associated with Christmas. Other popular holiday plants include holly, mistletoe, red amaryllis, and Christmas cactus.

Municipalities often sponsor decorations as well. Christmas banner may be hung from street lights and Christmas trees placed in the town square. In the U.S., decorations once commonly included religious themes. This practice has led to many lawsuits, as some say it amounts to the government endorsing a religion. In 1984, the US Supreme Court ruled that a city-owned Christmas display, even one with a Nativity scene, does not violate the First Amendment.

Although Christmas decorations, such as a tree, are considered secular in many parts of the world, the Kingdom of Saudi Arabia bans such displays as symbols of Christianity.

In many countries, businesses, schools, and communities have Christmas parties and dances in the weeks before Christmas. Christmas pageants may include a retelling of the story of the birth of Christ. Groups may visit neighborhood homes to sing Christmas carols. Others do volunteer work or hold fund-raising drives for charities.

On Christmas Day or Christmas Eve, a special meal of Christmas dishes is usually served. In some regions, particularly in Eastern Europe, these family feasts are preceded by a period of fasting. Candy and treats are also part of Christmas celebration in many countries.

Many people also send Christmas cards to their friends and family members. Many cards are also produced with messages such as "season's greetings" or "happy holidays", so as to including senders and recipients who may not celebrate Christmas .

Because of the focus on celebration, friends, and family, people who are without these, or who have recently suffered losses, are more likely to suffer from depression during Christmas. This increases the demand for counseling services. It is widely believed that suicides and murders spike during the holiday season. However, the peak months for suicide are May and June. Because of holiday celebrations involving alcohol, drunk driving-related fatalities increase.

Christmas is typically the largest annual stimulus for many nations. Sales increase dramatically in almost all retail areas and shops introduce new products as people purchase gifts, decorations, and supplies. In the U.S., the Christmas shopping season now begins on Black Friday, the day after Thanksgiving. The economic impact of Christmas continues after the holiday. During Christmas sales and New Year's sales, stores sell off excess inventories. More businesses and stores close on Christmas Day than any other day of the year. In the United Kingdom, the Christmas Day (Trading) Act 2004 prevents all large shops from trading on Christmas Day. Many religious Christians, as well as anti-consumerists, decry the commercialization of Christmas. They accuse the Christmas season of being dominated by money and greed at the expense of the holiday's more important values. Frustrations over these issues and others can lead to a rise in Christmas time social problems.

Most economists agree, however, that Christmas produces a deadweight loss under orthodox macroeconomic theory, due to the surge in gift-giving. This loss is calculated as the difference between what the gift giver spent on the item and what the gift receiver would have paid for the item. It is estimated that in 2001 Christmas resulted in a $4 billion deadweight loss in the U.S. alone. Because of complicating factors, this analysis is sometimes used to discuss possible flaws in current macroeconomic theory.

In North America, film studios release many high-budget movies in the holiday season, including Christmas films, fantasy movies or high-tone dramas with rich production values. This helps the studio capture holiday crowds and position themselves for the Academy Awards. Christmas is the most lucrative season for the industry aside from summer. Christmas-specific movies generally open in late November or early December as their themes and images are not nearly as popular once the season is over. Home video release is often delayed until the following Christmas season.

Christmas was not among the earliest festivals of the Church. Irenaeus and Tertullian omit it from their lists of feasts; Origin, glancing perhaps at the discreditable imperial *Natalitia*, asserts that in the Scriptures sinners alone, not saints, celebrate their birthday; Arnobius can still ridicule the "birthdays" of the gods.

The first evidence of the feast is from Egypt. About A.D. 200, Clement of Alexandria (Strom., I, xxi in P.G., VIII, 888) says that certain Egyptian theologians "over curiously" assign, not the year alone, but the day of Christ's birth, placing it on 25 Pachon (20 May) in the twenty-eighth year of Augustus. [Ideler (Chron., II, 397, n.) thought they did this believing that the ninth month, in which Christ was born, was the ninth of their own calendar.] Others reached the date of 24 or 25 Pharmuthi (19 or 20 April). With Clement's evidence may be mentioned the "De paschs computus", written in 243 and falsely ascribed to Cyprian (P.L., IV, 963 sqq.), which places Christ's birth on 28 March, because on that day the material sun was created. But Lupi has shown (Zaccaria, Dissertazioni ecc. del p. A.M. Lupi, Faenza, 1785, p. 219) that there is no month in the year to which respectable authorities have not assigned Christ's birth. Clement, however, also tells us that the Basilidians celebrated the Epiphany, and with it, probably, the Nativity, on 15 or 11 Tybi (10 or 6 January). At any rate this double commemoration became popular, partly because the apparition to the shepherds was considered as one manifestation of Christ's glory, and was added to the greater manifestations celebrated on 6 January; partly because at the baptism-manifestation many codices (e.g. Codex Bez) wrongly give the Divine words as *sou ei ho houios mou ho agapetos, ego semeron gegenneka se* (Thou art my beloved Son, this day have I begotten thee) in lieu of *en soi eudokesa* (in thee I am well pleased), read in Luke 3:22. Abraham Ecchelensis (Labbe, II, 402) quotes the Constitutions of the Alexandrian Church for a *dies Nativitatis et Epiphania* in Nicaan times; Epiphanius (Har., li, ed. Dindorf, 1860, II, 483) quotes an extraordinary semi-Gnostic ceremony at Alexandria in which, on the night of 5-6 January, a cross-stamped Korê was carried in procession round a crypt, to the chant, "Today at this hour Korê gave birth to the Eternal"; John Cassian records in his "Collations" (X, 2 in P.L., XLIX, 820), written 418-427, that the Egyptian monasteries still observe the "ancient custom"; but on 29 Choiak (25 December) and 1 January, 433, Paul of Emesa preached before Cyril of Alexandria, and his sermons (see Mansi, IV, 293; appendix to Act. Conc. Eph.) show that the December celebration was then firmly established there, and calendars prove its permanence. The December feast therefore reached Egypt between 427 and 433.

In Cyprus, at the end of the fourth century, Epiphanius asserts against the Alogi (Hær., li, 16, 24 in P. G., XLI, 919, 931) that Christ was born on 6 January and baptized on 8 November. Ephraem Syrus (whose hymns belong to Epiphany, not to Christmas) proves that Mesopotamia still put the birth feast thirteen days after the winter solstice; i.e. 6 January; Armenia likewise ignored, and still ignores, the December festival. (Cf. Euthymius, "Pan. Dogm.", 23 in P.G., CXXX, 1175; Niceph., "Hist. Eccl,", XVIII, 53 in P.G., CXLVII, 440; Isaac, Catholicos of Armenia in eleventh or twelfth century, "Adv. Armenos", I, xii, 5 in P.G., CXXII, 1193; Neale, "Holy Eastern Church", Introd., p. 796).

In Cappadocia, Gregory of Nyssa's sermons on St. Basil (who died before 1 January, 379) and the two following, preached on St. Stephen's feast (P.G., XLVI, 788; cf, 701, 721), prove that in 380 the 25th December was already celebrated there, unless, following Usener's too ingenious arguments (Religionsgeschichtliche Untersuchungen, Bonn, 1889, 247-250), one were to place those sermons in 383. Also, Asterius of Amaseia (fifth century) and Amphilochius of Iconium (contemporary of Basil and Gregory) show that in their dioceses both the feasts of Epiphany and Nativity were separate.

In 385, Silvia of Bordeaux (or Etheria, as it seems clear she should be called) was profoundly impressed by the splendid Childhood feasts at Jerusalem. They had a definitely "Nativity" colouring; the bishop proceeded nightly to Bethlehem, returning to Jerusalem for the day celebrations. The Presentation was celebrated forty days after. But this calculation starts from 6 January, and the feast lasted during the octave of that date. (Peregr. Sylv., ed. Geyer, pp. 75 sq.) Again (p. 101) she mentions as high festivals Easter and Epiphany alone. In 385, therefore, 25 December was not observed at Jerusalem. This checks the so-called correspondence between Cyril of Jerusalem (348-386) and

Pope Julius I (337-352), quoted by John of Nikiu (c. 900) to convert Armenia to 25 December (see P.L., VIII, 964 sqq.).

Cyril declares that his clergy cannot, on the single feast of Birth and Baptism, make a double procession to Bethlehem and Jordan. (This later practice is here an anachronism.) He asks Julius to assign the true date of the nativity "from census documents brought by Titus to Rome"; Julius assigns 25 December. Another document (Cotelier, Patr. Apost., I, 316, ed. 1724) makes Julius write thus to Juvenal of Jerusalem (c. 425-458), adding that Gregory Nazianzen at Constantinople was being criticized for "halving" the festival. But Julius died in 352, and by 385 Cyril had made no change; indeed, Jerome, writing about 411 (in Ezech., P.L., XXV, 18), reproves Palestine for keeping Christ's birthday (when He hid Himself) on the Manifestation feast. Cosmas Indicopleustes suggests (P.G., LXXXVIII, 197) that even in the middle of the sixth century Jerusalem was peculiar in combining the two commemorations, arguing from Luke 3:23 that Christ's baptism day was the anniversary of His birthday. The commemoration, however, of David and James the Apostle on 25 December at Jerusalem accounts for the deferred feast. Usener, arguing from the "Laudatio S. Stephani" of Basil of Seleucia (c. 430. — P.G., LXXXV, 469), thinks that Juvenal tried at least to introduce this feast, but that Cyril's greater name attracted that event to his own period.

At Rome the earliest evidence is in the Philocalian Calendar (P. L., XIII, 675; it can be seen as a whole in J. Strzygowski, Kalenderbilder des Chron. von Jahre 354, Berlin, 1888), compiled in 354, which contains three important entries. In the civil calendar 25 December is marked "Natalis Invicti". In the "Depositio Martyrum" a list of Roman or early and universally venerated martyrs, under 25 December is found "VIII kal. ian. natus Christus in Betleem Iudes". On "VIII kal. mart." (22 February) is also mentioned St. Peter's Chair. In the list of consuls are four anomalous ecclesiastical entries: the birth and death days of Christ, the entry into Rome, and martyrdom of Saints Peter and Paul. The significant entry is "Chr. Cæsare et Paulo sat. XIII. hoc. cons. Dns. ihs. XPC natus est VIII Kal. ian. d. ven. luna XV," i.e. during the consulship of (Augustus) Csar and Paulus Our Lord Jesus Christ was born on the eighth before the calends of January (25 December), a Friday, the fourteenth day of the moon. The details clash with tradition and possibility. The epact, here XIII, is normally XI; the year is A.U.C. 754, a date first suggested two centuries later; in no year between 751 and 754 could 25 December fall on a Friday; tradition is constant in placing Christ's birth on Wednesday. Moreover the date given for Christ's death (*duobus Geminis coss.*, i.e. A.D. 29) leaves Him only twenty eight, and one-quarter years of life. Apart from this, these entries in a consul list are manifest interpolations. But are not the two entries in the "Depositio Martyrum" also such? Were the day of Christ's birth in the flesh alone there found, it might stand as heading the year of martyrs' spiritual *natales*; but 22 February is there wholly out of place. Here, as in the consular *fasti*, popular feasts were later inserted for convenience' sake. The civil calendar alone was not added to, as it was useless after the abandonment of pagan festivals. So, even if the "Depositio Martyrum" dates, as is probable, from 336, it is not clear that the calendar contains evidence earlier than Philocalus himself, i.e. 354, unless indeed pre-existing popular celebration must be assumed to render possible this official recognition. Were the Chalki manuscript of Hippolytus genuine, evidence for the December feast would exist as early as c. 205. The relevant passage [which exists in the Chigi manuscript Without the bracketed words and is always so quoted before George Syncellus (c. 1000)] runs:

> He gar prote parousia tou kyriou hemon he ensarkos [en he gegennetai] en Bethleem, egeneto [pro okto kalandon ianouarion hemera tetradi] Basileuontos

> Augoustou [tessarakoston kai deuteron etos, apo de Adam] pentakischiliosto kai pentakosiosto etei epathen de triakosto trito [pro okto kalandon aprilion, hemera paraskeun, oktokaidekato etei Tiberiou Kaisaros, hypateuontos Hrouphou kai Hroubellionos. —(Comm. In Dan., iv, 23; Brotke; 19)

In Antioch, on the feast of St. Philogonius, Chrysostom preached an important sermon. The year was almost certainly 386, though Clinton gives 387, and Usener, by a long rearrangement of the saint's sermons, 388 (Religionsgeschichtl. Untersuch., pp. 227-240). But between February, 386, when Flavian ordained Chrysostom priest, and December is ample time for the preaching of all the sermons under discussion. (See Kellner, Heortologie, Freiburg, 1906, p. 97, n. 3). In view of a reaction to certain Jewish rites and feasts, Chrysostom tries to unite Antioch in celebrating Christ's birth on 25 December, part of the community having already kept it on that day for at least ten years. In the West, he says, the feast was thus kept, *anothen*; its introduction into Antioch he had always sought, conservatives always resisted. This time he was successful; in a crowded church he defended the new custom. It was no novelty; from Thrace to Cadiz this feast was observed — rightly, since its miraculously rapid diffusion proved its genuineness. Besides, Zachary, who, as high-priest, entered the Temple on the Day of Atonement, received therefore announcement of John's conception in September; six months later Christ was conceived, i.e. in March, and born accordingly in December.

Finally, though never at Rome, on authority he knows that the census papers of the Holy Family are still there. [This appeal to Roman archives is as old as Justin Martyr (Apol., I, 34, 35) and Tertullian (Adv. Marc., IV, 7, 19). Julius, in the Cyriline forgeries, is said to have calculated the date from Josephus, on the same unwarranted assumptions about

Zachary as did Chrysostom.] Rome, therefore, has observed 25 December long enough to allow of Chrysostom speaking at least in 388 as above (P.G., XLVIII, 752, XLIX, 351). "For the first coming of Our Lord in the flesh [in which He has been begotten], in Bethlehem, took place [25 December, the fourth day] in the reign of Augustus [the forty-second year, and] in the year 5500 [from Adam]. And He suffered in His thirty-third year [25 March, the parasceve, in the eighteenth year of Tiberius Csar, during the consulate of Rufus and Rubellio]."

Interpolation is certain, and admitted by Funk, Bonwetsch, etc. The names of the consuls [which should be Fufius and Rubellius] are wrong; Christ lives thirty-three years; in the genuine Hippolytus, thirty-one; minute data are irrelevant in this discussion with Severian millenniarists; it is incredible that Hippolytus should have known these details when his contemporaries (Clement, Tertullian, etc.) are, when dealing with the matter, ignorant or silent; or should, having published them, have remained unquoted (Kellner, op. cit., p. 104, has an excursus on this passage.)

St. Ambrose (de virg., iii, 1 in P. L., XVI, 219) preserves the sermon preached by Pope Liberius I at St. Peter's, when, on *Natalis Christi*, Ambrose' sister, Marcellina, took the veil. This pope reigned from May, 352 until 366, except during his years of exile, 355-357. If Marcellina became a nun only after the canonical age of twenty-five, and if Ambrose was born only in 340, it is perhaps likelier that the event occurred after 357. Though the sermon abounds in references appropriate to the Epiphany (the marriage at Cana, the multiplication of loaves, etc.), these seem due (Kellner, op. cit., p. 109) to sequence of thought, and do not fix the sermon to 6 January, a feast unknown in Rome till much later. Usener, indeed, argues (p. 272) that Liberius preached it on that day in 353, instituting the Nativity feast in the December of the same year; but Philocalus warrants our supposing that if preceded his pontificate by some time, though Duchesne's relegation of it to 243 (Bull. crit., 1890, 3, pp. 41 sqq.) may not commend itself to many.

In the West the Council of Saragossa (380) still ignores 25 December (see can. xxi, 2). Pope Siricius, writing in 385 (P. L., XII, 1134) to Himerius in Spain, distinguishes the feasts of the Nativity and Apparition; but whether he refers to Roman or to Spanish use is not clear. Ammianus Marcellinus (XXI, ii) and Zonaras (Ann., XIII, 11) date a visit of Julian the Apostate to a church at Vienne in Gaul on Epiphany and Nativity respectively. Unless there were two visits, Vienne in A.D. 361 combined the feasts, though on what day is still doubtful. By the time of Jerome and Augustine, the December feast is established, though the latter (Epp., II, liv, 12, in P.L., XXXIII, 200) omits it from a list of first-class festivals. From the fourth century every Western calendar assigns it to 25 December. At Rome, then, the Nativity was celebrated on 25 December before 354; in the East, at Constantinople, not before 379, unless with Erbes, and against Gregory, we recognize it there in 330. Hence, almost universally has it been concluded that the new date reached the East from Rome by way of the Bosphorus during the great anti-Arian revival, and by means of the orthodox champions. De Santi (L'Orig. delle Fest. Nat., in Civiltæ Cattolica, 1907), following Erbes, argues that Rome took over the Eastern Epiphany, now with a definite Nativity colouring, and, with as increasing number of Eastern Churches, placed it on 25 December; later, both East and West divided their feast, leaving Ephiphany on 6 January, and Nativity on 25 December, respectively, and placing Christmas on 25 December and Epiphany on 6 January. The earlier hypothesis still seems preferable.

6

Dussehra/Durga Puja

> We are made for cooperation, like feet, like hands, like eyelids, like the rows of the upper and lower teeth. To act against one another then is contrary to Nature, and it is acting against one another to be vexed and turn away.
>
> —*Marcus Aurelius*

Dussehra/Durga Puja is most important festival, inviting intense religious ethos of every Hindu. The Durga Puja is celebrated in various parts of India in different styles. But the one basic aim of this celebration is to propitiate Shakti, the Goddess in Her aspect as Power, to bestow upon man all wealth, auspiciousness, prosperity, knowledge (both sacred and secular), and all other potent powers. Whatever be the particular or special request that everyone may put before the Goddess, whatever boon may be asked of Her, the one thing behind all these is propitiation, worship and linking oneself with Her. There is no other aim. This is being effected consciously or unconsciously.

Durga Puja or Navaratri commences on the first and ends on the tenth day of the bright half of Aswayuja (September-October). It is held in commemoration of the victory of Durga over Mahishasura, the buffalo-headed demon. In Bengal Her image is worshipped for nine days and then cast into water. The tenth day is called Vijaya Dasami or Dussera (the "tenth day"). Processions with Her image are taken out along the streets of villages and cities.

The mother of Durga (that is, the wife of the King of the Himalayas) longed to see her daughter. Durga was permitted by Lord Shiva to visit her beloved mother only for nine days in the year. The festival of Durga Puja marks this brief visit and ends with the Vijaya Dasami day, when Goddess Durga leaves for Her return to Mount Kailas. This is the view of some devotees.

In Bengal, Durga Puja is a great festival. All who live away from home return during the Puja days. Mothers reunite with their sons and daughters, and wives with their husbands. The potter shows his skill in making images, the painter in drawing pictures, the songster in playing on his instrument, and the priest in reciting the sacred books. The Bengalis save money throughout the year only to spend everything during the Puja days. Cloth is freely distributed to the Brahmins. The woman of Bengal welcomes the Goddess with a mother's love and sends away the image on the last day, with every ceremony associated with a daughter's departure to her husband's home and with motherly tears in her eyes. This signifies the parting of Durga from Her beloved mother.

Durga Puja is the greatest Hindu festival in which God is adored as Mother. Hinduism is the only religion in the world which has emphasised to such an extent the motherhood of God. One's relationship with one's mother is the dearest and the sweetest of all human relations. Hence, it is proper to look upon God as mother.

Durga represents the Divine Mother. She is the energy aspect of the Lord. Without Durga, Shiva has no expression and without Shiva, Durga has no existence. Shiva is the soul of Durga; Durga is identical with Shiva. Lord Shiva is only the silent witness. He is motionless, absolutely changeless. He is not affected by the cosmic play. It is Durga who does everything.

Shakti is the omnipotent power of the Lord, or the Cosmic

Energy. The Divine Mother is represented as having ten different weapons in Her hands. She sits on a lion. She keeps up the play of the Lord through the three attributes of Nature, namely, Sattwa, Rajas and Tamas. Knowledge, peace, lust, anger, greed, egoism and pride, are all Her forms.

Devi worship is, therefore, worship of God's glory, of God's greatness and supremacy. It is adoration of the Almighty. It is unfortunate that Devi is ignorantly understood by many as a mere blood-thirsty Hindu Goddess. No! Devi is not a vicious demoness nor is She the property of the Hindus alone. Devi does not belong to any religion. Devi is that conscious power of God. The words Devi, Shakti, etc., and the ideas of different forms connected with these names are concessions granted by the sages due to the limitations of the human intellect; they are by no means the ultimate definitions of Shakti.

The original or Adi Shakti is beyond human comprehension. Bhagavan Krishna says in the *Gita*: "This is only My lower nature. Beyond this is My higher nature, the life-principle which sustains the universe".

Sri Rama worshipped Durga at the time of the fight with Ravana, to invoke Her aid in the war. This was on the days preceding the Vijaya Dasami day. He fought and won through Her Grace.

In yore days, Kings used to undertake ambitious expeditions on the day of the Vijaya Dasami. Those kings who did not go on such expeditions used to go out hunting in the deep forests. In Rajputana, India, even up to this date, people arrange mock attacks on some fort on Vijaya Dasami.

This day, however, has much to do with the life of Sri Rama. Nowhere in the history of the world can we find a parallel to the character of Sri Rama as a man, son, brother, husband, father or king. Maharishi Valmiki has exhausted the entire language in describing the glory of Sri Rama. And, we shall be rightly celebrating the Dussera if we make honest efforts to destroy the demon of our ego, and radiate peace and love wherever we go. Let us all resolve to become men of sterling character. Let us resolve and act.

Dussera can also be interpreted as "Dasa-Hara", which means the cutting of the ten heads of Ravana. So, let us resolve today to cut the ten heads—passion, pride, anger, greed, infatuation, lust, hatred, jealousy, selfishness and crookedness—of the demon, Ego, and thus justify the celebration of Dussera.

Religious observances, traditional worship and observances at times have more than one significance. Apart from being the adoration of the Divine, they commemorate stirring events in history, they are allegoric when interpreted from the occult standpoint and, lastly, they are deeply significant pointers and revealing guides to the individual on his path to God-realisation.

Outwardly, the nine-day worship of Devi is a celebration of triumph. This nine days' celebration is offered to the Mother for Her successful struggle with the formidable demons led by Mahishasura. But, to the sincere spiritual aspirant, the particular division of the Navaratri into sets of three days to adore different aspects of the Supreme Goddess has a very sublime, yet thoroughly practical truth to reveal. In its cosmic aspect, it epitomises the stages of the evolution of man into God, from Jivahood (the state of individualisation) to Shivahood (the state of Self-realisation). In its individual import, it shows the course that his spiritual practice should take.

The central purpose of existence is to recognise your eternal identity with the supreme Spirit. It is to grow into the image of the Divine. The supreme One embodies the highest perfection. It is spotless purity. To recognise your identity with That, to attain union with That, is verily to grow into the very likeness of the Divine. The aspirant, therefore, as his initial step, has to get rid of all the countless impurities, and the demoniacal elements that have come to cling to him in his embodied state. Then he has to acquire lofty virtues and auspicious, divine qualities. Thus purified, knowledge flashes upon him like the brilliant rays of the sun upon the crystal waters of a perfectly calm lake.

This process demands a resolute will, determined effort, and arduous struggle. In other words, strength and infinite power are the prime necessity. Thus it is the Divine Mother who has to operate through the aspirant.

Let us now consider how, on the first three days, the Mother is adored as supreme power and force, as Durga the Terrible. You pray to Mother Durga to destroy all your impurities, your vices, your defects. She is to fight with and annihilate the baser animal qualities in the spiritual aspirant, the lower, diabolical nature in him. Also, She is the power that protects your spiritual practice from its many dangers and pitfalls. Thus the first three days, which mark the first stage or the destruction of impurity and determined effort and struggle to root out the evil tendencies in your mind, are set apart for the worship of the destructive aspect of the Mother.

Once you have accomplished your task on the negative side, that of breaking down the impure propensities and old vicious habits, the next step is to build up a sublime spiritual personality, to acquire positive qualities in place of the eliminated demoniacal qualities. The divine qualities that Lord Krishna enumerates in the Gita, have to be acquired. The aspirant must cultivate and develop all the auspicious qualities. He has to earn immense spiritual wealth to enable him to pay the price for the rare gem of divine wisdom. If this development of the opposite qualities is not undertaken in right earnest, the old demoniacal nature will raise its head again and again. Hence, this stage is as important in an aspirant's career as the previous one. The essential difference is: the former is a ruthless, determined annihilation of the filthy egoistic lower self; the latter is an orderly, steady, calm and serene effort to develop purity. This pleasanter side of the aspirant's Sadhana is depicted by the worship of Mother Lakshmi. She bestows on Her devotees the inexhaustible divine wealth or Deivi Sampath. Lakshmi is the wealth-giving aspect of God. She is purity itself. Thus the worship of Goddess Lakshmi is performed during the second set of three days. Once the aspirant succeeds in routing out the evil propensities, and develops Sattwic or pure, divine qualities, he becomes competent to attain wisdom. He is now ready to receive the light of supreme wisdom. He is fit to receive divine knowledge. At this stage comes the devout worship of Mother Saraswathi, who is divine knowledge personified, the embodiment of knowledge of the Absolute. The sound of Her celestial *veena* awakens the notes of the sublime utterances of the *Upanishads* which reveal the Truth, and the sacred monosyllable, Om. She bestows the knowledge of the supreme, mystic sound and then gives full knowledge of the Self as represented by Her pure, dazzling snow-white apparel. Therefore, to propitiate Saraswathi, the giver of knowledge, is the third stage.

The tenth day, Vijaya Dasami, marks the triumphant ovation of the soul at having attained liberation while living in this world, through the descent of knowledge by the Grace of Goddess Saraswathi. The soul rests in his own Supreme Self or Satchidananda Brahman.

This arrangement also has a special significance in the aspirant's spiritual evolution. It marks the indispensable stages of evolution through which everyone has to pass. One naturally leads to the other; to short-circuit this would inevitably result in a miserable failure. Nowadays many ignorant seekers aim straight at the cultivation of knowledge without the preliminaries of purification and acquisition of the divine qualities. They then complain that they are not progressing on the path. How can they? Knowledge will not descend until the impurities have been washed out, and purity is developed. How can the pure plant grow in impure soil?

Therefore adhere to this arrangement; your efforts will be crowned with sure success. This is your path. As you destroy one evil quality, develop the virtue opposite to it. By this process you will soon bring yourself up to that perfection which will culminate in identity with the Self which is your goal. Then all knowledge will be yours: you will be omniscient, omnipotent and you will feel your omnipresence. You will see your Self in all. You will have achieved eternal victory over the wheel of births and deaths, over the demon of worldliness. No more pain, no more misery, no more birth, no more death! Victory, victory be yours!

Glory to the Divine Mother! Let Her take you, step by step to the top of the spiritual ladder and unite you with the Lord!

The Essentials of Durga Puja: The decorated puja platform with all the required essentials. Specific items are needed for each day of Durga Puja. There is a detailed method to worshiping Goddess Durga that are mentioned in the scriptures. Items which are needed for the ritual worship of the goddess should be collected beforehand so that the ritual is performed smoothly. The list of essentials of Durga Puja are: Items needed for Kalparambho, the ritual performed before the commencement of the puja and Mahasna:

Food Offerings : Panchashasha (grains of five types—rice, mung or whole green gram, til or sesame, mashkalai or any variety of whole black leguminous seed, job or millet), panchagobbo (five items obtained from the cow—milk, ghee or clarified butter, curd, cow dung and gomutra), curd, honey, sugar, three big noibiddos, one small noibiddo, three bowls of madhupakka (a mixture of honey, curd, ghee and sugar for oblation), bhoger drobbadi (items for the feast), aaratir drobbadi mahasnan oil, dantokashtho, sugar cane juice, an earthen bowl of atop (a type of rice), til toilo (sesame oil).

Water Offerings: Ushnodok (lukewarm water), coconut water, sarbooushodhi , mahaoushodhi, water from oceans, rain water, spring water, water containing lotus pollen.

Puja Items: Sindur (vermillion), panchabarner guri (powders of five different colours—turmeric, rice, kusum flowers or red aabir, rice chaff or coconut fibre burnt for the dark colour, bel patra or powdered wood apple leaves), panchapallab (leaves of five trees—mango, pakur or a species of fig, banyan, betal and Joggodumur or fig), pancha ratna (five types of gems—gold, diamond, sapphire, ruby and pearl), panchakoshay (bark of five trees—jaam, shimul, berela, kool, bokul powdered in equal portions and mixed with water), green coconut with stalk, three aashonanguriuk (finger ring made of kusha).

Cloth Offerings: Gamcha or a piece of cloth to cover the pot, a dhoti for Vishnu, a sari each for bodhon and Chandi.

Decorative Items: Ghat or a pot, kundohari , a mirror, four arrows, tekatha or a triangular frame of wood, horitoki flowers (myrobalan), chandmala (garland with circular decorations), aashon (a mattress of jute or hay).

Other Items : Water camphor and perfumed sandal wood paste. soil—extracted from elephant tusks, from the teeth of the pig, from the horns of the ox, from the bank of rivers Ganga and Saraswati, from both the banks of a river, from a place where four roads intersect, from palaces, from the ant hill, from the mountains, Vishnu toilo.

During Durga puja or Durga Puja (commonly called in West Bengal), the idols of Goddess Durga are worshipped for nine days in beautifully decorated 'pandaals'. It is a public festival. On the tenth day, the 'Visarjan' or immersion of idols in sea waters is performed. During this time, in various parts of India, the 'Ram-Leela' is performed. Ram-Leela is a stage inaction of Ramayana, the story of Lord Rama. Durga puja has come to be associated with a grand exhibition of cultural functions.

In towns and villages, the evenings are replete with jatra, theatre, song, music, dance programmes, sports, physical and cultural competitions etc which everyone is free to attend. Community feasts are held. The immersion ceremony (vijaya), provides an impressive finale.

Navratri is a festival of worship, dance and music celebrated over a period of nine nights. Devotees perform the 'devi-sthaapna' in their homes wherein they invite the Goddess and perform 'pooja-path' for nine days. Gujaratis perform their traditional dances 'Garba' & 'Dandiya-Raas' during Navratri. The women-folk dance in a circle, singing 'Garbas' or traditional songs.

'Dandiya-Raas' is played with wooden sticks or 'dandiyas'. Apart from Gujrat, Garbas are performed in other states & cities like Mumbai. Young men-women wear colourful traditional dresses and play Garba with great enthusiasm.The mood of Navratri is very colourful & unique.

The annual mela or festival takes place in the Kullu Valley—also known as the Valley of the Living Gods, in North India. The festival celebrates the triumph of the God Ram over evil. The Rath Yatra of the idol of Lord Ragunath is led by the Kullu Raja and village deities, and is known as the running of the Gods. The procession starts a week of religious ceremonies, cultural activities, socializing and shopping at the huge bazaar, or market, that comprises most of the mela ground.

In Kullu, Dussehra commences on the tenth day of the rising moon, i.e. on 'Vijay Dashmi' day itself and continues in seven days. The birth of Dussehra in Kullu lay in royal fads and it nourished on religious, social and economic factors and ultimately came to be well established, because of the inborn love of the hill-men for fun, frolic, displayed in community singing and dancing. Numerous stalls offer a verity of local wares. This is also the time when the International Folk Festival is celebrated.

In Mysore, Dussehra is easily the most popular festival. It is celebrated on a grandiose scale here. Elephants are decked up with robes and jewelery and taken in processions through the streets of the city. In fact, many people visit Mysore from all over the country to watch this colorful event. There is also a floating festival in the temple tank at the foot of Chamundi Hill and a procession of chariots around the temple at the top. The Dussehra of Mysore is a 10-day long festival. On the day of Dussehra, a procession of caparisoned elephants carrying the idol of goddess Chamundi is taken through the city. The festival is celebrated in a grand style with scores of cultural performances in the great Durbar Hall of the Maharaja's Palace. On Vijaydashami, the 10th day of the festival, a colorful procession featuring caparisoned elephants winding through the gaily-decorated streets of the city, mark the occasion.

Bommai Kolu is traditionally a women's festival that Tamilians celebrate during Dasshera. Every year, a series of steps is set up and kolu bommai or dolls are displayed. These dolls typically depict gods or village scenes and weddings. A kolu can be as simple or as elaborate as one likes. The woman of the house invites other women to come inspect the kolu, eat a few snacks, exchange a little gossip and go home with a couple of small goodies.

During this time, the girls and women make rounds from house to house during those nine days of Navrathri. Sundal is a delicious confection made from bean sprouts and coconut that is traditionally served at kolu. Women set up decorated planks in a corner and place on it all the dolls in the house. This beautiful clay figurines of gods and goddesses are worshipped during Navaratri, viewing art as Divinity. Women traditionally exchange gifts of coconuts, clothes and sweets. The ninth day is also the day of the Ayudha Puja. After the slaying of Mahisasura and other demons by Chamundeswari, there was no more use for her weapons. So the weapons were kept aside and worshipped. This Ayudha puja is being celebrated since ancient times. The importance of Ayudha Puja on this occasion may also be due to the fact that on the Vijayadasami day, Arjuna took back his weapons which he had hidden in a Vani tree in order to lead a life in disguise for the promised period of exile. It is believed that one who begins or renovates his learning to work on the Vijayadasami day will secure a grand success as Arjuna did in Kurukshetra war.

The Ayudha Puja is a worship of whatever implements one may use in one's livelihood. On the preceding evening, it is traditional to place these implements on an altar to the Divine. If one can make a conscious effort to see the divine in the tools and objects one uses each day, it will help one to see one's work as an offering to God. It will also help one to maintain constant remembrance of the divine. In India it is customary for one to prostrate before the tools one will use before starting one's work each day; this is an expression of gratitude to God for helping one to fulfil one's duties.

The tenth day or Vijayadasami is also the day of Vidyaramba or beginning of study when children usually begin to learn the alphabets. On the Vijayadasami day after a Puja in the morning, the Books and implements are removed from the room and this ceremony is called 'Puja Eduppu'. The time for the break up of the puja marks the beginning of learning and work.

The Goddess Saraswathi is worshipped as the Goddess of Learning, the deity of Gayathri, the fountain of fine arts and science, and the symbol of supreme vedantic knowledge.

On the Durgashtami day, a ceremony called Poojavaipu is performed in the evening in Kerala. In a village, generally, it is done only in certain households, in temples and also sometimes in the village schools. The Brahmin houses and the houses which enjoy reputation for learning, mainly take the lead in celebrating the festival. The members of other houses in the village attend the ceremony performed in these houses or institutions. In a well-decorated room, books and grandhas (holy books) are tastefully arranged with a picture or an image of Goddess Saraswathi in front. In certain poaches weapons and implements are kept by the side of books and garandhas. Then a Puja is performed to Saraswathi during which fruits, beaten rice, roasted paddy (malar), jaggery etc, are offered to Her. These offerings are distributed among those present when the Puja is over.

Just before the Pujavaipu, all studies and work which mainly require skill, are suspended. The following day is known as Mahanavami and it is totally devoted to the worship of Saraswathi. Pooja is performed both in the morning and in the evening. Many more items such as rice, payasam, thirali, etc are also offered to Devi.

The ten-day Saraswati festival, also known as Dussehra or Navaratri, is held September-October. It's celebrated throughout India but takes on special significance in Kerala. Young children are taken to the temples and, before an image of a goddess-celebrated in Kerala as Saraswati, the goddess of wisdom and learning—they are introduced to the letters of the alphabet.

In ancient times kings used the feast of Dasara to cross the frontier and fight against their neighboring kingdoms. This border crossing is known as "Simollanghan". Thus Dasara also marks the beginning of the war season.

This was also the day to worship the weapons. According to legend, Pandav went to dwell in the forest. On the way he hid his weapons in the hole of a "shami" tree. After one year he returned from the forest and on Dussehra day he took again his weapons and worshipped the shami tree and the weapons. Hence the custom of worshipping weapons on this feast.

People decorate the entrances of their homes with torans, flower studded strings, and worship the tools of trade, vehicles, machinery, weapons and even books. As the evening falls, the villagers cross the border, and worship the Shami tree. The leaves of the Apta tree are collected and exchanged among friends and relatives as gold.

Durga's mode of journey to the earth is detailed in scriptures. The modes, an elephant, a horse, palanquin, boat all signify luck or omen which influence the life on earth.Goddess Durga visits the earth for only four days but seven days prior to puja starts the Mahalaya. From this day starts 'Devipaksha' when people pray for their demised relatives and take holy dip in the Ganges. This ritual is known as 'Tarpan'. Puja Rule according to Bengali calender. Days are counted based on sunrise and sunset while 'Tithi' depends on the rising and setting of the moon. Sandhi Puja is performed counting 'Tithi'. Sasthi, Saptami, Nabami and Dashami pujas are performed after sunrise even if they fall in the previous evenings.This year the goddess arrives on a boat and departs on an elephant. Goddess Durga's arrival on a boat signifies good harvest, growth and prosperity while her departure on an elephant indicates greenery and prosperity through out the year. Dates : Festivities commence on the first night in the month of Ashwin (September / October). Nine nights are spent in worship and the tenth day is devoted to goddess Durga, who occupies a special position in the Hindu pantheon of gods and goddesses.

The Goddess is worshipped as a kumari or young girl, and reveals herself in her true form Mahasaptami (the seventh day of the moon). On Mahastami (eighth day) and Mahanavami (ninth day) the celebrations reach a fever pitch. On Dashami (tenth day) the idol of Durga is immersed in water. The ten-armed goddess dazzles the devotees with her splendour and appearance of fiery valour during her short stay every year. In the older days of zamindars (landed aristocracy) there used to be a Barwari pooja financed by the local zamindar who usually had a huge Nat Mandir or Mandap (out-hall) for pooja purposes, where the entire village congregated. All found employment of some kind—from the Brahmins performing the rites to various artisans of lower castes. Even women had their share of work in the preparations. The time of immersion is a sad occasion and the Devi is repeatedly requested to return to shower bliss on devotees whenever invoked.

Rituals: Durga pooja is celebrated extensively in North India where beautiful idols of the Mother Goddess are worshipped in elaborate pandals for nine days, and on the tenth day, these are carried out in procession for visarjan (immersion) in a river or pond. The face of the goddess remains covered until the bodhon (unveiling) ritual is performed on Sasthi—the sixth day of the moon.

The Goddess is worshipped as a kumari or young girl, and reveals herself in her true form Mahasaptami (the seventh day of the moon). On Mahastami (eighth day) and Mahanavami (ninth day) the celebrations reach a fever pitch. On Dashami (tenth day) the idol of Durga is immersed in water. The ten-armed goddess dazzles the devotees with her splendour and appearance of fiery valour during her short stay every year.

It is the time of the Durga Puja, celebrating the ten-armed goddess of fertility and the third embodiment of the Devi, Durga. It was Durga who vanquished the buffalo-demon Mahishasura. The festivities start with the first day called Mahalaya. It is also the day of the beginning of the countdown to the Durga Puja, which is celebrated in most households apart from the gaily-decorated puja mandaps that are erected in almost every locality. It is a common belief that Ma Lakshmi brings peace and prosperity to the households that celebrate the puja.

Goddess Durga is called by various names on each day of the Navaratri festival:

Day 1: Shaila Putri

Day 2: Brahmacharini

Day 3: Chandraghanta

Day 4: Kooshmanda

Day 5: Scandamaata

Day 6: Kaatyayini

Day 7: Kaalaraatri

Day 8: Mahagowri

Day 9: Siddhidaatri

She is worshipped on all the days with special pooja. The fifth day, Lalithapanchami is considered a very auspicious day. On this day, Sharada pooja is done, where everyone worships his or her books and anything connected to learning. On Durgashtami, Durga Havana is performed, and on Mahanavami, Ayudha Pooja is performed. On this day, people worship their respective tools of work, and their vehicles too.

It is believed that if Goddess Durga is worshipped during Navaratri with devotion and dedication, the devotee will be bestowed with Her blessings, which will bring about prosperity in all that he/she does.

The various kinds of Poojas conducted during Navaratri are:

- Sharada Pooja
- Pustaka Pooja
- Lalitapanchami Vrata

- Durga Pooja
- Durgadeeta Namaskara
- Chandika Parayana
- Navadurga Poojane
- Durga Havana
- Chandika Havana
- Laxminarayana Hradaya Parayana
- Kumkumarchane
- Ayudha Pooja
- Yantra Vaahana Pooja.

In Kerala, Durga Puja signifies the beginning of formal education for every child aged 3-5 years. While puja goes on in the temple for all ten days, it is only the concluding three days which are really important. Ashtami is the day of Ayudya Puja, when all the tools at home are worshiped. Custom dictates that no tools be used on this day. On navami, day, Goddess Saraswati is honored by worshiping the books and records at home.Thousands throng the Saraswati temple at Kottayam during this period to take a dip in the mysterious holy pond whose source is yet unknown. Large gatherings are also seen at the famous temples at Thekkegram (Palghat), in which there are no idols— only huge mirrors. A devotee finds himself bowing before his own reflection which indicates that God is within us.

Hindus are a minority in Jammu and Kashmir but they celebrate their festivals with pomp and show. These days, festivities are subdued, though. The favorite deities of Kashmir are Lord Shiva and Serawali Ma Durga, the one who rides the tiger. Pundits and Muslims alike vouch that Navratri is important. No big pandals here, each Hindi house-hold does the pooja at home. All the adult members of the household fast on water. In the evenings, fruit may be taken. As elsewhere, Kashmiris grow barley in earthen pots. They believe that if the growth in this pot is good, there is prosperity all year. The most important ritual for Kashmiri Pandits is to visit the temple of guardian goddess Kheer Bhawani on all nine days. On the last day of Navratri, an aarti is held at the temple after which people break their fast. On Dussehra day, Ravana's effigy is burnt.

Durga Pooja has some fond memories related to childhood. Initial ones are those of my native place. Later, we were not so frequent in visiting the village during Durga Pooja and it had not remained that interesting either. But at one point of time, it was almost a custom in our family that almost everyone would gather in our village during this time. Needless to say the place looked really cheerful then. Even the married daughters of the families would not stay at their in-laws place during Durga Pooja. They will come there with their children and stay here, most of the times accompanied by their husbands too all along. And it was not the case with just our family, but almost all the families in the locality. The Pooja of our village was quite famous in the villages nearby.

7

Diwali

> Count your assets. If you have a clear conscience, a good liver, three good friends and a happy home; if your heart has kept its youth and your soul its honesty—cheer up!—you are still one of life's richest millionaires.

Diwali (also known as Deepawali) is a prominent Hindu festival. Known as the "Festival of Lights," it symbolises the victory of good over evil, and lamps are lit as a sign of celebration and hope for mankind. Celebrations focus on lights and lamps, particularly traditional *diyas*. Fireworks are associated with the festival in some regions of the country.

Deepawali is celebrated for five consecutive days in the Hindu month of Ashwina. It usually occurs in October/November, and is one of the most popular and eagerly awaited festivals of India. Hindus, Jains and Sikhs alike regard it as a celebration of life and use the occasion to strengthen family and social relationships. For Jains it is one of the most important festivals, and beginning of the Jain year. It is also a significant festival for the Sikh faith.

The date of Diwali is based on the Hindu calendar, which has solar sidereal years and lunar months. Although the festival is worshipped on exactly the same set of days across India, it falls in different months depending on the version of the Hindu calendar being used in the given region. The

Amanta ("ending on the no-moon") version of the Hindu Calendar has been adopted as the Indian national calendar. According to this calendar, which is prevalent in southern India and Maharashtra, Deepawali falls in the middle of the month of Ashwayuja. According to the *Purnimanta* ("ending on the full-moon") version prevalent in northern India, the 5-day celebration is spread over the last three days of the month of Ashwayuja and the first two days of the new month of Kartika. According to this calendar, the festival of Deepawali marks the new year's day of this calendar and is therefore an especially significant festival. Diwali is also known as festival of lights.

The festival marks the victory of good over evil. The Sanskrit word Deepawali means array of lights that stands for victory of brightness over darkness. As the knowledge of Sanskrit diminished, the name was popularly modified to Diwali, especially in northern India. On the day of Diwali, many wear new clothes, share sweets and light firecrackers. The North Indian business community usually starts their financial new year on Diwali and new account books are opened on this day.

Diwali is celebrated over five days in most of North India. All the days except Diwali are named using the designation in the Indian calendar. A lunar half-month is 15 days. Diwali as a new-moon day, marks the last day of a 15-day period. Diwali has emerged as one of the most famous Hindu festivals. An integral part of Diwali decorations, Rangoli is a colorful pattern drawn on the floor.

Sikhs also celebrate Diwali to commemorate the laying of the foundation stone for the Golden Temple in 1577. It is also known as Bandi Chhorh Divas. The Mughal emperor Jehangir arrested the Sikh Guru Hargobind and imprisoned him in Gwalior. Later Jehangir relented and released the Guru. The Guru asked that 52 rulers imprisoned with him should also be released. To the joy of the Sikhs the Guru returned to Amritsar on Diwali and it prompted the followers to celebrate the day with joy and happiness.

On Diwali the Sikhs illuminate their Gurdwaras and homesare with Deewé (earthen oil lamps) or candles. Early in the morning, Sikh pilgrims take a dip in the sacred tank while reciting Japji Sahib, and then pray at the Golden Temple. Circumambulation of the tank is done.

According to Jain tradition the chief disciple of Mahavira, Ganadhar Gautam Swami also attained complete knowledge on this very day, thus making Diwali a really special occasion for the Jains to celebrate. Diwali is first mentioned in Jain books as the date of the nirvana of Lord Mahavira. The oldest use of the word "Diwali/Dipavali" occurs in Harivamsha-Purana written by Acharya Jinasena, composed in Shaka Samvat 705. The sample of text containing the word Diwali is below:

The way Jains celebrate Diwali is different in many respects. There is a note of asceticism in whatever the Jains do, and the celebration of Diwali is not an exception. The Jains celebrate Diwali during the month of Kartik for three days. During this period, among the Shvetambaras, devoted Jains observe fasting and chant the Uttaradhyayan Sutra, which contain the final pravachans of Lord Mahavira, and meditate upon him. The Jain year starts with Pratipada following Diwali. Vira Nirvana Samvat 2532 starts with Diwali 2005. The Jain businessmen traditionally started their accounting year from Diwali.

Diwali is celebrated in various parts of the world, in countries such as Britain, The Netherlands, Suriname, Canada, Guyana, Mauritius, Fiji, Japan, Indonesia, Malaysia, Myanmar, Nepal, Singapore, Sri Lanka, South Africa, Trinidad and Tobago, Thailand, United Arab Emirates, Australia, much of Africa, and the United States. With more and more Indians now migrating to various parts of the world, the number of countries where Diwali is celebrated has been gradually increasing. While in some countries it is celebrated mainly by Indian expatriates, in others it has become part of the general local culture. In most of these countries Diwali is celebrated on the same lines as described in this article with some minor variations. Some important variations are worth mentioning. In Malaysia, Diwali is known as "Hari Deepawali," and is celebrated during the seventh month of the Hindu solar calendar. It is a federal public holiday. In many respects it resembles the traditions followed in the Indian subcontinent.

In Nepal, Diwali is known as *Tihar* and celebrated during the October/November period. Here, though the festival is celebrated for five days, the traditions vary from those followed in India. On the first day, cows are given offerings, in appreciation of the food they have given and agricultural work they have performed. On the second day, dogs and all living animals are revered and offered special food. On the third day, celebrations follow the same pattern as in India, with lights and lamps and much social activity. On the fourth day Yama, the Lord of Death, is worshipped and appeased. On the fifth and final day, brothers and sisters meet and exchange pleasantries.

Diwali is celebrated in the Caribbean Islands as well. Especially in Trinidad and Tobago, Diwali is marked as a special occasion and celebrated with much fanfare.

Diwali is an annual stimulus for the Indian economy. Indians purchase gold, gifts, decorations, crackers and household appliances during this festival. Companies offer huge discounts during the Diwali season to attract customers, which helps the economy and also helps the poor. It also helps the community in hunger since this festival shares it food. It also brings tourists to the country.

Deepawali Celebration

The *First day* is called *Dhanteras* or *Dhantrayodashi* which falls on the thirteenth day of the month of Ashwin. The word "Dhan" means wealth. As such this day of the five-day Diwali festival has a great importance for the rich mercantile community of Western India. Houses and Business premises are renovated and decorated. Entrances are made colourful with lovely traditional motifs of Rangoli designs to welcome the Goddess of wealth and prosperity. To indicate her long-awaited arrival, small footprints are drawn with rice flour and vermilion powder all over the houses. Lamps are kept burning all through the nights. Believing this day to be auspicious women purchase some gold or silver or at least one or two new utensils. "Lakshmi-Puja" is performed in the evenings when tiny diyas of clay are lighted to drive away the shadows of evil spirits. "Bhajans"-devotional songs-in praise of Goddess Laxmi are sung and "Naivedya" of traditional sweets is offered to the Goddess. There is a peculiar custom in Maharashtra to lightly pound dry coriander seeds with jaggery and offer as Naivedya.

In villages cattles are adorned and worshipped by farmers as they form the main source of their income. In south cows are offered special veneration as they are supposed to be the incarnation of Goddess Lakshmi and therefore they are adorned and worshipped on this day.

A very interesting story about this day is of the sixteen year old son of King Hima. As per his horoscope he was doomed to die by a snake-bite on the fourth day of his marriage. On that particular fourth day of his marriage his young wife did not allow him to sleep. She laid all the ornaments and lots of gold and silver coins in a big heap at the entrance of her husband's boudoir and lighted innumerable lamps all over the place. And she went on telling stories and singing songs. When Yam, the god of Death arrived there in the guise of a Serpent his eyes got blinded by that dazzle of those brilliant lights and he could not enter the Prince's chamber. So he climbed on top of the heap of the ornaments and coins and sat there whole night listening to the melodious songs. In the morning he quietly went away.

Thus the young wife saved her husband from the clutches of death. Since then this day of Dhanteras came to be known as the day of *Yamadeepdaan* and lamps are kept burning throughout the night in reverential adoration to Yam, the god of Death.

The *Second day* is called *Narka-Chaturdashi* or *Choti Diwali* which falls on the fourteenth day of the month of Ashwin. The story goes that the demon king Narakasur ruler of Pragjyotishpur after defeating Lord Indra had snatched away the magnificent earrings of Aditi, the Mother Goddess and imprisoned sixteen thousand daughters of the gods and saints in his harem. On the day previous to Narakachaturdashi, Lord Krishna killed the demon and liberated the imprisoned damsels and also recovered those precious earrings of Aditi. As a symbol of that victory Lord Krishna smeared his forehead with the demon king's blood. Krishna returned home in the very early morning of the Narakachaturdashi day. The womenfolk massaged scented oil to his body and gave him a good bath to wash away the filth from his body. Since then the custom of taking bath before sunrise on this day has become a traditional practice specially in Maharashtra. In South India that victory of the divine over the mundane is celebrated in a very peculiar way. People wake up before sunrise prepare blood by mixing Kumkum in oil and after breaking a bitter fruit that represents the head of the demon King that was smashed by Krishna, apply that mixture on their foreheads. Then they have an oil bath using sandalwood paste.

In Maharashtra also, traditional early baths with oil and "Ubtan" (paste) of gram flour and fragrant powders are a must. All through the ritual of baths, deafening sounds of crackers and fireworks are there in order that the children enjoy bathing. Afterwards steamed vermiceli with milk and sugar or puffed rice with curd is served. Another legend is about King Bali of the nether world mighty power had become a threat to the gods. In order to curb his powers Lord Vishnu in the guise of a Batu Waman- a small boy- visited him and begged him to give him only that much land which he could cover with his three steps. Known for his philanthropy King Bali proudly granted him his wish. That very moment that small boy transformed himself into the all-powerful Lord Vishnu. With his first step Lord Vishnu covered the entire heaven and with the second step the earth and asked Bali where to keep his third step. Bali offered his head. Putting his foot on his head Vishnu pushed him down to the underworld. At the same time for his generosity Lord Vishnu gave him the lamp of knowledge and allowed him to return to earth once a year to light millions of lamps to dispel the darkness and ignorance and spread the radiance of love and wisdom.

Diwali is a five day Hindu festival which occurs on the fifteenth day of Kartika. Diwali means "rows of lighted lamps" and the celebration is often referred to as the Festival of Lights. During this time, homes are thoroughly cleaned and windows are opened to welcome Laksmi, goddess of wealth. Candles and lamps are lit as a greeting to Laksmi. Gifts are exchanged and festive meals are prepared during Diwali. The celebration means as much to Hindus as Christmas does to Christians.

The *Third day* of the festival of Diwali is the most important day of *Lakshmi-Puja* which is entirely devoted to the propitiation of Goddess Lakshmi. This day is also known by the name of *Chopada-Puja.* On this very day sun enters his second course and passes Libra which is represented by the balance or scale. Hence, this design of Libra is believed to have suggested the balancing of account books and their closing. Despite the fact that this day falls on an amavasya day it is regarded as the most auspicious.

The day of Lakshmi-Puja falls on the dark night of Amavasya. The strains of joyous sounds of bells and drums float from the temples as man is invoking Goddess Lakshmi in a wondrous holy "pouring-in" of his heart. All of a sudden that impenetrable darkness is pierced by innumerable rays of light for just a moment and the next moment a blaze of light descends down to earth from heaven as golden-footed Deep-Lakshmi alights on earth in all her celestial glory amidst chantings of Vedic hymns. A living luminance of Universal Motherhood envelopes the entire world in that blessed moment of fulfillment of a long-awaited dream of the mortal. A sublime light of knowledge dawns upon humanity and devotion of man finally conquers ignorance. This self enlightenment is expressed through the twinkling lamps that illuminate the palaces of the wealthy as well as the lowly abodes of the poor. It is believed that on this day Lakshmi walks through the green fields and loiters through the bye-lanes and showers her blessings on man for plenty and prosperity. When the sun sets in the evening and ceremonial worship is finished all the home-made sweets are offered to the goddess as *Naivedya* and distributed as *Prasad*. Feasts are arranged and gifts are exchanged on this day gaily dressed men, women and children go to temples and fairs, visit friends and relatives. Everything is gay, gold and glitter!

The *Fourth day* is *Padwa* or *Varshpratipada* which marks the coronation of King Vikramaditya and Vikaram-Samvat was started from this Padwa day.

Govardhan-Puja is also performed in the North on this day. As per *Vishnu-Purana* the people of Gokul used to celebrate a festival in honour of Lord Indira and worshipped him after the end of every monsoon season but one particular year the young Krishna stopped them from offering prayers to Lord Indra who in terrific anger sent a deluge to submerge Gokul. But Krishna saved his Gokul by lifting up the Govardhan mountain and holding it over the people as an umbrella.

Govardhan is a small hillock in Braj, near Mathura and on this day of Diwali people of Punjab, Haryana, Uttar Pradesh and Bihar build cowdung, hillocks, decorate them with flowers and then worship them.

This day is also observed as Annakoot meaning mountain of food. In temples specially in Mathura and Nathadwara, the deities are given milkbath, dressed in shining attires with ornaments of dazzling diamonds, pearls, rubies and other precious stones. After the prayers and traditional worship innumerable varieties of delicious sweets are ceremoniously raised in the form of a mountain before the deities as "Bhog" and then the devotees approach the Mountain of Food and take Prasad from it. Goddess Lakshmi is worshipped in every Hindu household and her blessings sought for success and happiness. This day is looked upon as the most auspicious day to start any new venture.

In many Hindu homes it is a custom for the wife to put the red tilak on the forehead of her husband, garland him and do his "Aarathi" with a prayer for his long life. In appreciation of all the tender care that the wife showers on him, the husband gives her a costly gift. This Gudi Padwa is symbolic of love and devotion between the wife and husband. On this day newly-married daughters with their husbands are invited for special meals and given presents.

The *Fifth and final day* of Diwali Festival is known by the name of *Bhayya-Duj* in the Hindi-speaking belt *Bhav-Bij* in the Marathi-speaking communities and in Nepal by the name of "*Bhai-Taka*". As the legend goes Yamraj, the God of Death visited his sister Yami on this particular day. She put the auspicious tilak on his forehead, garlanded him and led him with special dishes and both of them together ate the sweets, talked and enjoyed themselves to their heart's content, while parting Yamraj gave her a special gift as a token of his love and in return Yami also gave him a lovely gift which she had made with her own hands. That day Yamraj announced that anyone who receives tilak from his sister will never be thrown. That is why this day of Bhayyaduj is also known by the name of *Yama-Dwitiya* Since then this day is being observed as a symbol of love between sisters and brothers. It became also imperative for the brother to go to his sister's house to celebrate Bhayyaduj.

Diwali on the whole has always been the festival with more social than religious connotations. It is a personal, people-oriented festival when enmities are forgotten, families and friends meet, enjoy and establish a word of closeness. As a festival of light and beauty it encourages artistic expressions through home-decorations stage-plays, elocution competitions singing and dancing programmes, making gift items and making delectable sweets thereby discovering new talents of younger people. As a result innumerable communities with varying cultures and customs mingle together to make Diwali celebrations a very happy occasion for all.

8

Ganesh Chaturthi

> A man of a right spirit is not a man of narrow and private views, but is greatly interested and concerned for the good of the community to which he belongs, and particularly of the city or village in which he resides, and for the true welfare of the society of which he is a member.
>
> —*Jonathan Edwards*

Ganesh Chaturthi is one of the most popular of Hindu festivals. This is celebrated as the birthday of Lord Ganesha. It is the day most sacred to Lord Ganesha. It falls on the 4th day of the bright fortnight of Bhadrapada (August-September). It is observed throughout India, as well as by devoted Hindus in all parts of the world. Clay figures of the Deity are made and after being worshipped for two days, or in some cases ten days, they are immersed into water.

Lord Ganesha is the elephant-headed God. He is worshipped first in any prayers. His Names are repeated first before any auspicious work is begun, before any kind of worship is begun. He is the Lord of power and wisdom. He is the eldest son of Lord Shiva and the elder brother of Skanda or Kartikeya. He is the energy of Lord Shiva and so He is called the son of Shankar and Umadevi. By worshipping Lord Ganesha mothers hope to earn for their sons the sterling virtues of Ganesha.

Legend goes thus:— Once upon a time, the Goddess Gauri (consort of Lord Shiva), while bathing, created Ganesha as a pure white being out of the mud of Her Body and placed Him at the entrance of the house. She told Him not to allow anyone to enter while she went inside for a bath. Lord Shiva Himself was returning home quite thirsty and was stopped by Ganesha at the gate. Shiva became angry and cut off Ganesha's head as He thought Ganesha was an outsider.

When Gauri came to know of this she was sorely grieved. To console her grief, Shiva ordered His servants to cut off and bring to Him the head of any creature that might be sleeping with its head facing north. The servants went on their mission and found only an elephant in that position. The sacrifice was thus made and the elephant's head was brought before Shiva. The Lord then joined the elephant's head onto the body of Ganesha.

Lord Shiva made His son worthy of worship at the beginning of all undertakings, marriages, expeditions, studies, etc. He ordained that the annual worship of Ganesha should take place on the 4th day of the bright half of Bhadrapada.

Without the Grace of Sri Ganesha and His help nothing whatsoever can be achieved. No action can be undertaken without His support, Grace or blessing.

In his first lesson in the alphabet a Maharashtrian child is initiated into the Mantra of Lord Ganesha, *Om Sri Ganeshaya Namah.* Only then is the alphabet taught.

His Mantra is *Om Gung Ganapathaye Namah.* Spiritual aspirants who worship Ganesha as their tutelary Deity repeat this Mantra or *Om Sri Ganeshaya Namah.*

The devotees of Ganesha also do Japa of the Ganesha Gayatri Mantra. This is as follows.

Tat purushaaya vidmahe
Vakratundaaya dheemahi
Tanno dhanti prachodayaat.

Lord Ganesha is an embodiment of wisdom and bliss. He is the Lord of Brahmacharins. He is foremost amongst the celibates.

He has as his vehicle a small mouse. He is the presiding Deity of the Muladhara Chakra, the psychic centre in the body in which the Kundalini Shakti resides. He is the Lord who removes all obstacles on the path of the spiritual aspirant, and bestows upon him worldly as well as spiritual success. Hence He is called Vighna Vinayaka. His Bija Akshara (root syllable) is *Gung,* pronounced to rhyme with the English word "sung". He is the Lord of harmony and peace.

Lord Ganesha represents Om or the Pranava, which is the chief Mantra among the Hindus. Nothing can be done without uttering it. This explains the practice of invoking Ganesha before beginning any rite or undertaking any project. His two feet represent the power of knowledge and the power of action. The elephant head is significant in that it is the only figure in nature that has the form of the symbol for *Om*. The significance of riding on a mouse is the complete conquest over egoism. The holding of the *ankusha* represents His rulership of the world. It is the emblem of divine Royalty.

Riding on a mouse, one of nature's smallest creatures and having the head of an elephant, the biggest of all animals, denotes that Ganesha is the creator of all creatures. Elephants are very wise animals; this indicates that Lord Ganesha is an embodiment of wisdom. It also denotes the process of evolution—the mouse gradually evolves into an elephant and finally becomes a man. This is why Ganesha has a human body, an elephant's head and a mouse as His vehicle. This is the symbolic philosophy of His form.

He is the Lord of Ganas or groups, for instance groups of elements, groups of senses, etc. He is the head of the followers of Shiva or the celestial servants of Lord Shiva.

The Vaishnavas also worship Lord Ganesha. They have given Him the name of Tumbikkai Alwar which means the divinity with the proboscis (the elephant's trunk).

Lord Ganesha's two powers are the Kundalini and the Vallabha or power of love. He is very fond of sweet pudding or balls of rice flour with a sweet core. On one of His birthdays He was going around house to house accepting the offerings of sweet puddings. Having eaten a good number of these, He set out moving on His mouse at night. Suddenly the mouse stumbled—it had seen a snake and became frightened—with the result that Ganesha fell down. His stomach burst open and all the sweet puddings came out. But Ganesha stuffed them back into His stomach and, catching hold of the snake, tied it around His belly.

Seeing all this, the moon in the sky had a hearty laugh. This unseemly behaviour of the moon annoyed Him immensely and so he pulled out one of His tusks and hurled it against the moon, and cursed that no one should look at the moon on the Ganesh Chaturthi day. If anyone does, he will surely earn a bad name, censure or ill-repute. However, if by mistake someone does happen to look at the moon on this day, then the only way he can be freed from the curse is by repeating or listening to the story of how Lord Krishna cleared His character regarding the Syamantaka jewel. This story is quoted in the *Srimad Bhagavatam.*

Ganesha and His brother Lord Subramanya once had a dispute as to who was the elder of the two. The matter was referred to Lord Shiva for final decision. Shiva decided that whoever would make a tour of the whole world and come back first to the starting point had the right to be the elder. Subramanya flew off at once on his vehicle, the peacock, to make a circuit of the world. But the wise Ganesha went, in loving worshipfulness, around His divine parents and asked for the prize of His victory.

Lord Shiva said, "Beloved and wise Ganesha! But how can I give you the prize; you did not go around the world?"

Ganesha replied, "No, but I have gone around my parents. My parents represent the entire manifested universe!"

Thus the dispute was settled in favour of Lord Ganesha, who was thereafter acknowledged as the elder of the two brothers. Mother Parvati also gave Him a fruit as a prize for this victory.

On the Ganesh Chaturthi day, meditate on the stories connected with Lord Ganesha early in the morning, during the Brahmamuhurta period. Then, after taking a bath, go to the temple and do the prayers of Lord Ganesha. Offer Him some coconut and sweet pudding. Pray with faith and devotion that He may remove all the obstacles that you experience on the spiritual path. Worship Him at home, too. You can get the assistance of a pundit. Have an image of Lord Ganesha in your house. Feel His Presence in it.

Don't forget not to look at the moon on that day; remember that it behaved unbecomingly towards the Lord. This really means avoid the company of all those who have no faith in God, and who deride God, your Guru and religion, from this very day.

Take fresh spiritual resolves and pray to Lord Ganesha for inner spiritual strength to attain success in all your undertakings.

May the blessings of Sri Ganesha be upon you all! May He remove all the obstacles that stand in your spiritual path! May He bestow on you all material prosperity as well as liberation!

Ganesha — the elephant-deity riding a mouse — has become one of the commonest mnemonics for anything associated with Hinduism. This not only suggests the importance of Ganesha, but also shows how popular and pervasive this deity is in the minds of the masses.

From then onwards, this festive occasion has grown in acceptance and today, commands the respect of millions of citizens all over Maharashtra. Lokmanya Bal Gangadhar Tilak brought Ganesha as a deity out on the streets. It was a unique move by this freedom fighter, which he achieved with the Ganpati visarjana or immersion procession, wherein the mass output of several Ganesh mandals is taken out on a parade on the final day of the Ganesh festival and taken to be immersed. This process was started in 1892 and is now prevalent virtually all over Maharashtra, with special emphasis on Bombay and Pune. Lokmanya Tilak attached this mass celebration to increase national awareness about the Freedom movement. Herein, neighbourhood Ganeshas are worshipped and brought to immersion sites, where huge crowds gather to bid him an emotional and frenzied farewell.

In Pune, as the sun sets over darkening rivers, the images are taken out in boats and as each one is immersed, a cry is raised asking him to return the next year. It is an emotional and public farewell to their beloved god as parthiva (of the earth), who like the Phoenix, will rise once again the following year. A special puja is performed for Ganesha. The worship of the deity involves getting a corner ready to receive the god. Ganesha is invited with a special phrase and with material and verbal offerings, the puja begins. It involves the Panchamrit (five nectars), which includes milk, curd, ghee, honey and jaggery, with which the god's icon is bathed, cleansing in between with water.

Ganesha is then given a red garment and the sacred thread—saying it is silver. He is then smeared with red sandal paste and offered red or yellow flowers. A lamp is lit, bells chime and food is offered in six symbolic mouthfuls—not to the god's body, but to his five panchapranas or 'vital breaths' and the one beyond—the absolute.

During the festival, puja is performed twice every day—once in the morning and again in the evening. Ganesha is offered special leaves and flowers, 21 of each and white durva grass. The idol is formally installed on the first day and given life in the presence of Brahma, Vishnu and Shiva, and the Vedas. Touching the idol with blades of durva grass, he is brought to life step by step and made to go through 15 of the 16 rites of passage that each Hindu goes through in his lifetime. (The sixteenth one, which is for death, is omitted.)

The Ganesha mantra is chanted, followed by a Ganesha prayer. The last puja done, the family or congregation gathers around and rice grains are placed on the head of the idol, which is moved, symbolically unseating him. As a matter of interest there are about 91 different figures of Ganesha according to research done by several scholars. The details of their make up may vary from figure to figure, but with no change in the main set-up. It is the enigma of certain striking variations in details that the sublime in the figures of Ganesha has to be sought for.

Environmentalists too have questioned the dumping of the idols made increasingly with chemicals which pollute the lakes and seas. On September 2004, the Chennai High Court imposed a temporary ban on such immersions. Every year there are at least a couple of casualties associated with accidents (while dumping the idols) or clashes associated with this.

On the day of the festival, it is placed on raised platforms in homes or in elaborately decorated outdoor tents for people to view and pay their homage. The priest, usually clad in red silk dhoti and shawl, then invokes life into the idol amidst the chanting of mantras. This ritual is the pranapratishhtha. After this the shhodashopachara (16 ways of paying tribute) follows. Coconut, jaggery, 21 modakas (rice flour preparation), 21 durva (trefoil) blades and red flowers are offered. The idol is anointed with red unguent (rakta chandan).

According to Swami Sivananda on the Ganesh Chaturthi day, meditate on the stories connected with Lord Ganesha early in the morning, during the Brahmamuhurta period. Then, after taking a bath, go to the temple and do the prayers of Lord Ganesha. Offer Him some coconut and sweet pudding. Pray with faith and devotion that He may remove all the obstacles that you experience on the spiritual path. Worship Him at home, too. You can get the assistance of a pundit. Have an image of Lord Ganesha in your house. Feel His Presence in it.

Don't forget not to look at the moon on that day; remember that it behaved unbecomingly towards the Lord. This really means avoid the company of all those who have no faith in God, and who deride God, your Guru and religion, from this very day.

Take fresh spiritual resolves and pray to Lord Ganesha for inner spiritual strength to attain success in all your undertakings.

May the blessings of Sri Ganesha be upon you all! May He remove all the obstacles that stand in your spiritual path! May He bestow on you all material prosperity as well as liberation!

The festival ends with the ceremony of immersion of the idols in the sea or rivers and wells. This ceremony which is called Ganesha-Visarjan which means immersion of Ganesha is as popular as the festival proper. During the immersion ceremony huge crowds move in a procession carrying idols of Ganesha towards the places of immersion. These processions which take place with great fanfare, begins in the afternoon and continue till the late hours of the night.

Ganesh Chaturthi is celebrated as the birthday of Lord Ganesh on the fourth day (Chaturthi) of the bright fortnight of Bhadrapada month of Hindu calendar. It is among the most celebrated of the festivals in India, and perhaps the only one involving general public (others only involve families and friends and are celebrated privately).

It is interesting to note that the festival was not celebrated until the times of Lokamanya Bal Gangadhar Tilak, who used it a great means to unite Hindus all over India and educate them the evils of colonization.

The festivities include fund-raising, building all kinds of innovative forms Ganesh idols, organizing public performances of music and dance, cooking grand feasts and making a lot of noise. The festivities end when the idol of the year is immersed in water (*visarjan*), accompanied by loud shouts of *Ganapati Bappa Moraya*!

Names of Ganesha

Ekadant (one-toothed)

- To scribe the Mahabharat Katha Ganeshji removed one of his tusks to carve a quill from it. He then scribed the epic on palm leaves as the sage Ved Vyas recited it. The scribing took three years!
- In south India there is a belief that when ploughing first began on earth, it was Lord Ganeshji who first ploughed using one of his tusks.
- In the Uttar Ramayan, Brahmand Puran and Padma Puran there is a reference of a battle between Ganeshji and Parshuram. During the duel, the latter's axe fractured one of Ganeshji's tusks According to the Brahmand Puran, it was his left tusk.

There are other names related to his body and virtues. A few commonly known are listed below:

- Lambodar—from the long—'lambo', tummy—'udar'.
- Gajkarna—from the large elephant 'Gaja' ears—'karna.'
- Kapil—from his ruddy complexion.
- Vikat—heavy-bodied.
- Bhalchandra—having a Chandra (moon) on his forehead—'bhal.'

— Dwaimatur—one who has 'dwi'—two, 'mata'—mother; Parvati—who gave birth to him and Malini—a demoness who nurtured him.
— Vakratund—one who breaks the ego of he who behaves anti-socially ('Vakra').
— Mudgal—In south India, a special 'Mudgal Puran' extols Ganapati's glory. It cites 32 names, while 'Shardatilak' lists 51 names.
— Vigneshwar—One who removes mayic obstacles—'vignas'

9

Guru Govind Singh Jayanti

Guru Govind Singh was the tenth and the final Guru in the holy tradition initiated by that great saint Guru Nanak. Devji Maharaj, who was the propounder of Sikh religion. Richly had Guru Govind Singh inherited the legacy of the fearless martyrdom of his father—Guru Tegh Bahadur. Guru Tegh Bahadur, with a view to instilling courage and confidence among the Kashmiri Hindus to withstand Aurangzeb's fanatical tyranny and threats to Islamize them, challenged the Moghal emperor to convert him first. And the great Guru preferred to have his head roll down in Chandni Chowk of Delhi rather than sacrifice his faith, Govind Singh was just a boy of nine years at that time. On coming to know of his father's terrible end he exclaimed: "He saved with his blood the honor of Hindu Dharma. Oh, what a remarkable act in this Kaliyuga! He preferred to give up his life, but not his faith!"

Guru Gobind Singh (1666-1708 A.D.) lived during an extremely dangerous time. His father, Guru Tegh Bahadur, had sacrificed his life to protect the freedom of worship by Hindus, who were being threatened with conversion or death by zealous Muslim rulers. Abduction of women and pillage of goods were rampant, but the people were too timid and terrorized to resist. In the midst of this political situation, Guru Gobind Singh gained great stature as both Saint and soldier a leader of firm spiritual principles and intense devotion to God, and at the same time, fearless dedication to protecting all people from oppression and injustice through the practice of Kshatradharma. In 1699, He dramatically initiated five men from the lower castes as His Five Beloveds (Panj Piaras), blessing them with great courage as well as nearness to God. They became models for the Khalsa (the Order of the Pure), which Guru Gobind Singh created to stand on the frontline against injustice. The Khalsa were held to a very strict moral and spiritual discipline and under Guru Gobind Singh's courageous inspiration, helped turn the tide against Mughal oppression in India. In addition to his spiritual and military leadership, Guru Gobind Singh was a gifted intellectual and had many poets in his court. He was inspired to write many powerful spiritual compositions that infused a martial spirit in the people.This included the Jaap Sahib, but He did not include them in the Sikh scripture, the *Guru Granth Sahib*. His writings have instead been collected in a separate volume, called the Dasam Granth. Upon His passing away, He instructed his Sikhs to regard the *Guru Granth Sahib* as their teacher. 'Granth' literally means 'volume' (especially, a Holy volume). 'Sahib' is a term of reverence used for anything sacred. The *Guru Granth Sahib* is the perpetual guru of the Sikhs today. The prasad of Ugadi/Gudi Padwa is the bitter leaves of the neem tree with jaggery. There are special foods prepared for this festival. In the southern states, puligore-a sour tamarind rice dish, bobbatlu, holige-sweet stuffed bread and Ugadi Pachadi made of jagerry, raw mango pieces, neem flowers and tamarind is prepared. In Maharastra, shrikhand, a fragrant yogurt dessert, with poori—a fried puffy bread is prepared.

The celebration is generally similar for all Gurpurabs; only the hymns are different. The birthday celebration usually lasts three days. Generally two days before the birthday, *Akhand Path* (a forty-eight-hour non-stop reading of the *Guru Granth Sahib* is held in the Gurdwaras.

The day prior to the birthday, a procession is organised which is led by the *Panj Pyaras* (Five Beloved Ones). They head the procession carrying the Sikh flag, known as the *Nishan Sahib* and the *Palki* (Palanquin) of Siri Guru Granth Sahib. They are followed by teams of singers singing hymns, brass bands playing different tunes, 'Gatka' teams (Martial Arts) display their swordmanship, and devotees sing the chorus. The procession pours into the streets of the town which are covered with buntings and decorated gates for this special occasion. The leaders also spread the message of Guru Nanak.

10

Guruparab

Guruparab is not a single festival or occasion. These are holy days and are associated with anniversaries of the many of the Sikh Guru's birth or death, martyrdom day and anniversary of the installation of the *Adi Granth Sahib*. People from Sikh religion celebrate Guruparabs. Some Guruparabs are local events celebrated only where the original event took place. Some are celebrated universally.

Some of the important Gurpurab's are the birth anniversaries of Guru Nanak, the founder of Sikhism (Oct.-Nov.) and of Guru Gobind Singh, the last Guru (Dec.-Jan.).

Celebrations are done by reading of the holy verses in the *Guru Granth Sahib* and by holding processions where the 'Guru Granth Sahib' is carried in procession through the town. The holy book is placed on a van strewn with flowers and has a troop of five armed guards around it.

Teachings of Guru Nanak: He was not only the founder of the Sikh religion, he was a great poet, philosopher, humanist and a powerful social reformer, a teacher of mankind. Nanak said that one need not become a sanyasi sacrificing one's family, to please God. Those who practice devotion, whose mind is pure and who have sympathy, patience and honesty, are in no way inferior to a sanyasi. He considered that all human beings were highborn; no one was low.He stressed, "Do not ask someone's caste; those whose devotion is accepted by God are good people. God appreciates those who have conquered the 'I' and 'greed'. Nanak washes the feet of those who concentrate their minds on God, the source of truth".

Celebrations: The akhand path or the continuous reading of Granth Saheb, the sacred book of the Sikhs, begins three days before Guru Nanak Jayanti. The sacred scripture is read non-stop from beginning to end. The Akhand Path culminates on the day of the Guru Purab and the holy book is then taken out in a procession. It is beautifully decorated with flowers and carried on a float. Children participate in the procession and march to the tune of local band playing religious hymns. Five armed guards who are called the panj pyare lead the procession. At the head of the procession is the Nishan Saheb or the Sikh flag.

A few days before Guru Parab, people take out Prabhat Pheris or the early morning processions from the Gurdwaras. They go around their locality singing shabd or the religious hymns. Later in the day, special kirtans are arranged in the Gurdwaras. The devotees attend langar or the common meals where everyone eats the same food irrespective of caste, class, or creed. Devotees offer their services for cooking food, cleaning the Gurdwara or carrying out other chores. This is called the Kar Seva.

In the evening, the Gurdwaras are illuminated and people visit them in large numbers. People also illuminate their homes with candles and earthen lamps.

11

Holi

"Holi" is the festival of colours, merry-making and gaity. The festival of Holi is celebrated on the day after the full moon in early March every year. Originally a festival to celebrate good harvests and fertility of the land, Holi is now a symbolic commemoration of a legend from Hindu Mythology.

The *Holi Festival* is known as the "Festival of Color" and is a celebration of Lord Krishna and God's Creations. The colorful festival of *Holi*, literally means 'burning', is celebrated on the full moon day in the month of Phalguna and heralds the onset of spring season. *Holi* is the time when people from all castes and social strata come together forgetting all past differences and grievances.

Originally the festival was primarily for the Shudras who were otherwise not allowed to participate in festivals. This is specially significant in the rural areas where in many places, there still exists a clear demarcation between each caste and community.

In ancient India too, this festival was celebrated as a day when people forgot caste and gender differences and were allowed many liberties, otherwise forbidden. In fact Holi bears close resemblance to the important ancient festival called Vasantotsava.

The story centres around an arrogant king who resents his son Prahlada worshipping Lord Vishnu, and attempts to kill his son but fails each time. Finally, the king's sister Holika who is said to be immune to fire, sits with the boy in a huge fire. However, the prince Prahlada emerges unscathed, while his aunt burns to death. Holi commemorates this event from mythology, and huge bonfires are burnt on the eve of Holi as its symbolic representation.

Again, this festival is also associated with the immortal love of Lord Krishna and Radha, and hence, Holi is spread over 16 days in Vrindavan as well as Mathura—the two cities with which Lord Krishna shared a deep affiliation. Apart from the usual fun with coloured powder and water, Holi is marked by vibrant processions which are accompanied by folk songs, dances and a general sense of abandoned vitality.

The festival's preamble begins on the night of the full moon (i.e. Purnima). Bonfires are lit on street corners to cleanse the air of evil spirits and bad vibes, and to symbolize the destruction of the wicked Holika, for whom the festival was named. The following morning, the streets fill with people running, shouting, giggling and splashing. Ganja-based bhang and thandai add to the uninhibited atmosphere. Promptly at noon, the craziness comes to an end and everyone heads to either the river or the bathtub, then inside to relax the day away and partake of candies. In the afternoon an exhausted and contented silence falls over India. Although Holi is observed all over the north, it's celebrated with special joy and zest at Mathura, Vrindavan, Nandgaon, and Barsnar. These towns once housed the divine Krishna.

Each area celebrates Holi differently; the Bhil tribesmen of western Madhya Pradesh, who've retained many of their pre-Hindu customs, celebrate Holi in a unique way. In rural Maharashtra, where the festival is known as *Rangapanchami* it is celebrated with dancing and singing. In the towns of

Rajasthan — especially Jaisalmer — the music's great, and clouds of pink, green, and turquoise powder fill the air. The grounds of Jaisalmer's Mandir Palace are turned into chaos, with dances, folk songs, and colored-powder confusion.

Holi or Holika, also called holikotsava, is an extremely popular festival observed throughout India. It is especially marked by unmixed gaiety and frolics and is common to all sections of the people. This festival is very ancient. Known originally as *'Holika'* it has been mentioned in very early religious works such as Jaimini's *Purvamimamsa-sutras* and *Kathaka-grihya-sutras*. It must have therefore existed several centuries before Christ. It was at first actually a special rite performed by married women for the happiness and well-being of their families and the full moon (Raka) was the deity worshipped by them.

According to the stories in the Puranas and various local legends, this day is important for three reasons.

- It was on this day that Lord Siva opened his third eye and reduced Kamadeva (the god of love, Cupid or Eros) to ashes.
- It was on this day that Holika, the sister of the demon king Hiranyakasyapu, who tried to kill the child devotee Prahlad by taking him on her lap and sitting on a pyre of wood which was set ablaze. Holika was burnt to ashes while Prahlad remained unscathed!
- It was again on this day that an ogress called Dhundhi, who was troubling the children in the kingdom of Prithu (or Raghu) was made to run away for life, by the shouts and pranks of the mischievous boys. Though she had secured several boons that made her almost invincible, this—noise, shouts, abuses and pranks of boys—was a chink in her armour due to a curse of Lord Siva. The day itself came to be called 'Adada' or 'Holika' since then.

Practically, there are no religious observances for this day like fasting or worship. Generally a log of wood will be kept in a prominent public place on the Vasantapanchami day (Magha Sukla Panchami), almost 40 days before the Holi Festival. An image of Holika with child Prahlada in her lap is also kept on the log. Holika's image is made of combustible materials whereas Prahlada's image is made of non-combustible ones. People go on throwing twigs of trees and any combustible material they can spare, on to that log which gradually grows into a sizable heap. On the night of Phalguna Purnima, it is set alight in a simple ceremony with the Raksoghna Mantras of the *Rigveda* (4.4.1-15; 10.87.1-25 and so on) being sometimes chanted to ward off all evil spirits. The next morning the ashes from the bonfire are collected as prasad (consecrated material) and smeared on the limbs of the body. Singed coconuts, if any are also collected and eaten.

In some houses the image of Kamadeva is kept in the yard and a simple worship is offered. A mixture of mango blossoms and sandalwood paste is partaken as the prasad.

As elsewhere in India, Instead of the gay and frenzied celebrations, Bengal observes this festival in a quiet and dignified manner as Dolapurnima or Dolayatra (the festival of the swing). The festival, said to have been initiated by the king Indradyumna in Vrindavana, is spread over 3 or 5 days, starting from the Sukla Chaturdasi of Phalguna. A celebration in honour of Agni and worship of Govinda in image on a swing are the important features. The fire kindled on the first day is to be preserved till the last day. The swing is to be rocked 21 times at the end of the festival.

The day is also celebrated as the birthday of Sri Krishna Chaitanya (A.D. 1486-1533), mostly in Bengal, as also in Puri (Orissa), Mathura and Vrindavan (in Uttar Pradesh).

Holi or *Phagwah* (Bhojpuri), is an annual and popular Hindu spring festival. It takes place over two days in the latter part of March or early April. On the first day, a bonfire is lit at night to signify burning Holika. On the second day, known as *Dhulandi*, people go around until afternoon throwing coloured powder and water at each other, although the powder stings the eyes. A special drink called 'thandai' or bhang is also consumed sometimes, which actually contains small amounts of ganja (*Cannabis sativa*). People invite each other to their houses for feasts and celebrations later in the evening. *Rangapanchami* occurs a few days later on a Panchami (fifth day of the full moon), marking the end of festivities involving colours.

This festival occurs at the onset of spring. This period, during which the weather changes, is prone to cause viral fever and cold. Thus, the playful throwing of the coloured powders has a medicinal significance as the coloured powders are made of Neem, Kumkum, Haldi, Bilva, and other medicinal herbs prescribed by Âyurvedic doctors. Amongst India's innumerable festivals, Holi ranks as the most colourful. It celebrates the arrival of spring and death of demoness Holika, it is a celebration of joy and hope. Holi provides a refreshing respite from the mundane norms as people from all walks of life enjoy themselves. In a tight knit community, it also provided a good excuse for letting off some steam and settling old scores, without causing physical injury.

Twin towns of Nandagaon (where Lord Krishna grew up) and Barsana (where Shri Radha grew up), near Mathura, are the epicentre of the celebrations. Lord Krishna, while growing up in Vraj, popularised the festival with his ingenious pranks. Gopies of Vraj responded with equal enthusiasm and the festivities have continued ever since. Role reversal, feminism etc. are accepted customs for the duration of the festival! Men and women of Vraj clash in a colourful display of battle of the sexes. Celebrations start a week earlier than rest of India. Men of Nandagaon raid Barsana with hopes of raising their flag over Shri Radhikaji's temple. They receive a thunderous welcome as the women of Barsana greet them with long wooden sticks. The men are soundly beaten as they attempt to rush through town to reach the relative safety of Shri Radhikaji's temple. Men are well padded as they are not allowed to retaliate. In this mock battle the men try their best not to be captured. Unlucky captives can be forcefully lead away, thrashed and dressed in female attire before being made to dance.

The next day, men of Barsana reciprocate by invading Nandagaon. Clouds of pink and white powder mark the frenzy of activity taking place in it's narrow streets. A naturally occurring orange-red dye, Kesudo, is used to drench all participants. Today, the women of Nandagaon beat the invaders from Barsana. It is a colourful site.

The next day, the temples in Vrindavan celebrate the festival with great guesto. The renowned temple of Bakai-Bihari, the beloved lord of the 15th century saint Haridas, is at the centre of the festivities. Clouds of pink and white descend upon the pilgrims, as the Lord of Vrindavan plays Holi with all his beloved visitors. The festival moves on to other parts of Vraj. Soon enough, it is Dhulati and entire India celebrates the joys of spring as the "festival of colour".

Gulal-Kund in Vraj is a beautiful little lake, set in a delightful groves near the Goverdhan mountain, in the Mathura district. Here the festival is commemorated on a more regular basis. Pilgrims who visit the holy land of Vraj, can see the reenactments of Holi throughout the year at this lake. Local boys, acting in the Krishna-Lila drama troupes reenact the scenes of holi for the pilgrims.

Royal courts all over North India refined the festival in to an art form of its own. Rajput warriors of the Rajasthani courts used to show off their equestrian skills during the festival. Rajput men would ride their steeds through the white and pink clouds of colour, throwing colour powders on each other. Even the members of the royal families were not immune from being drenched by colour. The entire court would be drenched in saffron water and an orange-red dye of the "kasuda" flowers. Pushti-Marga temples, spread throughout North and Western States of India, celebrate the festival in a way reminiscent of rajput courts. The Deity, and the laity, are liberally sprinkled with perfumes, saffron water, kesudo, and covered in sandalwood aswell as the white and pink powder, abil and gulal. Joyous celebration is accompanied by classical music, poetry and folk songs appropriate for the occasion. Deity's white clothes' are soon transformed into a mass of colour as gold and silver syringes spray colourful water on all participants.

The celebrations officially usher in the pleasant season of love, spring. In the Pushti-Marga temples, the festivities last for almost a month. Beginning on the day of Vasant-Panchami, the festivals last till the day after Holi. This helps prolong the season of joy.

As the lust was won over by the Eternal Bliss of Lord Shiva the Kamadahana or Holi festival is celebrated as an event associating with the Bliss of God. The Holi bonfire is in commemoration of this event. The ash of kama's body settled over the Lord Shiva. So following kamadahana during Holi, people put the powders on themselves and others remembering this victory over lust. To this day, people offer sandalwood paste to Kamadeva to relieve from his stinging burns and mango blossoms that he loved on Holi.

The celebration of Holi is very ancient in its origin. And by its very origin, it celebrates an ultimate triumph of the 'good' over the 'evil'. While, a feast of colors associated with the Holi, is the face of this celebration, the original reason of celebrating Holi, lies in its soul. And this gives us the 'why' of this ancient festival.

Thabal Chongba, a popular Manipuri folk dance, is associated with this festival. The literal meaning of Thabal is 'moonlight' and Chongba means 'dance', thus 'dancing in the moonlight'. Traditionally conservative Manipuri parents did not allow their daughters to go out and meet any young men without their consent. Thabal Chongba therefore provided the only chance for girls to meet and talk to the boys. In earlier times, this dance was performed in the moonlight accompanied by folk songs. The only musical instrument used was a dholakor drum. It is performed in every locality on all the six days of the festival. Instead of a fire, a hut is built and then set ablaze. The next day, boys go in groups to play gulal with the girls. And in return for playing with them, the girls extract money from the boys.

Another significant feature of the festival in Manipur is the groups of devotees from different areas who gather at the Shree Govindaji Temple in Imphal. Dressed in the traditional white and yellow turbans, they sing songs in praise of Krishna and Chaitanya Mahaprabhu, play gulal and dance in front of the temple. On Halangkar, the last day of the festival, hundreds of devotees gather at the temple as usual and march together towards the Vijay Govindaji Temple about three kms. west of Imphal where various cultural activities are performed. This brings to an end the Yaosang festival.

12

Id

Muslims constitute a substantial segment of India's population. Besides this Muslims dominated the polity and governance of the country during medieval period. As such Indian culture is highly influenced by Islamic culture. Id is the major festival of Muslims. Here, we have been giving description of Iid.

I

ID-UL-FITR (RAMZAN ID)

Coming with the new moon, this festival marks the end of Ramzan (Ramdan), the ninth month of the Hizriyear. It was during this month that the holy Koran was revealed. Muslims keep a fast every day during this month and on the completion of the period, which is decided by the appearance of the new moon, Id-ul-Fitr is celebrated with great eclat. Prayers are offered in mosques and *Idgahs* and elaborate festivities are held.

II

ID-I-MILAD (BARAH-WAFAT)

The Prophet was born on the twelfth day of *Rabi-ul-Awwal*, the third month of the Muslim year. His death anniversary also falls on the same day, the word '*barah*' standing for the twelve days of the Prophet's sickness. During these days, sermons are delivered in mosques by learned men, focusing on the life and noble deeds of the Prophet. In some parts of the country, a ceremony known as *sandal* rite is performed over the symbolic footprints of the Prophet engraved in stone. A representation of '*buraq*', a horse on which the Prophet is believed to have ascended to heaven, is kept near the footprints and anointed with sandal paste or scented powder, and the house and casket containing these are elaborately decorated. Elegies or '*marsiyas*' are sung in memory of the last days of the Prophet. The 12th day or the *Urs* proper is observed quietly, in prayers and alms giving

III

ID-UL-ZUHA

Id-ul-Zuha also called Bakrid, Id-ul-Zuha, is a festival of great rejoice. Special prayers and exchange of greetings and gifts marked the Id-ul-Zuha (Bakrid), the festival of sacrifice, celebrated with traditional fervour and gaiety in India. Id-ul-Zuha is a reminder of Prophet Ibrahim's readiness to sacrifice his son for God's sake. It also marks the completion of Haj (pilgrimage to Mecca). On this day, special 'Dua' is recited by thousands of muslims for peace and prosperity.

It is a commemoration of Hazrat Ibrahim's great test of obedience to Allah, who ordered him to sacrifice the person dearest to him. Ibrahim decided to sacrifice his son Ismail, at Mina, near Mecca. As the great religious leader was on the point of applying the sword to the throat of his dear son, it was revealed to him that the exercise was merely a test of his faith in Allah, and that he could sacrifice a ram instead. On Bakrid, the Muslims go to the mosques in the morning to offer prayers to Allah. and then sacrifice the animal at home. Bakr means 'sheep', and on Bakrid, the affluent sacrifice one animal per member of the family, and distribute two-thirds of the meat among the poor. A full-grown camel, cow, goat or sheep, free from any disease, is sacrificed. Bakrid is also a day for feasting and visiting friends to say Id Mubarak.

It is one of the grandest Muslim festivals, and is also known as *Bakrid*. It fails on the 10th day of the Muslim month Zil-Hijja. There is an interesting story about the celebration. Once Hazrat Ibrahim was ordered by Allah in a dream to sacrifice his dearest thing. To Ibrahim his son was the dearest, So, he decided to sacrifice his son on the altar of Allah. He sought the permission of the members of the family and blindfolded himself so that at the time of sacrifice his love for the son may not deter him from the act. He struck with his sword, but when he removed the fold from his eyes, to his great pleasure and surprise, he found that he had sacrificed a ram instead of his son. Since, then a ram, or goat or a camel is sacrificed and distributed among the neighbours and relatives.

In fact, the sacrifice of a ram or goat also symbolizes that man's position in the creation is far more high than any beast, and any sacrifice, however great, is a small thing for the sake of religion and Allah. The sacrificial ram or goat is reared with great care and is kept quite healthy and fat And the man who does the sacrifice must. be a man of a character and deeply religious.

This Muslim festival of sacrifice, Id-ul-Zuha (Arabic) or Bakrid in India is celebrated all over the country. On this day Muslims sacrifice a goat or Bakr (Urdu) to commemorate the sacrifice of Prophet Ibrahim, who willingly agreed to kill his son at the behest of God. According to Islamic belief, to test Ibrahim's faith, Allah commanded him to sacrifice his son Ismail. He agreed to do it but found his paternal feelings hard to suppress. So he blind—folded himself before putting Ismail on the altar at the mount of Mina near Mecca. When he removed his bandage after performing the act, he saw his son standing in front of him, alive. On the altar lay a slaughtered lamb. This festival coincides with the Haj pilgrimage in Mecca.

Prayers are offered in the mosques and the sacrificial meat is then distributed after the Id prayers. Special delicacies are prepared and served among family and friends on the occasion. Legend has it that Allah commanded Hazrat Ibrahim (Abraham) to sacrifice his son Ismail on Mount Mina near Mecca. Ibrahim, unable to see himself kill his son, blindfolded himself and carried out the pronouncement of God. When he took off the blindfold, a lamb lay slaughtered on the altar and his son stood there unharmed.

Ibrahim understood then that this willingness on Ibrahim's part to give up his only son was what God sought, and not the sacrifice of human flesh and blood. The legend ascertains that all God requires of man is a surrender of his will and self. Like Ibrahim, who willingly surrenders his beloved son to God, a true follower of Islam is expected to sacrifice something that is dear to him.

The animal sacrifices made during Bakr-Id are mainly to provide food to the poor and to commemorate the noble act of Ibrahim. This spirit of sacrifice is what truly underlines the spirit of Bakr-Id. Incidentally, the day also coincides with the day when the holy Quran was declared complete. Bakr-Id is celebrated from the tenth to the twelfth day in the Islamic month of Dhul Hijjah. Every year, while pilgrims to the Mount of Mina make animal sacrifices as part of the pilgrimage rituals, Muslims the world over celebrate Bakr-Id in a similar fashion.

Every true Muslim who possesses wealth equal to or more than 400 grams of gold or is capable of affording two square meals a day, is expected to sacrifice an animal. A goat, sheep, camel or any other four-legged animal is slaughtered during one of the three days of the festival, and the meat is distributed. The sacrificial offering is divided in three parts—one for the self, another for friends, and the third, most importantly, for the needy. The sacrifice can be offered at any time before the afternoon of the third day.

Festivities mark the first day, when people wear new clothes, offer prayers at the mosque, and greet friends and relatives. Special prayers are offered on all three days. It is said that the celebrations are carried on over three days to ensure that the entire Muslim community partakes in the noble of act of giving and sharing.

Bakr-Id is celebrated all over India with much fervour, as it is in the rest of Islamic world. The name Bakr-Id, however, is most popular in India. In Arabic, the feast is usually referred to as Id-ul-Azha or Id-ul-Zuha.

Besides Hinduism, India is also the home of innumerable other faiths and the religious and cultural diversity of this nation is manifested in the large number of non-Hindu festivals.

The tombs of many Sufi saints attract devotees of all religious persuasions, especially during the urs or death anniversaries. The best known urs are centred at tombs in towns like Ajmer, Delhi, Manakpur, Nagore and Dongri.

The Id-ul-Azha commemorates the ordeal of Hazrat Ibrahim, who had been put to a terrible test by God when he was asked to sacrifice whatever was dearest to him and he decided to sacrifice the life of his son. As he was on the point of applying the sword to his son's throat, it was revealed to him that this was meant only to test his faith, and it was enough, if instead he sacrifices only a ram in the name of Allah. This is celebrated on the tenth day of *Zilhijja,* when the *Haj* celebrations at Mecca are rounded off by the sacrifice of goats or camels. In India, too, goats and sheep are sacrificed all over the country and prayers (Namaz) are offered.

13

Karwa Chauth

> It is the mark of a superior man that, left to himself, he is able endlessly to amuse, interest and entertain himself out of his personal stock of meditations, ideas, criticisms, memories, philosophy, humor, and what not.
>
> —*George Jean Nathan*

Karwa Chauth is considered one of the most important fasts observed by the married Hindu women. On this day the women pray for the welfare and long life of their husbands. The festival is followed mainly in the northern parts of the country. Married women eat food early in the morning, before sunrise. They are not supposed to eat or even drink water during the day. In the evening the ladies listen to the Karwa Chauth Katha (the legend). The fast is over after the moonrise.

Karva Chauth originated as a social and seasonal festival, but somewhere down the line the festival deviated from its original form. The word Karva Chauth, is composed of Karva—meaning a clay pot—and Chauth (from char meaning four) corresponding to the fourth day after the Full Moon in Kartik month (of Hindu calendar) following the Autumnal Equinox.

This time of the year is just after the harvest of Kharif (monsoon) crops and people are usually in a festive mood.

They like to remember and meet their relatives and friends, and exchange gifts with them. Diwali is a similar seasonal festival—in addition to having religious significance—that is nine days after Karva Chauth. The idea behind Karwa Chauth is very sweet and noble. In olden days girls were married at a very early age and used to go and live with their in-laws in other (often very remote) villages. Everyone would be a stranger there for the new bride. If she had any problems with her husband or in-laws, she would have no one to talk to or seek support from. Modes of communication/ transport were not very developed and hence it was not easy for her to approach her parents and relatives.

Thus the custom started that, at the time of marriage, when bride would reach her in-laws, she would befriend another woman (of similar age) there who would be her friend (kangan-saheli) or sister (dharam-behn) for life. It would be like god-friends or god-sisters. Their friendship would be sanctified through a small Hindu ceremony right during the marriage. Once the bride and this woman had become god-friends or god-sisters, they would remain so throughout their lives.. They would also treat each other like real sisters. During any difficulty later in life, involving even the husband or in-laws, these women would be able to confidently talk or seek help from each other.

Thus Karva Chauth started as a festival to celebrate this friendship (relationship) between the once-brides and their god-friends (god-sisters). Praying and fasting for the sake of husband came later and is secondary. It was probably added, along with other mythical tales, to enhance the festival. In any case, husband would always be associated with this festival, because the day on which this holy friendship between two god-sisters started was essentially the day of bride's marriage to him. Thus praying and fasting for husband by his wife during a celebration of her relationship with the god-friend would be quite logical.

The pooja preparations start a day in advance. Married women buy the shringar or the traditional adornments and the other pooja items like the karwa, matthi, heena etc. Early in the morning they prepare food and have it before sunrise. The morning passes by in other festive activities like decorating hand and feet with heena, decorating the pooja thali and meeting friends and relatives.

In the late afternoon women gather at a common place like temple or a garden or someones' place who has arranged the pooja. An elderly lady or the pujarin narrates the legend of Karwa Chouth.

The essentials of this gathering and listening of the Karwa chauth story, a special mud pot, that is considered a symbol of lord Ganesha, a metal urn filled with water, flowers, idols of Ambika Gaur Mata, Goddess Parwati and some fruits, mathi and foodgrains. A part of this is offered to the deities and the storyteller.

Earlier an idol of Gaur Mata was made using earth and cowdung. Now just an idol of Goddess Parwati is kept. Every one lights an earthen lamp in their thalis while listening to the Karwa story. Sindoor (vermillion), incense sticks and rice are also kept in the thali.

At this time the women wear heavy saris or chunries in red , pink or other bridal colors, and adorn themselves with all other symbols of a married women like, nose pin, tika, bindi, chonp, bangles, earrings etc.

Once the moon rises, the women see its reflection in a thali filled with water, or through a dupatta or a sieve. They offer water to the moon and seek blessings. They pray for the safety, prosperity and long life of their husbands. This marks the end of the day long fast.

Karwa Chauth falls about nine days before Diwali. It is the most important fast observed by Hindu women of North India. On this day married Hindu women offer prayers seeking the welfare, prosperity, and a long life of their husbands.The fast is very difficult to observe as it starts before sunrise and ends only after offering prayers and worshipping the moon, which usually rises at about 8.45 p.m. No food or water is to be taken after 4 a.m. or after sunrise. The fast is broken once the moon is sighted and special rituals and prayers marking the day have been offered.

In the evening women dress up in special clothes, usually red or pink coloured and apply *bindis* on their foreheads. New brides wear their bridal outfits and others wear outfits woven with gold. Bangles and other jewellery are worn and special henna patterns are applied on the hands. The fasting women in a neighbourhood usually gather in a group and narrate mythological stories illustrating the importance of fasting on Karwa Chauth. After the moon rises, the women try to spot its reflection in water. Then they pray for their husband's safety and long life, and finally break their fast.

'Karwa Chauth' is a ritual of fasting observed by married Hindu women seeking the longevity, well-being and prosperity of their husbands. It is popular amongst married women in the northern and western parts of India, especially, Haryana, Punjab, Rajasthan, Uttar Pradesh and Gujarat.

The term 'Chauth' means the 'fourth day' and 'Karwa' is an earthen pot with a spout—a symbol of peace and prosperity—that is necessary for the rituals. Hence the name 'Karwa Chauth'.

The fast of Karwa Chawth truly sets the merry tone of the fun and frolic, festivity and feasting that come in good measure during Diwali — the biggest festival of the Hindus.

In India, a marriage is considered to be a bond of a lifetime. This marital bond is considered very sacred. Karwa Chauth festival falls about nine days before diwali on the Kartik ki Chauth some time in October or November. It is the most important fast observed by the women of North

India. A woman keeps such a fast for the well-being of her husband, who becomes her protector after she leaves her parents home. Her husband provides her with food, shelter, clothing, respectability, comfort and happiness.

It is said that in a village, seven brothers and one sister was staying with their parents (moneylender). The sister was youngest among them. That's why everybody adored her.

When she was 10 or 12 years of age they married her. After marriage on first karwa chauth, she came to her mother's house. Her mother-in-law affectionately sent sargai for her. She put mehndi on her hands along with her mother and bhabhis (brother's wife) and did sargai in the morning before sunrise and kept nirjal fast (without taking water). By the evening the brothers got worried that how can their small sister live without food and water till night. They consulted among themselves and decided that we will create artificial moon for our sister.

Two brothers went to the forest and burnt cowdung coal. The other two brothers went home and said let's go sister the moon has risen. All her bhabhis (brother's wife's) kept quite. Sister said "let's go Bhabhi the moon has risen, lets worship the moon and offer ark (water is offered to the moon) to it. All the Bhabhi said "So early only your moon could have risen, You go."

She was not only young but also simple hearted, she really thought everyone's moon rises separately.

She hurriedly took the pooja material to the terrace. There in the forest one brother was standing with a sieve in front of the cowdung coalfire, so from distance she thought that the moon is rising from behind bushes.

She offered her worship and ark to the moon .As soon as she started eating Puya's, she received a message from her in laws that her husband has become seriously ill suddenly.

On hearing this, the Girl's father and brothers along with her rushed to her in law's house. There her husband was seriously ill. Every body was worried.

Vaidyas (Doctors) were called but nobody could understand the illness. Then the family enquired from priests and Astrologers. They told them that this has happened because the girl has eaten puya's, after seeing the artificial moon. Now the only solution is that till the next year karwa chauth, the girl take good care of her husband, then keep fast on Karwa Chauth and exchange karwa with Gaur Maata and make her say "le suhaagan karwa le","de suhagaan karwa de". Then her husband will be well and will live long. On hearing this, the girl decided to take good care of her husband for one year.

Next year Karwa chauth arrived, her mother sent sargai for her. As per the tradition, she did sargai and kept fast. Her mother also sent material for baya, karwa and money.

In the evening, all married ladies dressed up wore chunari, making preparation for the pooja, she waited to exchange karwa with Gaur Maata.

When the first Gaur Maata arrived. The girl held her feet and pleaded her:

" O'Gaur Maata, Please exchange karwa with me."

After lot of pleading Gaur Maata sat with her and said

"Sister of seven brothers karwa le",

"Jo bhukhi naa reh sake (who can't stay hungry) karwa le",

"Jo payasi naa reh sake (who can't stay thirsty) karwa le",

"Jo Chalni meh chaand dakhe (One who see moon in sieve) karwa le."

She begged her again and again to say "Le Suhaagan

Karwa Le" Gaur Maata said, "I won't say this. My other sisters will come, you make them say." And after saying this, she went away.

After some time 2nd Gaur Maata came and she also went away saying what the earlier one had said. In this way they came one by one when the ninth Gaur Maara came, the girl was worried. When she begged her again and again and held her feet, then Gaur Maata said," when my youngest sister will come, you ask her , I will not say. My sister is scary looking but good at heart, don't let her go, make her say it." After some time 10th Gaur maata came. She had dark complexion, had big teeth, horrible face and was wearing lot of jewelry. When she heard the small girl pleadings, she sat down with her to exchange karwa and like other Gaur Maata's said

"Sister of seven brothers karwa le",

"Jo bhukhi naa reh sake (who can't stay hungry) karwa le",

"Jo payasi naa reh sake (who can't stay thirsty) karwa le",

"Jo Chalni meh chaand dakhe (One who see moon in sieve) karwa le."

The girl fell on her feet and said "O' Mother please forgive my mistakes, Please say "Le suhaagan karwa le". If you will say this , my husband will live. I will always worship you. Please bless me.

On girls repeated pleading, Gaur Maata felt pity for her and said-Let it be so and said "Le suhaagan karwa le" and the girl said "de suhaagan karwa de". Then, the same thing was repeated by both of them in reverse order. When they said this ten times Girls husband was well again. Everybody touched Gaur Maata's feet".

The story of Karva is well known. Her husband was

caught by a crocodile. Karva bound the crocodile with a cotton yarn. She then asked Yama to send the crocodile to hell. Yama refused. Karva threatened to curse Yama. Yama, afraid of being cursed by Pativrat wife, sent the crocodile to hell. Karva and her husband enjoyed many years of wedded bliss. The fact that Yama was afraid of being cursed by a devoted wife showed the power a good faithful woman. There is great festivity on this day. Early in the morning, before sunrise, the women bathe, wear new clothes and eat a meal of select grains and fruit. For the rest of the day, they abstain from food and even water, though the more strict rules of observance are not always kept.

They pray to Shiva and Parvati, hoping that their own married lives will be as successful as that of the divine couple. In every neighbourhood, women gather together in the afternoon to perform a puja and to recite the story of 'Karva Chauth'. Most women are dressed in beautiful red or pink clothes and traditional jewelry. Moonrise is eagerly awaited. Once the moon is sighted, women gather on the terrace and pray for their husband and family's welfare, an elderly woman in the house narrates the story of Karva Chauth, and all the fasting women end their fast with a sip of water. It is a day of celebration, decoration and exchanging the Karwa Chauth gifts. On this occasion, the woman keeping the fast receives lots of gifts from all family members and friends. Traditional karwa chauth gift include that of 'sargi' given by Mother-in-laws that consists of various types of sweetmeats, and sometime clothes and 'Baya' given by parents of their son-in-law. This Baya contains few Mathris, Almonds, and some gifts. This is one Indian festival, which has great significance and also brings the family together.

This is indeed a very tough fast to observe as it starts before sunrise and ends after worshipping the moon, which usually rises at about 8.45 p.m. No food or water is to be taken after 4 a.m. or after sunrise. Nowadays, this fast is kept even in modern educated homes, becoming a symbol of the attachment that a woman has for her husband.

A sari (in the baya) is a must for the first Karva Chauth of a girl. One thing to be taken care of is that the baya reaches the girl's in-laws home, where the girl has gone during the course of the day, before the evening. The baya is given to the mother-in-law after the manasna. If the mother-in-law is not present, then the eldest lady in the house is presented with the baya. Sometimes, the elder one chooses to take only the perishable items, and leaves cash and clothes for the mother-in-law.

14

Krishna Janmashtami

Janmashtami is the birthday of Lord Krishna, the re-incarnation of Lord Vishnu who gave us the vital message through the *Bhagwat Gita*—the guiding principles for every Hindu. Janmashtami is celebrated with full vigor all over the country. Janmashtami is celebrated in various parts of India to mark the birth of Lord Krishna. It is observed on the Ashtami day of the Shravan month according to the Hindu calendar. The temples of Vrindavan witness an extravagant and colourful celebration on this occasion. Raslila is performed to recreate incidents from the life of Krishna and to commemorate his love for Radha. Lord Vishnu is invoked in his human incarnation as Krishna on his birth anniversary in the festival of Janmashtami. The idol of the infant Krishna is bathed at midnight and is placed in a cradle. Devotional songs and dances mark the celebration of this festive occasion all over Northern India.

On this day, in some parts of India, especially Maharashtra, youths celebrate it by breaking clay pots called 'Dahi-Handi', filled with curd and butter suspended high above the ground, young men and children form human pyramid to reach the pot and break it. This custom follows the habit of Lord Krishna who used to steal butter in this manner from villagers along with his friends. The reason for this is that Gokul; the place where lord Krishna spent his childhood used to generate a lot of milk and the people used to sell it in Mathura, thus depriving their children from milk and butter which is very essential for young boys and girls.

In Maharashtra, Janmashtami witnesses the exuberant enactment of the god's childhood endeavors to steal butter and curd from earthen pots beyond his reach.

Krishna Janmashtami is observed on the eighth day of the dark half (*Krishna Paksha*) of the month of Bhadrapadha in the Hindu calendar, when the Rohini Nakshatram is ascendent. The Hindu calendar being lunar, these two events [the day being the eighth of the waning moon (*Krishna-paksha Ashtami*) and the *Rohini Nakshatram* being ascendent] may overlap for only a few hours. In such an event, the festival may be celebrated on different (but successive) days by different people, depending on their local or family traditions.

The festival is celebrated differently in North India. The temples at Vrindavan and Mathura witness a colourful, even boisterous celebration on this occasion, and festivities at these places may extend for several days. Devotional songs and dances mark the celebration. The Rasa Lila is performed to recreate incidents from the life of Krishna and commemorate his love for Radha.

While the Rasa Lila recreates the youthful Krishna's dalliance with the milkmaids of his native land, the "Dahi-Handi" tradition of Maharashtra re-enacts his childhood pranks, wherein Krishna and his young friends helped themselves to butter and other goodies in the houses of their neighbours. Clay pots called "Dahi-Handi", filled with curd and butter, are suspended high above the ground. To a constant chorus of "Govinda, Govinda" from all those present, teams of young men form human pyramids to reach the pot and break it, to the merriment of the youths and of the assembly. The festival is thus celebrated with great joy and communal togetherness by one and all.

Janmashtami celebrates the birth of one of the most famous Gods of Hindu religion, Bhagwan Krishna, on the eighth day (Ashtami) in the month of Sravana or Savana. Lord Sri Krishna was born on the 'Rohini' nakshatram (star). It is generally celebrated in the month of August-September according to the Christian Calendar. Legend has it that Sri Krishna was born on a dark, stormy and windy night to end the rule and atrocities of his maternal uncle, Kansa.

The festival of Janmashtami is considered a very pious day by Hindus. Lot of bhajan singing, hymn chanting and poojas are performed this day. Devotees queue all the major Krishna temples to seek his blessings. People perform elaborate poojas during the festival. They keep day long fast. Functions and prayer meetings are organised to share the glory of their favourite God. The general pooja process begins early in the morning with devotees giving a bath or abhishek to Bal Gopal's idol with gangajal, ghee, water, honey and curd. The idol is then adorned with new clothes (preferably in yellow colour), stone or other precious jewellery. Next, the idol of lord is offered bhog, the contents of bhog may vary. Fruits, kheer, pedha, milk, and milk products are made. There are devotees who offer chappan bhog (56 dishes) to Bal Gopal. Thereafter, special Krishna pooja is performed. The cradle containing the divine infant's idol is rocked, conch is blown. Devotees sing Krishna arti, some people read out 108 names of lord. They get totally immersed in the name and praise of Gopal. After the entire pooja is over, devotees break their fast by having panchamrit. The time of breaking the fast may vary, this is so, because the time of performing pooja also differs from place to place. While some devotees choose to perform pooja at midnight and break fast, others perform pooja in the evening and have food.

Janamashtami in Mathura

The celebration of Janmashtami is at its peak in the city

of Mathura-birth place of Lord Krishna. The city is about 145 kms from Delhi. Lord is said to have been born around 5000 years back to put an end to the evils of demons. The city of Mathura adorns a complete festive look and the devotional mood reaches its pinnacle. The main celebration takes place at the actual place of birth, now converted into a big temple known as Krishna Janma Bhoomi Mandir. Lord's idol is kept in a room also known as the 'Garbha Griha'. Devotees keep a day-long fast and break it at midnight after the birth time of Bhagwan Krishna. All through the day devotees remain immersed in the chanting of Shlokas and name of the Lord. Songs and hymns are also sung in the glory of Sri Krishna. The Birth of Lord Krishna at midnight is followed by performance of pooja and other ceremonies. The idol of Lord Krishna is bathed with milk and curd and then rocked in the cradle. A popular belief of the inhabitants is that any wish made while rocking the cradle is fulfilled on this day. The entire Mathura echoes with the sound of the conch (shankh) and ringing of bells. Devotees pray and welcome the lord with slogans of 'Jai Shri Krishna'. After the prayers have been performed, Panchamrit, a mixture of honey, gangajal, curd, ghee is distributed. Lord is fed with the customary prasad of 'Chhapan Bhog' (Fifty six dishes). Devotees break their fast with 'Prasad' of the Lord. Lot of eatables made of milk and milk products are relished by the devotees. Kheer, Laddoo, Butter, Shrikhand and Singhare ki Poori are few of the main dishes prepared on the day. Performance of Rasleelas Rasleelas, a kind of dance drama are performed at various places in Mathura city both by professionals as well as amateurs. Rasleela is performed by young boys between the age of 10-13 years. The artist acting as Krishna takes the divine form for devotees who touch his feet in reverence. Jhanki (Tableau) Jhankis, cribs or scenes depicting the various stages of Life of Lord Krishna are a common sight during Janmashtami all over Mathura city. Jhankis depict various important activities of Lord Krishna right from the childhood like—Janmlila, Shankarlila, Putanalila and Naglila. Jhulanotsav and Ghatas. Another important feature of celebrations in Mathura city are Jhulanotsav and Ghatas. These are specially held only in Mathura City.

During Jhulanotsav, Swings are put in courtyard of temples and houses to welcome Lord Krishna's birth. It symbolizes cradling of Lord Krishna. Ropes of swings are decorated with flowers to give a festive look. The celebration of Sri Krishna's birth will be incomplete without Ghatas, another month-long unique feature, wherein all the temples of Mathura City are decorated with the same colour according to the theme selected. Even The idol of Lord Krishna is adorned with the Clothes of same colour. Devotees put their and heart and soul in decorating the temples and their house to welcome the birth of Lord Krishna. An estimated 8 lakh devotees visit the birth city Mathura during Janmashtami. The number, however, keeps growing every year. One finds it difficult to find an accommodation during festival days, so devotees get prior reservations made.

Janamashtami in Vrindavan

Vrindavan is quite a famous place for pilgrimage in North India. Just about 15 kms from Mathura, the birthplace of Lord Krishna, it houses nearly 5000 temples both ancient as well as modern. The holy town of Vrindavan is where Lord Krishna spent his formative years. The town situated on the banks of river Yamuna is also known for the famous rasleelas that Lord Krishna performed with his beloved gopis. During Janmashtami, the entire city gets immersed in the spirit of devotion. Euphoric celebrations among the devotees is a common sight. The sound of bhajans and chanting echo in the city. Rasleelas and staging of various plays It is said that the city of Vrindavan starts celebrating Janmashtami 7-10 days before the actual date of the festival. This is done by staging various plays and rasleelas at different places in the city. Professional artists enact various episode of Lord krishna's life. These plays are a huge drawers of devotees. Celebrations *at main Temples in Vrindavan Although* there are around 5000 temples in Vrindavan but the main temples are Banke Bihari Temple, Rangnathji Temple, Shri krishna Balram Temple, Radharaman Temple, ISCKON Temple etc. These temples have an itenarary for the entire day, with timings fixed for various ceremonies and poojas all day long. Darshans are open for devotees even during Abhishek (holy bath) of lord Krishna.

According to legend in Vrindavan, Madhuban is the exact place where Lord Krishna is said to have performed rasleelas with his beloved Gopis more than 5000 years ago. A famous folklore associated with the place is that Lord Krishna till date ascends to perform rasleela with the gopis. Anyone venturing into the place during night either dies or becomes insane. Thus no localite ventures into Madhuban during night. The place becomes alive during Janmashtami with rasleelas being performed in the premises during the daytime. Fasting *by devotees Fasting* is another ritual followed by all the devotees religiously every year. Devotees observe all day long last and break it at midnight after the arrival of Lord Krishna. It is believed by devotees that fasts act as an offering that humans can make to the Lord and bring them closer to him. Devotees cook various dishes of milk and milk products to mark the occasion. This is so because Lord Krishna was quite fond of milk and butter. Popular dishes include Kheer, Pedha, Shrikhand and Singhare ki poori.

Janmashtami in Dwarka

Dwarka, meaning 'Door to Moksha (Salvation)' is a popular city of Gujarat. It was established by Lord Krishna with his elder brother Balram. The city is also known as Golden City. It was built by divine architect Vishwakarma in two days. The city is said to have been made up of diamonds and crystal, with palaces made of gold, emeralds and other precious stones. It was the abode of Lord Krishna for nearly a 100 years. After Lord Krishna's death, the city is believed to have been submerged in the sea.

The celebration of Janmashtami in the main Dwarkadhish temple is very famous in India. Devotees from all over India throng the city of Dwarka during Janamashtami. The celebration on Janmashtami follows the daily routine or *'Nitya Kram'* of Lord Krishna. Rituals are performed by Aboti brahmins, who are special brahmins performing these rituals for the past many centuries now. The festival day begins with mangla arti performed in the morning. Mangla arti is always performed at 7 in the morning. Beginning with *'Banta Bhog'* (of milk and milk products) offered to Lord Krishna, followed by cleansing of his face with water, brushing of the idol's teeth. Then the first darshan of the day is allowed to the devotees.

Janmashtami by ISKCON

International Society for Krishna Consciousness organization was founded by Swami Prabhupada, an ardent devotee of Lord Krishna. At the age of 69, Swami Prabhupada left for United States. In 1965, ISKCON was established with its headquarter in New York. ISKCON is a monotheist faith organisation that believes Lord Krishna is supreme to all the other deities in Hinduism. The organisation is famous all over the world. ISKCON took the western countries by storm with its mantra chanting of "Hare Krishna Hare Krishna, Krishna Krishna Hare Hare; Hare Rama, Hare Rama Rama Rama Hare Hare".

Almost every year, Janmashtami is celebrated over two days by various communities of Hindus. Lord Krishna is believed to have been born at midnight so while Shaivyas celebrate it on the second day after midnight when Vasudevji took him to Gokul, The Vaishnavs choose to celebrate the festival on the first day. ISKCON too celebrates Janmashtami on the second day ie. the day after the birth of Lord Krishna.

ISKCON, celebrates Janmashtami festival at its various centres all over the world. Main celebrations are held in the prominent cities of United States including New York. Discourses and lectures are organised to mark the festival and spread the accomplishments of Lord Krishna.

An offering of 108 dishes to Lord Krishna known as 'Bhog' takes place at midnight and thereafter it is distributed among devotees. Viewing or darshan of the idol of Lord Krishna takes place. The idol is beautifully decorated with flowers. The platform on which the idol is kept is also equally laden with flowers. Thereafter, Abhishek (bathing) of the Lord takes place with milk, milk products and fresh fruit juices. This is followed by Bhajans (devotional songs) sung with various musical instruments in the glory of the Lord, dances are performed by devotees to rejoice the birth of Lord. Finally plays or dramas are held enacting the various phases and leelas of lord Krishna's life. Reading of Scriptures From Bhagawad Gita especially the episode of Birth of Lord Krishna is a special feature during Janmashtami.

Group Chanting of the Hare Krishna slogan takes place continuously and for a longer period than usual days. This is done to appease the Lord.

15

Mahavir Jayanti

According to the *Digambara* school of Jainism, Lord Mahavira was born in the year 615 BC, but the *Swetambaras* believe that he was born in 599 BC. Both sects however agree that he was the son of Siddhartha and Trisala. Legend has it that he was conceived by Devananda, wife of a Brahmin named Rishabhdeva. It is believed that the gods, ingeniously, transferred the embryo to the womb of Trisala. It is said that the expectant mother had sixteen auspicious dreams before the child was born (only 14 according to the Swetambaras). Astrologers intepreting these dreams, stated that the child would be either an emperor or a *Teerthankara*.

This religious event is largely observed by the Jains by visiting sacred sites and worshipping the *Teerthankara*. The event holds special significance in Gujarat and Rajasthan due to the ancient shrines at Girnar and Palitana in Gujarat. Mahavir Jayanti is also celebrated at Parasnath Temple in Kolkata and at Pawapuri in Bihar.

Mahavira, also known as Vardhamana, is the last one in the galaxy of Twenty-four Teerthankaras (Jain Prophets). He was born in the year 599 B.C. and has been acclaimed as one of the greatest prophets of peace and social reformation that Bharat has ever produced. He was born to a pious couple, Siddhartha and Priyakarani or popularly Trishala

Devi - who were deeply permeated with the philosophy of jainism preached by Parswanatha, the 23rd Teerthankara. Siddhartha was the king of Kaundinyapura on the outskirts of Vaishali (near Patna in Bihar).

Even as a boy, Mahavira came to be associated with many episodes of absolute fearlessness which earned him the name 'Mahavira'. He grew up as a prince, excelling in physical prowess as well as intellectual acumen. However, he renounced the pleasures and luxuries of the place, as also the power and prestige of kingship, and undertook a life of intense penance for more than twelve years. He calmly bore not only the rigors of nature but the torments from the ignorant and mischievous among his own countrymen also. He finally became self-illumined. But not content with his own personal salvation, he chose to become a great human redeemer.

He looked around and found the society corrupted by the distortions of the true concept of Dharma. Violence in the form of animal sacrifice had overshadowed the true spirit of yajna and yaga. Spiritual values had been supplanted by superstitions and lifeless rituals and dogmas. Propitiating various Gods and Goddesses was considered as a means of acquiring religious merit - Punya - to the exclusion of the true spiritual significance of these Vedic practices. Mahavira, with his penetrating insight born out of self-realization, struck mercilessly at these perversions. He simplified the religious procedures and concentrated on righteous conduct.

Mahavira's simple and convincing method of appealing to the highest and noblest impulses in the living breast soon won him a large following. He would, for example, pose the following question in order to bring home the grand message of non-injury to every living being: "Can you hold a red-hot iron rod in your hand merely because some one wants you to do so?" The listeners would instantly reply, "No, never". Then Mahavira would ask them, "Then, will it be right on your part to ask others to do the same thing just to satisfy your desire? If you cannot tolerate infliction of pain on your body or mind by others' words and actions, what right have you to do the same to others through your words and deeds?" Mahavira would then sum up his message: "Do unto others as you would like to be done by. Injury or violence done by your to any life in any form, animal or human, is as harmful as it would be if caused to your own self."

Mahavira's emphasis on this 'Unity of Life' forms one of the highest saving principles of human life. The modern civilization, which seeks to exploit and destroy every other kind of living species in order to satiate the never ending cravings of man, is landing the entire human species itself in a deadly peril.

As one deeply conversant with the needs, capacities and aptitudes of human being, Mahavira initiated a simple five-fold path for the householders: Ahimsa (Non-injury - physical or mental - to others), Asteya (non-stealing), Brahmacharya (temperance in sexual pleasures) and Aparigraha (non-acquisition of property).

Mahavira's injunctions for the monks and nuns were however very exacting. Abstinence from every kind of physical comfort and material possession and absolute dedication to the highest ethical and spiritual discipline were enforced. Even to this day, 2500 years after the passing away of that great master, this pure and upright tradition of the monks has been maintained. Thousands of white clad Sanyasins and Sanyasinis and also nude monks move on foot from village to village and town to town, throughout the length and breadth of the country, carrying Mahavira's gospel of peace, non-injury and brotherhood among people.

Mahavira left his mortal coils at the age of 71 on the Deepavali day. But the lamp of peace which he lit continues to glow through the myriad lights of that Festival of Lights.

A Grand Celebration: On this auspicious day, grand chariot processions with the images of Mahavira are taken out, rich ceremonies are held in the temples, fasts and charities are observed, Jain scriptures are read, and at some places grand fairs are set up.

Mahavira, the great teacher and the twenty-fourth Tirthankara of Jainism was a contemporary of Lord Buddha. His mother Trisala or Priyakarini had a series of miraculous dreams heralding the birth of Mahavira. Vardhaman achieved enlightenment under an Ashoka tree after two and a half days fasting and meditation. Then he stripped himself of all his clothes and wore none there after, but Shvetambars believe that Indra then presented him a white robe.

After his enlightenment he gave away all his wealth and possessions and owned nothing. Mahavira underlined the importance of austerity and complete non-violence as the essential means of spiritual evolution and salvation.

Mahavir Jayanti is celebrated as the anniversary of Vardhman Mahavir, the founder of Jain religion. Commemorating his birthday on this day, Mahavir was the most revered religious leader in this century and was perceived as a reformer who vehemently opposed the ritualism and false beliefs. The twenty-fourth and last Jain Tirthankara, Mahavir was born in 599 BC and lived for 72 years. He was born of Sidhartha, the Raja of Kundalpura, and Queen Trishala, who was also known by the name Priyakarni.

His Divine Life: Prince Vardhamana became extremely penitent and resolved to give up everything worldly. He gave up attachment to his parents, friends and relatives. Distributing all his wealth among the poor, he went to the forest and became a monk. Mahavir practised rigorous austerities, including fasts that lasted many days. He meditated on the pure nature of the Soul. Mahavir lived a life of absolute truthfulness, a life of perfect honesty and a life of absolute chastity.

His Teachings: Mahavira taught that people can save their souls from the contamination of matter by living a life of extreme asceticism and by practising non-violence towards all living creatures. This advocacy of non-violence encouraged his followers - monastic and lay - to become strong advocates of vegetarianism. Mahavira's followers were aided in their quest for salvation by the five mahavatars. Attributed to Mahavira, these great vows were the renunciation of killing, of speaking untruths, of greed, of sexual pleasure, and of all attachments to living beings and non-living things.

Sects: The main sects now are the Digambaras and Shvetambaras, with the latter again divided into Deravasis and Sthanakvasis. While the Deravasis visit the temples and worship the statue of Mahavir, the Sthanakvasis emphasise the internalisation of the faith. Mahavir himself was against idol worship.

On the day of Mahavir Jayanthi (Birth anniversary), many members of the community make offerings of milk, rice, fruit, incense, lamps and water to the tirthankar. Some sections of the community even participate in a grand procession.

Mahavira is the last and the greatest Tirthankar of the Jain religion, and Mahavir Jayanti is the birth anniversary of Lord Mahavira, the 24th Tirthankara. Mahavir Jayanti is celebrated in the first day of Bhadrapad, when there is a grand cradle procession, and a general celebration of the auspicious day.

The two sects of Jainism, Svetambaras and Digambaras, however, do not come to a concencous on the date of His birth. . According to the Digambara sect, his birth took place in 615 BC, whereas the Svetembaras claim that it occurred in 599 BC.

About Mahavira, his Birth and Enlightenment: According to the Jain mythology, Mahavir had acquired all the necessery qualities to become a Tirthankara in His pervous life. Six months prior to his birth, the supreme powers created an atmoshphere congenial and condusive to Mahavira's birth, who was a great being. Gods and Goddesses came down to bestow their blessings on the Tirthankara's expecting mother, and to cater to her needs. Wealth was showered from the heavens, relieving everyone from poverty and extending the superior ambience.

Just before Mahavira was born, His mother had sixteen dreams. Mahavira was born at four in the morning, which is considered very auspicious in Jainism and Hinduism.

Her sixteen dreams were:

— A white elephant
— A lion
— Goddess Lakshmi with two elephants at her side showering flowers
— The moon lighting the universe with silvery beams
— A pair of jumping fish
— The radiant sun, a golden pitcher
— A lake full of lotus flowers
— A calm ocean of milk
— A celestial palace
— A throne of rubies and diamonds
— A celestial king ruling the earth
— A garland
— A white bull
— A fragrant Mandara flowers
— and a vase as tall as Mount Meru, filled with gems.
— And immediately after this, she felt a white elephant enter her through her mouth. She also didn't feel any pain associated with childbirth.

It is believed that at the exact moment of his birth, the life forms in all the three worlds were cheerful and content. Several gods and goddesses descended from the heavens to pay homage to the tirthankara. They bathed him ceremonially and named him Vardhaman, Vir, Mahavira, Ativira and Samvati. The child was of exceptional beauty and developed great physical and spiritual strength. At the age of thirty, Mahavira renounced the material world, and sat for meditation. After 12 years of meditation under an Ashoke tree, also called Jonesia Ashoka, he attained the ultimate enlightenment. The divine Gods witnessed this great event, and carried him in a pamaquin to a park where he was put on a five-tiered throne and acknowledged as Mahavira. Here he stripped himself of all his clothes. Instead of shaving his head, he tore his hair out from the roots, for he was above pain. According to the Digambaras, Mahavira wore no clothes thereafter, but the Svetambaras believe that Indra presented him with a white robe.

Mahavira preached non-violence and prohibited any kind of killing. He also believed that the most virtuous life is spent sitting still and fasting, as then a man does not run the risk of injuring life even involuntarily, by swallowing or treading upon insects. On his birth anniversary, every Jain resolves to follow his teachings

Many feel that Jainism is actually an ancient atheist religion. Lord Mahavira preached that no single superior being could either produce or maintain the world.

Those people who follow Jainism believe that the world does not start or end, as is suggested by many other religions.

Mahavira was a believer in simplicity and as such suggested followers of Jainism should follow very simple rules:

— *Aparigraha:* No greed (taking more than you deserve or need)

— *Astyea:* No theft

— *Brahmacharya:* Control of sexual pleasure
— *Ahimsa:* No hurting others either emotionally or physically.

Jainism aims to achieve pure and perfect autonomy. Based almost entirely on celestial principles, Jainism believes in eternity.

Mahavir Jayanti is celebrated widely throughout the Jain community. Due to the high numbers of Jains in Rajasthan and Gujarat, most celebrations are seen in these states.

However, those that follow Jainism travel to recognized Jain shrines to celebrate Mahavir Jayanti. In Gujarat, the shrines are located at Girnar and Palitana. Others flock to Mahavirji in Rajasthan.

Lord Mahavira was born in Vaishali, which also hosts a majestic celebration.

Mahavir Jayanti Celebration

— Temples that host Mahavir Jayanti festivals are decorated with flags to mark the birthday of Lord Mahavira.
— Each locality holds a traditional bath (*abhishek*) for a deity of Lord Mahavira.
— Following the bath, the deity is carried in a parade throughout the region.
— Each parade varies but generally includes drummers, horses, elephants, singers and lamps.
— Depending on the region, the parade ends at a temple, shrine or large communal area where people may pray and meditate.

Donations made during Mahavir Jayanti are made in the form of food, medicines or knowledge.

The birthday of Lord Mahaveer is called "Mahaveer

Janma Kalyanak" and also popularly known as Mahaveer Jayanti.

Five hundred and forty-three years before Vikrama Era (in 599 B.C.) Bhagwan Mahaveer, the twenty-fourth and the last Tirthankar was born at midnight on the thirteenth day of the bright half of the month Chaitra. He was in the womb of Devananda for 82 days and in the womb of Trishala for a period of 195 days and a half (in all nine months and seven and a half days).

The birth of this great saviour spread divine light in the whole universe. All beings were steeped in divine bliss. In accordance with the established convention, the thrones of the fifty-six goddesses presiding over all the directions, started receiving tremors and realising that it was the signal of the great event of the birth of the saviour,they all flew towards Bhagwan Mahaveer and his blessed mother. They bowed down to them, bathed them, applied scented pastes, dressed and decked them artistically. With their mission fulfilled, they returned to their respective abodes.

In West India: The festival is celebrated on a large scale in Gujarat and Rajasthan where many people practice Jainism. Festivities can be witnessed at Jain shrines in Girnar and Palitana in Gujarat, at Pawanpuri in Bihar and at Parasnath temple in Calcutta.

Lord Mahavir was conceived by Devananda, the wife of a Brahmin called Rishabhdeva. However, the Gods transferred the embryo to Trisala's womb. When astrologers were asked to interpret the dreams of the expectant mother, they predicted that the child would be either an emperor or a Teerthankar. Vardhaman Mahavir went on to become the 24th Tirthankara of the Jain religion. Rishabhadeva, the first Tirthankara, is believed to have founded Jainism. At the age of 30, Mahavir became a wandering ascetic and attained enlightenment after 13 years of meditation.

As the emphasis is on renunciation, liberation of man from the material world, there is no exhibition of pomp and gaiety on Jain festivals. Rather, devotees spend their time in quiet introspection. Mahavir Jayanti is largely spent in prayer. In some places, peaceful processions are taken out. Children enact scenes depicting different phases of Mahavir's life. It is considered an auspicious day to embark on new ventures or for social activities. Jain devotees visit sacred places and worship the Teerthankaras or the religious gurus.

"There is no doubt that Jainism prevailed even before Vardhaman or Parshvanath." In the 12th century A.D. King Kumarapala was won over to Jainism and made Gujarat a model Jam state. Today the followers of the lain religion form a community of more than one million and a half living in India.

Mahavir is the "Jina" or "Conqueror", under whose guidance his devotees are encouraged to conquer the karma-rebirth cycle, this being the goal of the lain religion. Mahavir was a kshatriya prince (warrior caste) of North Bihar in Northern India. At the age of 30 he became a wandering ascetic. Thirteen years later he reached illumination. His followers form four orders: monks (muni or sadhu), nuns (sadhvi), laymen (shravaka) and lay-women (shravika).

Digambaras and Shvetambaras: Around the year 80 A.D. the Jains split into two sects: Digambaras (space clothed) and Shvetambaras (clothed in white). Digambaras hold that sadhus must be naked as a sign of total renunciation. Other doctrines held by the Digambaras but rejected by the Shvetambaras are 1. Only men can obtain final liberation (moksha), women must be reborn as men. 2. The images of the Tirthankars must be represented with downcast eyes, nude and unadorned. 3. Mahavir never married. 4. Once the highest stage of knowledge is reached, a saint can sustain life without eating, and 5. By the 2nd century AD the entire canon of sacred books was lost.

Dash Laxanparva: The holiest feast of the Jains is Dashlaxanparva, which is celebrated by the Digambaras from the 5th to the 14th of the bright half of Bhadrapad. During these days there is an atmosphere of joy in every lain temple. Every day in the morning after taking bath all men and women go to worship in the temple. Then each day there is a lecture on each of the ten chapters of the holy book "Shritatvarth Sutra". These ten chapters dwell on the following ten duties (dharma): 1. Kshama (forgiveness), 2. Mardava (humility), 3. Arjava (simplicity and frankness). 4. Shaucha (cleanliness), 5. Satya (truthfulness), 6. Samyama (self-control), 7. Tap (austerity), 8. Tyag (renunciation). 9. Akimchanya (detachment), and 10. Bramhacharya (celibacy). On the day dedicated to "tyag" gifts are offered to social service institutions, and on the first day of the dark half of Ashvin, at the end of the celebration, all the men come together and embracing each other they ask pardon for the of-fences committed during the past year.

The 14th day of the bright half of Bhadrapad is known as Anant Chaturdashi (endless fourteenth). This is a very important day for the Jains, this being the last day of the Dashlaxanparva. According to Jam scriptures one can gain much merit by observing a vow on this day. The Jains of the Shvetambara sect celebrate the Paryushan Feast, from the 12th of the dark half of Bhadrapad to the 4th of the bright half of Ashvin.

Legend of Mahaveera: According to Swetambar sect of Jains, in 599 B.C. on Chaitra Shukla Trayodsahi i.e. the thirteenth day of the bright half of Chaitra (March-April), a child was born to King Siddhartha and queen Priyakarani or popularly known as Trishala Devi. Siddhartha was the king of Kaundinyapura near Patna in Bihar. The child who was named Mahaveera and also Vardhamana (which means ever advancing) and Sanmati, was destined to become one of the greatest prophets of Jainism. He was the last 24th

Teerthankara (Jain prophets) of the Jains. Vardhamana from his childhood was brave and fearless which earned him the name of 'Mahaveera', 'Maha' means great and 'Veera' means a hero. He grew up as a prince excelling in all arts of prowess and intellectual sphere. His parents being the followers of Jainsim preached by Parswanatha, the 23rd Teerthankara, Mahaveera was much influenced by its philosophy. It is seems 'Tirtha' literally means a ford, a means of crossing over. Metaphorically, it denotes a philosophy or a spiritual guide who helps to cross over the ocean of recurring births in this world. 'Kara' means one who makes. Mahaveera was very obedient to his parents. It is said at the age of eight to observed the twelve vows of Ahims etc. He also grew up to be a great statesman but he did not marry. He lived a life of truthfulness, honesty and chastity. He realised the transitory pleasures of the world and engrossed himself in Self-contemplation. He renounced the pleasures and luxurious of the palace and its kingship. He gave up attachment to his parents, relatives and friends and undertook a life of intense penance for more than twelve years. He knew that renunciation was the only means of attaining eternal bliss. During his long penance, he went through a rigorous life of austerities, fasted and meditated on the pure nature of the Soul. He was unmoved by the beautiful damsel whom God sent to test him. Again, he not only bore the inclements of Nature but the torments of his jealous opponents, his own countrymen but finally attain self-enlightenment. Mahaveera was not content with his own salvation. He wanted to become a true human redeemer. He found that the real concept of Dharma was mis interpreted and there was much corruption in the religious sphere also. In the name of religion animal sacrifices took place during Yagnas etc. He did not believe in rituals and spirituals that were distorted and were filled with more superstitions than reality. He remarked, worshipping Gods and Goddesses were more for attaining Punya or religious merit for oneself than practising goodness and understanding the true significance of the Vedic scriptures. He ruthlessly condemned the existing ill practices of the religious priests. Instead, he introduced simple codes of righteous conduct which appealed to all and he won a large number of followers. Mahaveera preached non-injury to other creatures and beings. He would ask "Can you hold a red-hot iron rod in your hand merely because some one wants you to do so?" The listeners would ofcourse answer "No never". Then, Mahaveera would ask them, "Then, will it be right on your part to ask others to do the same thing just to satisfy your desires? If you cannot tolerate infliction of pain on your body or mind by others' words and actions, what right have you to do the same to others through your words and deeds" His sermon was "Do unto others as you would like to be done by. Injury or violence done by you to any life in any form, animal or human, is as harmful as it would be if caused to your own self. "His message and emphasis was on 'Unity of Life' and Brotherhood. Before renunciation Mahaveera had distributed all his wealth to the poor with his own hands. When he went to the forest it seems he took off even the piece of cloth which he was wearing. Before he became a meak, he rooted out with his hands five tufts of hair from his head and turning to the North said, "Salutations to the Siddhas! "Mahaveera, the greatest Teerthankara spread his teachings to Magadha, Mithila and other distant places, and even many kings became his disciples. Even today, we find Jain whiteclad monks and Sanyasins spreading Mahaveera's teachings of Peace, non-injury and Brotherhood throughout the length and breadth of the country. Mahaveera lived for 72 years and entered into Nirvana in 527 B.C. on the Deepavali day but the lamp of Peace which he lit still continues to glow.

Look at traditional Mahavir Jayanti celebrations where the emphasis is on piety, self-control and a willingness to help the less fortunate.

Mahavir Jayanthi usually begins with the idol of Lord

Mahavir being given a ceremonial bath. This is followed by various offerings to the idol in the form of fruit, rice and milk. Incense sticks and lamps are lit in the temple which is also decorated with red and saffron flags on the occasion.

After the ceremonial bath called the abhishek, the idol is taken around the neighborhood by a large procession of devotees. Celebrations are particularly high profile in the ancient Jain shrines at Girnar and Palitana in Gujarat where thousands of pilgrims congregate.

16

Maha-Shivaratri

> You cannot run away from a weakness; you must some time fight it out or perish; and if that be so, why not now, and where you stand?
>
> —*Robert Louis*

Maha Shivratri falls on the 13th (or 14th) day of the dark half of 'Phalgun' (February-March). Literally, Shivaratri means "the night of Shiva". The ceremonies take place chiefly at night. This is a festival observed in honour of Lord Shiva and it is believed that on this day Lord Shiva was married to Parvati. On this festival people worship 'Shiva—the Destroyer'. This night marks the night when Lord Shiva danced the 'Tandav'. In Andhra Pradesh, pilgrims throng the Sri Kalahasteshwara Temple at Kalahasti and the Bharamarambha Malikarjunaswamy Temple at Srisailam. About *The Lord Shiva*—the word meaning auspicious—is one of the Hindu Trinity, comprising of Lord Brahma, the creator, Lord Vishnu, the preserver and Lord Shiva or Mahesh, the Destroyer and Recreater of life. Lord Shiva is known by many names like "Shankar", "Mahesh", "Bholenath", "Neelakanth", "Shambhu Kailasheshwar", "Umanath", "Nataraj" and others.

For few people, Shiva is "Paramatman", "Brahman", the Absolute, but many more prefer to see Shiva as a personal God given to compassion for his worshippers, and the dispenser of both spiritual and material blessings. Related to the Absolute concept is Shiva as "Yoganath" meaning the Lord of Yoga, wherein he becomes teacher, path and goal. As such he is the "Adi Guru" or the Highest Guru of 'Sannyasins' who have renounced the world to attain the Absolute. He is the most sought-after deity amongst the Hindus and they pray to him as the god of immense large-heartedness who they believe grants all their wishes.

Mahakal Shiva, as per the Vedas, manifested himself as "Lingum" to make mankind aware of the presence of Eternal Time. That day when Shiva manifested himself in the form of "Lingum" was the fourth day of the dark night in the month of 'Magha' i.e. February-March. Maha Shivratri continues to be celebrated forever and ever. In the Shanti Parva of the *Mahabharata*, Bhishma, whilst resting on the bed of arrows and discoursing on Dharma, refers to the observance of Maha Shivaratri by King Chitrabhanu. The story goes as follows—Once upon a time King Chitrabhanu of the Ikshvaku dynasty, who ruled over the whole of Jambudvipa, was observing a fast with his wife, it being the day of Maha Shivaratri. The sage Ashtavakra came on a visit to the court of the king. The sage asked the king the purpose of his observing the past. King Chitrabhanu explained that he had the gift of remembering the incidents of his previous birth. The king said to the sage that in his previous birth he was a hunter in Varanasi and his name was Suswara. His only livelihood was to kill and sell birds and animals. One day while roaming through forests in search of animals he was overtaken by the darkness of night.

Unable to return home, he climbed a tree for shelter. It happened to be a Bel (Vilva) tree. He had shot a deer that day but had no time to take it home. So he bundled it up and tied it to a branch on the tree. As hunger and thirst tormented him, he was kept awake throughout the night.

He shed profuse tears when he thought of his poor wife and children who were starving and anxiously waiting for his return. To pass away the time that night he engaged himself in plucking the Bel leaves and dropping them down onto the ground.

The next day he returned home and sold the deer and then bought some food for himself and his family. The moment he was about to break his fast a stranger came to him, begging for food. He served the food first to stranger and then had his own. At the time of his death, he saw two messengers of Lord Shiva. They were sent down to conduct his soul to the abode of Lord Shiva. He learnt then for the first time of the great merit he had earned by the unconscious worship of Lord Shiva during the night of Shivaratri. The messengers told him that there was a Lingam at the bottom of the tree. The leaves I dropped fell on the Lingam. His tears, which had shed out of pure sorrow for his family, fell onto the Lingam and washed it and he had fasted all day and all night.

Thus, he unconsciously worshiped the Lord. As the conclusion of the tale the King said that he lived in the abode of the Lord and enjoyed divine bliss for long ages and now he has reborn as Chitrabhanu. People observe a strict fast on this day. Some devotees do not even take a drop of water and they keep vigil all night. The Shiva Lingam is worshipped throughout the night by washing it every three hours with milk, curd, honey, rose water, etc., whilst the chanting of the Mantra "Om Namah Shivaya" continues. Offerings of Bael leaves are made to the Lingam as Bael leaves are considered very sacred and it is said that Goddess Lakshmi resides in them. Hymns in praise of Lord Shiva, such as the "Shiva Mahimna Stotra" of Pushpadanta or Ravana's "Shiva Tandava Stotra" are sung with great fervor and devotion. People repeat the 'Panchakshara' Mantra, "Om Namah Shivaya". He, who utters the names of Shiva during Shivratri, with perfect devotion and concentration, is freed from all sins. He reaches the abode of Shiva and lives there happily. He is liberated from the wheel of births and deaths.

On the day of Shivratri, the lingam is bathed with the five sacred offerings of a cow, called the panchagavya—milk, sour milk, urine, butter and dung. Thereafter the five foods of immortality—milk, clarified butter, curd, honey and sugar—are placed before the lingam. Dhatura and jati, though poisonous fruits, are believed to be sacred to Shiva and thus offered at his temple. Eleven is considered to be the sacred number of the Lord. Devotees keep a fast (vrat) on Shivratri and observe strict rules, for vardan (boon). Special celebration are held at important Shiva temples at Chidambaram, Kalahasi Khajuraho and Varanasi. Worship of Shiva is to release the worship perform the cycle of birth and rebirth. In Kashmir, the festival is held for 15 days; the thirteenth day is observed as Hearth, a day of fast followed by a family feast.

It is said, during the samudra manthan (the great churning of ocean) by the gods and demons, haalaa-hala, a poison came out of the ocean. It was so toxic, that it effects would have wiped out the entire creation. At this juncture, as per the advice of Vishnu, gods approached Mahadev and prayed him to protect life by consuming this poison. Pleased with their prayers, out of compassion for living beings, Lord Shiva drank this poison and held it in his throat by binding it with a snake. The throat became blue due to the poison and Shiva remained unharmed. The vaidyas advised gods to keep Lord Shiva awake during the night as part of the therapy. To amuse Shiva and to keep him awake, the gods took turn performing various dances and playing music. A vigil was thus kept by the gods in contemplation of Shiva. As the day broke out, Shiva, pleased with their devotion blessed them all. Since then, on this day and night—devotees fast, keep vigil, sing glories of Lord and meditate.

After creation was complete, Parvati asked Shiva of which rituals pleased him the most. The Lord replied that the 14th night of the new moon, during the month of Phalgun, is my most favourite day. It is known as Shivaratri. Parvati repeated these words to her friends, from whom the word spread over all creation.

Maha Shivratri, the night of the worship of Shiva, occurs on the 14th night of the new moon during the dark half of the month of Phalguna (Feb / March) when Hindus offer special prayer to the lord of destruction.

1. The absolute formless God, Sadashiv appeared in the form of "Lingodbhav Moorti" exactly at midnight on Maha Shivratri. That is why all Shiv devotees keep vigil during the night of Shivratri and do "Shivlingam abhishekham" (coronation of the phallic idol) at midnight.
2. Lord Shiva was married to Devi Parvati on Shivratri. Remember Shiva minus Parvati is pure Nirgun Brahman. With his illusive power, (Maya, Parvati) He becomes the "Sagun Brahman" for the purpose of the pious devotion of his devotees.
3. It is also believed that on Shivratri, Lord Shiva became Neelkantham by swallowing the deadly poison that came up from the ocean during the churning of "Kshir Sagar". The poison was so deadly that even a drop in His stomach, which represents the universe, would have annihilated the entire world. Hence, He held it in His neck, which turned blue due to the effect of poison. Shivratri is therefore also a day of thanksgiving to the Lord for protecting us from annihilation.

Kashmiri Pandits used to clebrate Shivratri festival over a period of 23 days. First six days (hurye okdoh to hurye shayam) were devoted to cleaning of the house and buying puja articles. Next 2-3 days were the days for devotional prayers. Dyara daham was designated for giving presents to married daughters and newly weds. Gadkah and Vager bah were special days for the worship of Bhairavas. Herath truvah is the day for Shiva worship. Herath Kharch (gift of money) is given by the eldest person to all members of the family on the following day. Herath truvah is the day for lord Shiva's worship. On Doon mavas, the prasad of walnuts and rice cakes (tomala-chuut) are distributed, in past, this often continued until Tila ashtami. The latter day also marks the end of winter, and is celebrated by burning kangris and singing the chorus of ja-tun-]tn'. On the social side, there used to be great joy all around. People wore new and their nicest clothes, and families would sit together and enjoy the game with sea shells.

Bhagwan Shiva is portrayed with ash on his forehead, and devotees of Lord Shiva frequently apply sacred ash to various parts of their body. This symbolizes two things. Everything that today has a form on the Earth once was ash in the ground and again will be reduced to nothing but ash. Therefore, the ash serves to remind us that all that we are, all that we do, all that we earn and acquire will only be reduced to ash one day, and therefore we should live our lives dedicated to God and dedicated to serving humanity, rather than to the accumulation of temporary possessions and comfort. When we apply the sacred ash or see it, we are reminded "Ah yes, it is only by the grace of Lord Shiva that I am still here today, and that I have not yet been turned to ash. It is His grace that my home, my family and my possessions are still with me and that they have not become ash. Therefore, I should remember Him, pray to Him and devote myself to Him."

Maha Shivratri, as the name suggests, is in the honour of Lord Shiva, the third lord of the Trinity (Bramha— the creator, Vishnu—the preserver and Shiva– the destroyer).

Lord Shiva is offered special food, made from fruits of the season, root vegetables and coconuts, during ritual worship. The Shivling (phallic symbol of the Lord) is bathed with the panchagavya (five sacred offerings of a cow including milk, sour milk, urine, butter and dung). Thereafter, milk, butter, curd, sugar and honey, (believed to be the foods granting immortality), are offered. Dhatura and jati, though poisonous fruits, are sacred to Shiva and therefore placed in front of him.

Unmarried girls are supposed to perform the Maha Shivratri pooja with great faith. They pray to the lord for eligible husbands. Moreover, married women pray to Lord Shiva for marital bliss and a long prosperous married life.

17

Makar Sankranti

> Honest differences of views and honest debate are not disunity. They are the vital process of policy-making among free men.
>
> —*Herbert Hoover*

The term "Sankranti" literally denotes state of transition. The festival of Makar Sankrant traditionally coincides with the beginning of the Sun's northward journey (the *Uttarayan*) when it enters the sign of Makar (the *Capricorn*). Uttarayana is considered holy and auspicious. This is most opportune time for all religious activities. Even, as per Hindu pantheon, one who dies in Uttaryana goes to heaven. It falls on the 14th of January every year according to the Solar Calendar (i.e. the first day of Magh as per Hindu calenders). This day has a very special significance because the day and night on Makar Sankrant are equal i.e. of 12 hours each. Makar Sankrati is celebrated as a festival right from the advent of the Aryans and is looked upon as the most auspicious day by the Hindus.

Mention is there of Makar Sakranti in a *Mahabharat* wherein it is told that the great warrior-hero, Bhishma Pitamaha even after being wounded and lying on the bed of arrows, lingered on till Uttarayan set in, to breathe his last. It is believed that the person who dies on this auspicious day of Sankrant escapes the cycle of birth and re-birth and that his soul mingles with the Almighty.

Again, different manners are observed for celebrating this festival in different parts of the country yet the use of til is found everywhere. Til or sesame seed contain lot of oil and they therefore have a quality of softness in them. Therefore, firstly the use of til in sweets is good for health and secondly being soft their exchange means exchange of love and tender feelings.

In Maharashtra on the Sankranti day people exchange multi-coloured tilguds made from til (sesame seeds) and sugar and til-laddus made from til and jaggery. Til-polis are offered for lunch and these are specialities of Maharashtra. Maharashtrian women are proud of their excellence in preparing these delicacies. While exchanging tilguls as tokens of goodwill people greet each other saying—"til-gul ghya, god bola" meaning "accept these tilguls and speak sweet words". The underying thought in the exchange of tilguls is to forget the past ill-feelings and hostilities and resolve to speak sweetly and remain friends. This is a special day for the women in Maharashtra when married women are invited for a get-together called "Haldi-Kumkoo" and given gifts of any utensil, which the woman of the house purchases on that day.

In Gujarat Sankrant is observed more or less in the same manner as in Maharashtra but with a difference that in Gujarat there is a custom of giving gifts to relatives. The elders in the family give gifts to the younger members of the family. The Gujarati Pundits on this auspicious day grant scholarships to students for higher studies in astrology and philosophy. This festival thus help the maintenance of social relationships within the family, caste and community.

In Punjab where December and January are the coldest months of the year, huge bonfires are lit on the eve of Sankrant and which is celebrated as *Lohari*. Sweets, sugarcane and rice are thrown in the bonfires, around which friends and relatives gather together. The following day, which is Sankrant is celebrated as *Maghi*. The Punjabi's dance their famous Bhangra dance till they get exhausted. Then they sit down and eat the samptions food that is specially prepared for the occasion.

In Bundelkhand and Madhya Pradesh this festival of Sankrant is known by the name *Sukart* or *Sakrat* and is celebrated with great pomp merriment accompanied by lot of sweets.

In South India Sankrant is known by the name of *Pongal*, which takes its name from the surging of rice boiled in a pot of milk, and this festival has more significance than even Diwali. It is very popular particularly amongst farmers. Rice and pulses cooked together in ghee and milk is offered to the family deity after the ritual worship. In essence in the South this Sankrant is a "Puja" (worship) for the Sun God.

In Uttar Pradesh, Sankrant is called *Kicheri*. Having bath on someoly river on this day is regarded as most pious. A mass of humanity can be seen bathing in the Sangam at Prayagraj where the rivers Ganga, Yamuna and Saraswati meet. At the confluence of these holy rivers every year Kumbh Mela is held for full one month.

The tribals in our country start their New Year from the day of Sankrant by lighting bonfires, dancing and eating their particular dishes sitting together. The Bhuya tribals of Orissa have their Maghyatra in which small home-made articles are put for sale.

There is also a fair in the Western Ghats at a place called Shabari Mala, where the temple of the Community Goddess is decorated with dazzling lights. The Goddess is worshipped by touchables and untouchables both and the "bhog" to the Goddess is cooked in the touchables and untouchables both. These tribals participate in the Mela and enjoy all together as if they belong to one single family. May be therefore, the experts pine that this festival of Makar Sankrant comes to us from those olden times when the caste system did not exist in India as it emphasises or communal harmony.

From Makar Sankranti onwards when the sun travels northwards, innumerable auspicious things start happening. Climate and atmosphere improve. Children born during this period are naturally progressive, well mannered, pleasant and of noble disposition. All such special reasons make the northward journey of the sun sacred and auspicious at Makar Sankranti.

This is the day when the sun begins its northward journey. It usually falls in the middle of January. For the people of the northern hemisphere, the northward path of the sun marks the period when the sun is getting closer and closer to them, when the days are getting longer, and it is becoming warmer and warmer. To Hindus, the sun stands for knowledge, spiritual light and wisdom. Makara Shankranti signifies that we should turn away from the darkness of delusion in which we live, and begin to joyously let the light within us shine brighter and brighter. We should gradually begin to grow in purity, wisdom, and knowledge, even as the sun does from this day.

In fact, the sun itself stands for all the ideals of the Pongal festival. Its message is that of light, unity, equality and true selflessness. These are the ideals of Karma Yoga. Hence, the sun is the greatest Karma Yogi. Does it ask any reward for all that it gives to us? If it stops shedding its light, we are doomed to death. If we learn this one lesson from the sun, our lives will shine with divine lustre like that of the sun.

In Karnataka, men, women and children attired in colourful tunics visit friends and relatives and exchange pieces of sugarcane, a mixture of fried *til*, molasses, pieces of dry coconut, peanuts and fried gram. The significance of this exchange is that sweetness should prevail in all the dealings. As part of the festival, cows and bulls are given a wash and the horns are painted with bright colours and decorated with garland, and are taken in a procession in the village to the accompaniment of pipes and drums. In the night a bonfire is lit and the animals are made to jump over the fire.

18

Muharram

It is remarkable to note that Muharram is the first month of the Islamic calendar. It is one of the four sanctified months of the year. Fighting in this month is looked down upon and is often put to the side in respect for Islam. Since the Islamic calendar is lunar, Muharram moves from year to year when compared to the Gregorian calendar.

The first day of Muharram is the start of the Islamic New Year. The Festival of Muharram takes place during this month in which Shia Muslims especially commemorate the Battle of Karbala. The commemoration reaches its climax on the tenth day of Muharram, known as Ashurah. This day is related to the time of Moses when he crossed the Red Sea escaping from the Pharaoh. Sunni Muslims often fast on this sacred day. Later, in the month of Ramadan it is recommended to fast so the day of Ashura is optional.

This month of Muharram also has traditions which have no support from Islamic teachings. For example, the celebration of the Muslim new year, and the partying and card giving, etc, associated with it is considered to be a bidah and even haraam to some. Muharram is so called because it was unlawful to fight during this month; the word is derived from the word 'haram' meaning forbidden. It is held to be the most sacred of all the months. This months is most sacred to the Shi'a community and the fast on the first ten days of the month to commemorate the slaying of Hussain, a grandson of Muhammed, by the Sunnis. The tenth day is called Ashura, meaning, 'the tenth', and it is a day of voluntary fasting. The Sunnis also fast on the tenth day because they believe that Adam and Eve, heaven and hell, life and death, fate and the pen were created on this day.

The Remembrance of Muharram is an important period of mourning in the Shiaite branch of Islam.

A banner (*aalam*) being carried in a procession during the Remembrance of Muharram in Bahrain. For the duration of the remembrance, it is customary for mosques to provide free meals (*nazar*) on certain nights of the month to all people. These meals are viewed as being special and holy, as they have been consecrated in the name of Husayn, and thus partaking of them is considered an act of communion with God, Husayn, and humanity. In Trinidad and Tobago all ethnic and religious communities participate in the event, locally known as "Hosay".

Many of the events associated with the remembrance take place in congregation halls known as "Hussainia".

The Tenth of Muharram and Ashurah: The Islamic year begins with Muharram ul Haram, the first month of the Hijri Calendar. While followers of other religions spend their opening month in worthless merriment, the first month of Islam teaches us lessons of admonition, good counselling, knowledge of Allah Ta'ala, sacrifice, selflessness, patience and seeking the pleasure of Allah Ta'ala.

The tenth day of Muharram (Ashurah) has many distinctive qualities and features. Allah Ta'ala created the heavens and the earth on this blessed day. On this day He gave His infinite blessings and bounties to many of His Prophets and delivered them from the clutches of their enemies.

Allah Ta'ala created Hazrat Adam (Alaihis-Salam) in this month, pardoned him of his mistake, and Hazrat Noah's

(Alaihis-Salam) Ark landed successfully on Mount Judi, and he saved Hazrat Ibrahim (Alaihis-Salam) from fire and rescued Hazrat Musa (Alaihis-Salam) from Pharaoh. On the first of Muharram offer 2 rakats Nafl prayer. In each rakat after Surah Fateha recite Surah Ikhlas 3 times. After the Salam pray to Allah Ta'ala for all your needs and desires. From the blessing of this prayer, Allah Ta'ala will appoint an angel for such a person. The angel will guide him or her to do only good deeds and prevent them in engaging in sinful acts.

On the eve of "Ashurah" offer 100 rakats Nafl. In each rakat recite Surah Ikhlas 3 times after Surah Fateha. After Salam recite first 'Kalimah' 100 times. Allah Ta'ala will forgive all the sins of such a person.

Dua-e-Ashurah - An Insurance for a Year's Life: Hazrat Imam Zainul Abidain (Radi Allah Anhu) reports that who ever recites this dua on the tenth of Muharram, any time after sunrise and before sunset, or listens to its recitation from someone else, Allah Ta'ala will certainly make it an insurance for a years' life for him, by keeping death away from him. However, if one is to become the victim of death in that year, they will by some strange coincidence not remember to recite it.

Nafl Salat for the Eve of Ashurah: On the eve of Ashurah offer 4 rakats Nafl Salat as follows: In every rakat after Surah Fateha recite "Ayetul Kursi" once and Surah Ikhlas 3 times. After completing this Namaz recite Surah Ikhlas 100 times. Allah Ta'ala will purify such a person of all their sins and grant them endless bounties and blessings in paradise.

The Fast of Ashurah: On the 9th and 10th of Muharram, one should fast. If it is not possible to fast on both days, then every effort should be made to fast on the 10th day of Muharram, as there is great reward for this fast. (Muslim Shareef).

The following are some of the desirable acts one should do on the day of Ashurah:

1. To observe fast on this day.
2. To give as much charity as you can afford.
3. To perform Nafl Salat prayers.
4. To recite Surah Ikhlas 1000 times.
5. To visit and be in the company of pious Ulema.
6. To place a hand of affection on an orphan's head.
7. To give generously to one's relatives.
8. To put surma in one's eyes.
9. To take a bath.
10. To cut one's nails.
11. To visit the sick.
12. To establish friendly ties with one's enemies.
13. To recite Dua-e- Ashurah
14. To visit the shrines of Awliyas and the graves of Muslims.

Hazrat Abdullah bin Masood (Radi Allah Anhu), a Companion of the Holy Prophet Muhammad (PBUH) reports the following saying of the Messenger of Allah Ta'ala, "Whosoever prepares ample food and drink for his family on this sacred day and delights in feeding them generously, Allah Ta'ala will increase His provisions for that year and place much blessings and good therein."

Imam Hussain (Radi Allah Anhu) and his companions were martyred on the tenth of this month.

Like any month in the Islamic Calendar there are in this first Islamic month, many anniversaries which are celebrated every where in the world.

Muharram festival commemorates the martyrdom of Hazrat Imam Hussain, the grandson of the Holy Prophet (peace be upon him). This festival starts at the 1st day of Muharram and lasts for 10 days until 10th of Muharram. Muharram is the first month of Islamic calendar.

During this month, while on a journey, Hazrat Imam Hussain, his family members and a number of his followers were surrounded by the forces of Yazid, the Muslim ruler of the time. During the siege, they were deprived of food and water and many of them were put to death. The incident happened at a place called Karbala in Iraq in 61st year after Hijra. This dispute was result of a disagreement among Muslims on the question of succession after the demise of Hazrat Ali, the fourth caliph. Some Muslims sects hold meetings where speeches are made on the happenings of Karbala and on the lives of martyrs. The Shias, however, observe this festival in a different fasion. As Muharram, the first month of the Muslim year, approaches, they put on black clothes, as black is regarded as a color of mourning. Majalis (assemblies) are held every day during the first nine days where shia orators relate the incident of the martyrdom of Hazrat Imam Hussain and his party in a great detail. On the 10th day of Muharram, large processions are formed and the devoted followers parade the streets holding banners and carrying models of the mausoleum of Hazrat Imam Hussain and his people, who fell at Karbala. They show their grief and sorrow by inflicting wounds on their own bodies with sharp metal tied to chain with which they scourge themselves. This is done in order to depict the sufferings of the martyrs. It is a sad occasion and everyone in the procession chants "Ya Hussain", with loud wails of lamentation. Generally a white horse beautifully decorated for the occasion, is also included in the procession, to mark the empty mount of Hazrat Imam Husain after his martyrdom.

During these first ten days of Muharram, drinking posts are also set up temporarily by the Shia community where water and juices are served to all, free of charge.

The 1st of Muharram is New Year's Day, and with it marks the beginning of the Islamic (Hijri) Calendar. Its real significance lies in the major turning point in the course of Islam. As told in the Noble Qur'ân: "Verily the number of months with Allah is twelve months (in a year), so was it ordained by Allah on the Day when He created the heavens and the earth; of them four are Sacred. That is the right religion, so wrong not yourselves therein ...".

Today itself, as we usher in the new year, many of us take the time to at least briefly reflect on the major lessons in the past year and anticipate new experiences in the fresh year of 1422 Hijrah. This is also the day that we should be reminded of the Prophet's last pilgrimage and the message that he wants us to carry in our hearts.

The prophet offered the noon and afternoon prayers in Arafah along with 100,000 worshippers, and the victory of Islaam over blasphemy became decisive and final. Thereafter, the Prophet mounted his camel, and delivered the historical sermon. In it, he had said: "... All mankind is from Adam and Eve, an Arab has no superiority over a non-Arab nor a non-Arab has any superiority over an Arab, also a white has no superiority over black nor a black has any superiority over white except by piety and good action. Learn that every Muslim is a brother to every Muslim and that the Muslims constitute one brotherhood. Nothing shall be legitimate to a Muslim which belongs to a fellow Muslim unless it was given freely and willingly. Do not, therefore, do injustice to yourselves...".

The period of mourning is observed in the first month of the Islamic calendar, and it commemorates the death of Hazrat Imam Hussain in the battle of Karbala. Muharram means 'respected'. It is the first month of the Islamic calendar.The first ten days of this month are observed as a period of mourning by Muslims, particularly by those belonging to the Shiah sect, in memory of the tragedy of 680

AD. Hazrat Imam Hussain, the grandson of Muhammad the Prophet was killed in the battle of Karbala. This event, called Muharram, is named after the month in which it took place. The tenth day, called Ashura, is observed as the day for a public expression of their grief and is the most important day of the month.

19

Nagpanchami

> The only people who achieve much are those who want knowledge so badly that they seek it while the conditions are still unfavorable. Favorable conditions never come.
>
> —*Clive Staples Lewis*

Hindus are nature worshippers. They believe that behind every object of the nature there is the presence of god.

Nag-Panchami is an important all-India festival and is celebrated on the fifth day of the moonlit-fortnight in the month of Shravan (July /August). This is the time when serpents invariably come out of their holes that get inundated with rain-water to seek shelter in gardens and many times in houses. As such they pose a great danger to man. May be therefore, snakes are worshipped on this day. Right from the times when mankind started acquiring some sort of culture, Sun and Snake have been invoked with prayers and ritual worship in most of the countries. In India even before the Vedic times, the tradition of snake-worship was in vogue.

During ancient times in India, there lived a clan by the name of "Nagas" whose culture was highly developed. The Indus Valley civilisation of 3000 B.C. gives ample proof of the popularity of snake-worship amongst the Nagas, whose culture was fairly wide-spread in India even before the Aryans came. After the Naga culture got incorporated into Hinduism, the Indo-Aryans themselves accepted many of the snake deities of the Nagas in their pantheon and some of them even enjoyed a pride of place in the Puranic Hinduism. The prominent Cobra snakes mentioned in the Puranas are Anant, Vasuki, Shesh, Padma, Kanwal, Karkotak, Kalia, Aswatar, Takshak, Sankhpal, Dhritarashtra and Pingal. Some historians state that these were not snakes but Naga Kings of various regions with immerse power.

The thousand-headed Shesh Nag who symbolises Eternity is the couch of Lord Vishnu. It is on this couch that the Lord reclines between the time of the dissolution of one Universe and creation of another. Hindus believe in the immortality of the snake because of its habit of sloughing its skin. As such Eternity in Hinduism is often represented by a serpent eating its own tail.

In Jainism and Buddhism snake is regarded as sacred having divine qualities. It is believed that a Cobra snake saved the life of Buddha and another protected the Jain Muni Parshwanath. To-day as an evidence of this belief, we find a huge serpent carved above the head of the statue of Muni Parshwanath. In medieval India figures of snakes were carved or painted on the walls of many Hindu temples. In the carves at Ajanta images of the rituals of snake worship are found. Kautilya, in his "Arthashastra" has given detailed description of the cobra snakes. Fascinating, frightening, sleek and virtually death-less, the cobra snake has always held a peculiar charm of its own since the time when man and snake confronted each other. As the cobra unfolded its qualities, extra-ordinary legends grew around it enveloping it in the garble of divinity. Most of these legends are in relation with Lord Vishnu, Shiv and Subramanyam.

The most popular legend is about Lord Krishna when he was just a young boy. When playing the game of throwing the ball with his cowherd friends, the legend goes to tell how the ball fell into Yamuna river and how Krishna vanquished

Kalia Serpent and saved the people from drinking the poisonous water by forcing Kalia to go away.

It is an age-old religious belief that serpents are loved and blessed by Lord Shiv. May be therefore, he always wears them as ornamentation around his neck. Most of the festivals that fall in the month of Shravan are celebrated in honour of Lord Shiv, whose blessings are sought by devotees, and along with the Lord, snakes are also worshiped. Particularly on the Nag-Panchami day live cobras or their pictures are revered and religious rights are performed to seek their good will. To seek immunity from snake bites, they are bathed with milk, haldi-kumkum is sprinkled on their heads and milk and rice are offered as "naivedya". The Brahmin who is called to do the religious ritual is given "dakshina" in silver or gold coins some times, even a cow is given away as gift.

In Bengal and parts of Assam and Orissa the blessings of Mansa, the queen of serpents are sought by offering her all the religious adoration. Protection from the harmful influence of snakes is sought through the worship of Mansa who rules supreme over the entire clan of serpents. On this occasion snake-charmers are also requisitioned to invoke the Snake Queen by playing lilting and melodious tunes on their flutes. In Punjab Nag-Panchami is known by the name of "Guga-Navami". A huge snake is shaped from dough, which is kneaded from the contribution of flour and butter from every household. The dough-snake is then placed on a winnowing basket and taken round the village in a colourful procession in which women and children sing and dance and onlookers shower flowers. When the procession reaches the main square of the village all the religious rites are performed to invoke the blessings of the snake god and then the dough snake is ceremoniously buried.

In Maharashtra, Hindu women take an early bath wear their "nav-vari"—nine yards-sarees, put on ornaments and get ready for the "puja" of Nag-Devata. Snake charmers are seen sitting by the roadsides or moving about from one place to another with their baskets that hold dangerous snakes that are their pets. While playing the lingering melodious notes on their flutes, they beckon devotees with their calls—"Nagoba-la dudh de Mayi" (give milk to the Cobra Oh Mother!) On hearing that call, women come out of their houses and then the snake-charmers take out of the snakes from their baskets. Women sprinkle haldi-kumkum and flowers on the heads of the snakes and offer sweetened milk to the snakes and pray. Cash and old clothes are also given to the snake-charmers. Bowls of milk are also placed at the places which are likely haunts of the snakes. Elderly women draw pictures of five-headed cobras on wooden planks, recite mantras and pray. The daughters wash the eyes of their fathers with rose flowers dipped in milk and then receive gifts from their fathers. In Hindu homes frying any thing on this day is forbidden by tradition.

The most fantastic celebrations of Nag-Panchami are seen in the village of Baltis Shirale which is 70 kilometres from Sangli and 400 kilometres from Mumbai. There people pray to live cobras that they catch on the eve of this pre-harvest festival. About a week before this festival, dig out live snakes from holes and keep them in covered earthen pots and these snakes are fed with rats and milk. Their poison-containing fangs are not removed because the people of this village believe that to hurt the snakes is sacrilegious. Yet it is amazing that these venomous cobras do not bite instead protect their prospective worshipers.

On the day of the actual festival the people accompanied by youngsters, dancing to the tune of musical band carry the pots on their heads in a long procession to the sacred-temple of goddess Amba and after the ritual worship the snakes are taken out from the pots and set free in the temple courtyard. Then every cobra is made to raise its head by swinging a white-painted bowl, filled with pebbles in front. The Pandit sprinkles haldi-kumkum and flowers on their raised heads.

After the puja they are offered plenty of milk and honey. After all the obeisance is rendered to the goddess and the ritual puja is over, the snakes are put back in the pots and carried in bullock-carts in procession through the 32 hamlets of Shirala village where women eagerly await outside their houses for "darshan" of the sacred cobras. One or two cobras are let loose in front of each house where men and women offer prayers, sprinkle puffed rice, flowers and coins over them, burn camphor and agarbattis and perform "aarti". Girls of marriageable age regard the cobras as blessings of good luck in marriage. Some courageous girls even put their faces near the cobra's dangerous fangs.

There is one popular legend telling how this festival started. Once Guru Gorakhnath while passing through his village saw a woman praying before a clay-cobra idol. He turned it into a living snake and told her not to be afraid of snakes. Since then this Baltis Shirale and its neighbouring regions worship snakes. Guru Gorakhnath's temple is on a nearby hillock. Tribals in the interior parts of Maharashtra perform acrobatics and magic shows on the streets. Crowds collect around them to see and touch the snakes which the tribals bring in their baskets to show them off. There are snake-temples in our country with idols of snake-gods. In these temples cobras are also reared and live snakes are worshipped on Nag-Panchami day.

Serpents are worshipped on Shravan Shukla Panchami. On this day, on both the sides of door 2 idols of serpents are made of cowdung. In this vow, on the Chaturthi day one should take food only once a day. One should fast on the Panchami day and should take food only in the evening..

One should make an idols of a 5 hooded serpents of silver, gold, mud or wood pens and using Turmeric and

Sandal wood pastes as ink. On the Panchami day porridge, Panchamrit (milk, curd, ghee, honey and sugar), lotus flowers, incense etc are offered and the god is accordingly worshipped. In serpents, Ananta, Vasuki, Shesh, Padma, Kambal, Karkotok, Ashvatar, Dhifrashta, Shankpal, Kaaliya, Takshak and Pingal these 12 serpent are the most important ones. Every month one serpent is prayed and worshipped and the (Brahman) person who performs the worship, should be offered food. On the day of Nag Panchami the Brahmin should be offered cows and gold. Some also offer a silver serpents on betel leaves. The person who performs worship of the serpents on Panchami day should not dig the ground. By observing this vow, one is freed from the fear of snakes and serpents and earns plenty of money.

Nag Panchami is celebrated across India in various ways. In Mumbai, cobras arc venerated and fed sweetened milk, usually by women. Tourists can hope to see more snake charmers than usual on the streets and could indulge in a little cobra feeding.

Nag Panchami is celebrated throughout India; however, more festivities are seen in the south than in the north. The village of Baltis Shirale, which is situated approximately 400 kilometers (approximately 250 miles) from Mumbai, conducts the most outstanding of all the celebrations. Reportedly, the largest collection of snakes in the world can be found in Baltis Shirale. Visitors from all over the world gather in the village to worship live snakes. Interestingly, despite no venom being removed from the snakes, no one has ever been bitten. Other popular areas of worship during the Nag Panchami include:

- Adiesha Temple in Andhra Pradesh
- Nagaraja Temple in Kerala
- Nagathamman Temple in Chennai
- Hardevja Temple in Jaipur.

Naga Panchami is a Hindu festival celebrated by Hindus in most parts of India. It is celebrated on Panchami in Shravan month. On this day, they worship Nâga Devata (Cobras). Cobras are considered devine in Hindu mythology. People go to temples and snake pits and they worship the snakes. They offer milk, and silver jewelry to the Cobras to protect them from all evils.

It is on the fifth day of the bright half of the Shravan that Naga Panchami, or the festival of snakes, is celebrated. The setting sun is witness to mile-long processions of gaily-decorated bullock carts, cheerfully trundling to the nearby Shiva temple. The excitement and merry-go-round of a fair takes over, lasting well into the night. The snakes that the men had captured from the deep forests the week before can now return to where they came from.

Snake worship no doubt owes its origin to man's natural fear of these reptiles. Hindu books are filled with stories and fables about snakes, and pictures and images of them meet you at every turn. Worshippers search for holes where snakes are likely to be found. When they have found a hole, they make periodic visits, placing before it milk, bananas, and other food that the snake is likely to fancy.

The Naga culture was fairly widespread in India before the Aryan invasion, and continues to be an important segment of worship in certain areas. After the invasion, the Indo-Aryans incorporated the worship of snakes into Hinduism, as is apparent in prevailing worship and mythology. The thousand-headed Ananta is Vishnu's couch and also holds up the earth, while snakes play an ornamental role in the case of Shiva.

Snake worship is more common in peninsular India than in the north. On this day, ploughing a field is forbidden. Legend has it that on this day, while tilling his land, a farmer accidentally killed some young serpents. The mother of these serpents took revenge by biting and killing the farmer and his family, except one daughter, who happened to be praying to the Nagas. This act of devotion resulted in the revival of the farmer and the rest of his family.

On this day, the women draw figures of snakes on the walls of their houses using a mixture of black powder, cow dung and milk. Then offerings of milk, ghee, water and rice are made. It is believed that in reward for this worship, snakes will never bite any member of the family.

On Nag Panchami day the victory of Krishna over the Kaliya snake is commemorated. For this reason Krishna is known as "Kaliya Mardan". Snakes are believed to like milk. As this is the day of the serpents, devotees pour milk into all the holes in the ground around the house or near the temple to propitiate them. Sometimes, a small pot of milk with some flowers is placed near the holes so that the snakes may drink it. If a snake actually drinks the milk, it is considered to be extremely lucky for the devotee. The festival is celebrated with much enthusiasm by all, especially women.

As most rivers in India are in spate during the month of Shriven, poisonous snakes come out of their subterranean abodes and creep about in plenty all over the place. Many also float on flooded rivers running through the countryside. Mortality from snakebites must have been considerable to prompt people to worship the nagas to seek protection from them. Because of the fear, nagas were elevated to a divine status by the Hindus. The serpents are believed to have the capability to change their shape at will. When in human form, they are depicted as beautiful women and handsome men.

Naga Panchami is observed in different ways in different parts of India. It is one of the most ancient fasts, and finds mention in the Puranas. It is believed to be one of the most auspicious days of the entire year. According to the Bhavishya Purana, when men bathe the snakes called Vasuki, Takshaka, Kaliya, Manibhadra, Airavata, Dhritarashtra, Karkotaka and Dhananjaya with milk on the fifth day of the bright fortnight of Shriven, they ensure freedom from danger for their families.

20

Onam

Onam is the most popular festival of Kerala. Onam portrays the fabulous cultural heritage of Kerala, its golden past, rich traditions. It is the spirit of Onam that attracts tourist not only across India but also from other parts of the world. High-spirited people of Kerala celebrate Onam with gaiety and fervor. The festival is celebrated for a period of ten days, starting from the first day Atham and continuing till tenth and the biggest day called Thiru Onam. It is the most famous festival of South India. All in Kerala celebrates Onam irrespective of their social status, religion, caste and age. According to legends it celebrates the return of King Mahabali, the kind demon king who once ruled the land. Intricate floral carpets called Pookalam mark the first day of the festival. The biggest and the most happening day in the carnival of Onam is Thiruvonam. There are lots of activities like sports and cultural events that take place all over the state on Onam. Number of sports and games events are also organized on the day. These are collectively called Onakalikal. Some of them are rigorous sports like Talappanthukali, Kutukutu and combats like Kayyankali and Attakalam.

This ten-day long festival, generally, falls in the month of Chingam (according to the Malayalam calendar) and is celebrated with much pomp and gaiety. Onam is also a harvest festival. It is celebrated at a time when everything appears so nice and good. The best part of the festival is it's secular flavor as people from all religious background takes part in it. It is more like a community festival. Onam reflects the faith of the people of Kerala; their belief in the legendary past, religion and power of worship. It shows the high spirit of the people who go out of the way to celebrate the festival in the prescribed manner and a grand fashion.

People decorate their homes with fresh flower mats known as 'Pookalam' to welcome the King Mahabali. They wear new dresses; visit the temples to offer their prayers to the Gods and performing traditional dances such as Thiruvathirakali and Thumbi Tullal. One of the most exciting facets of Onam is the unfolding of its rich and well-established culture and tradition. We see not just glimpses but a whole gamut of it in the ten-day-long carnival. The rich cultural heritage is portrayed beautifully in these ten days. Onam is the true picture of the passion of the people of Kerala and most popular festival among masses.

21

Pongal

> Culture is not just an ornament; it is the expression of a nation's character, and at the same time it is a powerful instrument to mould character. The end of culture is right living.
>
> —*W. Somerset Maugham*

Pongal is the first festival beginning off each new year in the Tamil Nadu. As the dates for this festival are calculated by the solar calander (i.e. Western), the dates of January 13-16 never change. Each day of this festival has a special significance, however, it is celebrated more grandly in the villages, while the city folk mainly celebrate on the second day only.

The first day of the festival is called *Bhogi*. On Bhogi all people clean out their homes from top to bottom, and collect all unwanted goods. In the evening, people will light bonfires and burn what can be burnt. In the village, the people lived in mud huts with thatched roves. The porches of these homes was fully covered by the thatch material, but somewhat elevated from the ground. This part of the home was taken apart and reconstructed on this day along with the front section of the walkway in front of their home. Both the porch and ground in front of their home was solid mud which had dried. So, to undo this, they put in water to soften it, and dug it out and rebuilt it. After rebuilding it, they took cow dung and added water to make a paste and spread this mixture evenly over the new fixtures to coat and sanitize them. This mixture was also spread on the floor of the hut. Although, the mixture had been spread on the floor, it did not at all smell fowl in any way.

The second day of the festival, *Surya Pongal*, is the day on which the celebrations actually begins, is the first day of the Tamil month Thai. On this day, Surya, the sun God is worshipped and women will wake early on this day to create elaborate kolum on the grounds in front of their doorway or home. Kolums are created with colored rice flour placed on the ground carefully by using one's hand. The picture shown to the right shows the beginnings of this. The women in the picture took several hours to finish that kolum. All people will wear their new dresses and use the new utensils or household items which replace the ones discarded the previous day. On this day the new rice is collected and cooked in pots until they over flow. It is this overflowing which means Pongal.

This overflowing of rice is a joyous occasion, and the children and adults as well will shout out 'Pongal-o Pongal!' Children will dance and make music to the tune of these words. The words have no real meaning but an expression of happiness that the new harvest is here and we should enjoy it! The rice is cooked and prepared as a dish called Pongal, which is rice with dhal and sugar. This Pongal variety is called *venpongal*, ven meaning white. Another variety is also prepared with dhal and jaggery (sweet), called *chakrai pongal*, chakrai meaning sweet. To accompany the venpongal, people eat brinjal (eggplant) sambar (stew), vadai, idli, and spicy accompaniments.

The third day is called *Mattu Pongal*, 'maatu' meaning cattle. This day is devoted to paying homage to cattle. Cows and Bulls are decorated with paint and bells and people pray to them. In fact, the cattle are decorated with bells on their neck, and kum placed on their head paid respect to them by bending down, like praying in temple, and touching their feet and foreheads, followed by an aarthi and offering the cattle prasadam (food offering, in this case, Pongal). In some villages in south India, there are bull fights of varying types.

The fourth day is termed as *Kaanum Pongal*. On this day, people travel to see other family members. On this day, the younger members of the family pay homage to the elders, and the elders thank them by giving token money. Another thing many do is leave food out on banana leaves for birds to take. Many South Indian people will take the first bit of rice cooked in any given day and set it outside for the crows to take, so this is not necessarily a habit only for Pongal. Some also go to temple.

The great diversity of Indian religious beliefs and the varied cultured traditions of the different states are very interesting and this is seen in the festival of Pongal.

"May the pot of prosperity boil over

May the Pongal that we cook,

the fragrance of turmeric

the taste of sugarcane, ginger and honey

Bring the joy of Pongal into our homes

May the blessings of the Sun God flood our lives.

With many other verses like this the people of Tamil Nadu greet the great festival of Pongal celebrated all over the South as Makar Sankranti, in Tamil Nadu it has an additional significance as Pongal welcomes the occasion of the incoming harvest.

The Puranas, usually prolific in legends connected with festivals, have little to say about this Pongal festival. It is in all probability a Dravidian harvest festival that has survived the preponderant influence of the Indo-Aryan religion in the South.

There is a beautiful Tamil composition of the ancient Sangam period which was known for the ancient Tamil Academics. This charming composition describes the joy of a love-born young woman on the return of her husband from the battlefield. Her happiness is likened to the month before Pongal. When, with the end of rains, the "kaya" flowers blossom, the tender 'Konrai' flowers shower their golden polen on the ground, the white "kandal" flowers blossom, the tender 'Konrai' plant is in full bloom and with receding clouds the female and male deer are making love in the fields. This poem describes the mood of anticipation and excitement of the people in Tamil Nadu which gets its main rains from the north-eastern monsoon in October and November and the harvest is gathered in the period just preceding this Pongal festival.

This festival of Pongal falls in the month of January after the winter solstice and as such this Pongal festival marks the favourable course of the Sun. It is a three-day festival and the fourth day is a day for outdoors and excursions.

Pongal is a festival when god is praised with a simple faith and sincerity. Old vices are all washed out and all that is good is welcomed in this New year. This festival is of all living things, of man, his beast and his crop and of the birds that fly in the sky making man look up to the heaven in joy and thankfulness to God for everything that He gives to man specially peace and happiness and the feeling of brotherhood.

The astronomical significance of the festival is that it marks the beginning of Uttarayana, the Sun's movement northward for a six month period. In Hinduism, Uttarayana is considered auspicious, as opposed to Dakshinaayana, or the southern movement of the sun. All important events are scheduled during this period. Makara Sankranti refers to the event of the Sun entering the zodiac sign of Makara or Capricorn.

22

Raksha Bandhan

> Natural abilities are like natural plants; they need pruning by study.
>
> —*Francis Bacon*

Raksha Bandhan (*the bond of protection* in Hindi) or *Rakhi* is a Hindu festival which celebrates the relationship between brothers and sisters. It is celebrated on the full moon of the month of Shravana.

Raksha Bandhan is marked by the tying of a rakhi, or holy thread by the sister on the wrist of her brother. The brother in return offers a gift to his sister and vows to look after her. The brother and sister traditionally feed each other sweets. It is not necessary that the rakhi can be given only to a brother by birth; any male can be "adopted" as a brother by tying a rakhi on the person, whether they are cousins or a good friend. Indian history is replete with women asking for protection, through rakhi, from men who were neither their brothers, nor Hindus themselves.

Alexander The Great and King Puru: One of the oldest legendary references to the festival of Rakhi goes back to 300 B.C. At this time Alexander the Great, was invading India. Alexander was shaken by the fury of the Indian king Puru in his first attempt. Upset by this, Alexander's wife, who had heard of the Rakhi festival, approached King Puru.

King Puru accepted her as his sister and when the opportunity came during the war, he refrained from fighting Alexander.

Vrita-Indra: The origin of this festival is usually traced back to the mythological incidents of Indra's fight with Vritra-Indra that resulted in Indra's loss. Then, his wife had tied a thread around his wrist and empowered it with divine powers to make sure Indra emerged victorious in the duel that followed.

Krishna and Draupadi: Another incident is the one that concerns Krishna and Draupadi, the wife of the Pandavas. She had torn a strip of silk off her sari and tied it around Krishna's wrist to stop the flow of blood Krishna was so touched by her action that he found himself bound to her by love. He promised to repay the debt and then spent the next 25 years doing just that. Draupadi inspite of being married to 5 great warriors and being a daughter of a powerful monarch only trusted and depended wholly on Krishna.

King Bali and Goddess Laxmi: According to another legend the Demon King Bali was a great devotee of Lord Vishnu. Lord Vishnu had taken up the task to guard his kingdom leaving his own abode in Vaikunth. Goddess Laxmi wished to be with her lord back in her abode. She went to Bali disguised as a Brahmin woman to seek refuge till her husband came back. During the Shravan Purnima celebrations, Laxmiji tied the sacred thread to the King. Upon being asked she revealed who she was and why she was there. The king was touched by her goodwill for his family and her purpose and requested the Lord to accompany her. He sacrificed all he had for the Lord and his devoted wife.

Thus, the festival is also called Baleva that is Bali Raja's devotion to the Lord. It is said that since then it has been a tradition to invite sisters in Shravan Purnima for the thread tying ceremony or the Raksha Bandhan

Rani Karnawati and Emperor Humayun: The ealiest origins of Raksha Bandhan in documented history can be traced to the medieval era. During this period the Rajputs were fighting Muslim invasions. Rakhi at that time was a spiritual symbol associated with protection of the sister. History has it that when Queen Karnawati the widow of the then King of Chittor realised that she could in no way defend the invasion of the Sultan of Gujarat, Bahadur Shah, she sent a rakhi to Emperor Humayun. The Emperor touched by the gesture, accepted the rakhi thereby accepting Queen Karnawati as a "sister" and immediately started off with his vast troops to protect Queen Karnavati.

Yama and the Yamuna: According to another legend, Raksha Bandhan was a ritual followed by Lord Yama (the Lord of Death) and his sister Yamuna. Yamuna tied rakhi to Yama and bestowed immortality. Yama was so moved by the serenity of the occasion that he declared thar whoever gets a rakhi tied from his sister and promised her protection will become immortal.

While Rakhsa Bandhan is celebrated all over the country, different parts of the country celebrate the festival in different ways with a different significance.

Perhaps the single most important way of celebrating Raksha Bandhan is by tying the rakhi. A sister ties a rakhi to the wrist of her brother. The tying of a rakhi signifies her asking of her brother for his protection and love for the sister. The brother is turn, accepts the rakhi, confirms his love and affection for his sister and shows this with gifts and money. It is a family event where all members of family, dressed in finery, gather and celebrate. The tying of rakhi is followed by a family feast.

Rakhi is celebrated as Rakhi Purnima in North India as well as in parts of Northwest India. The word "Purnima" means a full moon night.

While, in western India and parts of Maharashtra, Gujarat, Goa and Karnataka, this day is celebrated as Nariyal Purnima. On this day an offering of a coconut (nariyal) is made to the sea, as a mark of respect to Lord Varuna, the God of the Sea. Nariyal Purnima marks the beginning of the fishing season and the fisherman, who depend on the sea for a living, make an offering to Lord Varun so that they can reap bountiful fish from the sea.

In southern parts of India including Kerala, Andhra Pradesh, Tamil Nadu and Orissa this day is celebrated by the Brahmin community as Avani Avittam. On this day they change their sacred threads or Janeyu.

In central parts of India such as Madhya Pradesh, Chattisgarh, Jharkhand and Bihar this day is celebrated as Kajari Purnima. It is an important day for the farmers and women blessed with a son. On the ninth day after Shravana Amavasya, the preparations of the Kajari festival start. This ninth day is called Kajari Navami and varied rituals are performed by women who have sons until Kajri Purnima.

In parts of Gujarat, this day is celebrated as Pavitropana. On this day people perform the grand pooja or the worship of Lord Shiva. It is the culmination of the prayers done through out the year.is a unique Indian festival dedicated to the angelic love between a brother and a sister. Rakhi or Raksha Bandhan is the day of love, care and bonding signified by a thread that is tied around the wrist of the brother by his loving sister.

The festival of Rakhi is observed on the full moon day of the Hindu month of Shravan. Rakhis are generally made of silk with gold and silver threads and are beautifully embroidered with glitter and decorated with semi precious stones. It is also the time when gifts are exchanged, wishes given and blessings showered for a safe, secure and loving time ahead. Rakhi or Raksha Bandhan is known by many names like Vish Tarak—the destroyer of venom, Punya Pradayak—the bestower of boons, and Pap Nashak—the destroyer of sins.

The Rishis tied rakhi on the wrist of the people who came seeking for their blessings. The sages also use to tie this sacred thread to themselves to safe guard them from evil. Rakhi – thus – has always signified a bond of love, protection, security and unity. It is much more than just a celebration of brotherly love – Rakhi actually encompasses the broader arena of universal brotherhood and peace. Rakhi Celebrations. Rakhi is celebrated all over the world. Sister wait for their brothers with a warm heart, an auspicious Rakhi thali, rakhi thread, sweets and lovely rakhi gifts for their brothers. In case of long distance relationships, Rakhis are brought online and sent to brothers anywhere in the world. Brothers too send return gifts to their beloved sisters. With wishes and blessings, gifts and greetings, love and unity – Rakhi – the festival of love – is unique in its own way.

The strong bond represented by Rakhi has resulted in innumerable political ties among kingdoms and princely states. The pages of Indian history testify that the Rajput and Maratha queens have sent Rakhis even to Mughal kings who, despite their differences, have assuaged their Rakhi-sisters by offering help and protection at critical moments and honoured the fraternal bond. Even matrimonial alliances have been established between kingdoms through the exchange of Rakhis.

History has it that the great Hindu King Porus refrained from striking Alexander, the Great because the latter's wife had approached this mighty adversary and tied a Rakhi on his hand, prior to the battle, urging him not to hurt her husband.

Rakhi: Rituals like Rakhi, there is no doubt, help ease out various societal strains, induce fellow-feeling, open up channels of expression, give us an opportunity to rework on our role as human beings and, most importantly, bring joy in our mundane lives.

Shravan purnima's second festival is Raksha Bandhan. This is an ancient tradition. Bhavishya Purana refers to a battle between gods and demons, and Indra (the king of the gods) was feeling depressed. At that time Indra's wife Sachi took a thread, charged it with sacred verses or Mantras for protection and tied it on Indra's hand. Through the strength of this thread Indra conquered his enemies. Since then till today this festival is celebrated.

Through the passage of time festivals are undergoing modifications. Raksha Bandhan is also known as Rakhi. Rakhi has become a sacred festival for sisters and brothers. Sisters tie them to brothers. Priests tie them to people of his congregation. During the middle ages, if a woman tied a Rakhi on the hand of any man, then it became imperative for him, as his religious duty of the highest order, to protect that woman. That man would put his life at stake to protect the honour of that woman.

In those days, many Rajputs sacrificed their lives to protect their spiritual sisters. Humayun received a Rakhi from the queen Karmavati of Chittor and for that, Humayun carried out his sacred brotherly duty and protected her by opposing his own soldiers.

According to ancient traditions, it is customary to have protection threads that are charged with sacred verses (Mantras) and sanctified with rice, durva grass etc.; to have these tied by people who know the Vedas or by near and dear ones. This protection thread saves from sins on the one hand and removes diseases on the other hand. By tying this thread, protection is afforded for a full one year and all kinds of fears are removed.

Nowadays Rakhis are decorated with soft silky threads

of various colours, and also with ornaments, pictures, gold and silver threads etc. These Rakhis enhance the artistry of the people. Within these Rakhis reside sacred feelings and well wishes. It is also a great sacred verse of unity. Acting as a symbol of life's advancement and a leading messenger of togetherness.

Each person should celebrate with enthusiasm this sacred festival of Rakhi or Raksha Bandhan. (Raksha = protection. Bandhan = tie).

Two important festivals are celebrated during the bright fortnight in the month of Shravan. One is known as Upakarma and the other as Raksha Bandhan.

The annual "festival" of Raksha Bandhan, which is meant to commemorate the abiding ties between siblings of opposite sex, usually takes place in late August, and is marked by a very simple ceremony in which a woman ties a rakhi — which may be a colorful thread, a simple bracelet, or a decorative string — around the wrist of her brother(s). The word "raksha" signifies protection, and "bandhan" is an association signifying an enduring sort of bond; and so, when a woman ties a rakhi around the wrist of her brother, she signifies her loving attachment to him. He, likewise, recognizes the special bonds between them, and by extending his wrist forward, he in fact extends the hand of his protection over her. The thread-tying ceremony is sometimes preceded by the woman conducting *aarti* before her brother, so that the blessings of God may be showered upon him, and this is to the accompaniment of her enunciation or chanting of a mantra, which may be in Sanskrit or one of the other Indian languages. In Punjabi, for instance, the mantra says: "Suraj shakhan chhodian / Mooli chhodia beej / Behen ne rakhi bandhi / Bhai tu chir jug jee", which can be roughly translated as follows: "The sun radiates its sunlight / the radish seeds / I (the sister) tied the rakhi / brother, may you live long." After the conclusion of the ceremony, she places a sweet in her mouth, and he might return the gesture. The brother bestows a small gift upon his sister, generally in the form of a small sum of money, such as Rupees 51, 101, 251, or 501.

It is doubtless possible, from a feminist perspective, to view raksha bandhan as another expression of patriarchal culture, however well-intentioned. It is, after all, the brother who extends his protection to his sister, and the woman who, in a manner of speaking, agrees to place herself under the protection of her brother. Against such a reading, one could well argue that the festival seeks to celebrate simply the affectionate ties between siblings of opposite sex, and that the brother-sister nexus is, comparatively speaking, innocent. This is scarcely to say that the relationship is devoid of power, or that there are not habitual practices and customs which define the relationship. But the real significance of raksha bandhan may lie elsewhere. Though it has been common in most societies for the woman to leave her natal home at marriage for her husband's home, in India this is firmly entrenched as a social practice, and has often had undesirable consequences. Women who are subjected to harassment or life-threatening behavior on account of dowry by the husband's family have often been reluctant to return to their natal home, and similarly parents are reluctant to take back their married daughters on account of the immense stigma attached to the return of a married daughter.

There is ample evidence to suggest that the problem of dowry has unquestionably been aggravated by the social sanction placed upon married daughters residing in their natal home. Consequently, raksha bandhan can be viewed as an occasion for reasserting a woman's ties to her natal home. The brother conveys a message to his sister that she has not been abandoned by her biological kin; similarly, the woman conveys a message to her husband's family that she can well count upon her natal family to come to her assistance.

Though in principle raksha bandhan is an observance between biological siblings of the opposite sex, the practice often extends more generally to people of the opposite sex who are not biologically related, or who are not related as siblings. On raksha bandhan day, a number of women may tie the rakhi around the Prime Minister's wrist (unless the Prime Minister be a woman), and similarly soldiers can expect to have women tie rakhis around their wrists. Thus, from ads placed on the occasion of raksha bandhan in the *Times of India* (Mumbai, 25 August 1999), col. 3: "Let's break the traditions of Sisters sending Rakhis to their Brothers this time and approach the widows of Kargil Heroes with Rakhis to tie", and "Let us all send a Thread to our Brave Soldiers in Kargil so that they shred their Pakistan opponents. Satnam Kaur." Everywhere, especially in north and western India, females might tie a rakhi around the wrist of boys and men without sisters. A man might acquire a *muh boli behen*, that is a sister who in every respect is such except in biological fact; or a woman may tie a rakhi around the wrist of her male first cousin who is without sisters. Imagining a person of the opposite sex as a sibling is certainly one way of obscuring the problem of sexual desire, and Indian texts are rife with the observation that men should look upon women as their sisters and mothers.

Raksha bandhan is not entirely a pious affair, though sentimentality doubtless prevails. It has, thankfully, also become an occasion for some jest, humor, and mild ribaldry. Rakhi advertisements from the *Times of India*, Mumbai (25 August, 1999), suggest that some men construe "raksha bandhan" truly as an occasion for taking their responsibilities as a protective brother seriously, as in this advertisement which deploys the familiar metaphor of the sheltering banyan tree: "Your Brother Banyan Tree will protect 5 branches

Saroja, Vijaya, Laxmi, Thangam, Lalitha on auspicious Raksha Bandhan Day. A.R. Parshuram" (col. 3). A similar sentiment, with the sacred as its central trope, is expressed by this woman: "Dear Brother. Accept my blessing and affection through this sacred thread which tightens our relationship better" (col. 6).

The supposition that a sister stands in place of a mother comes across in some ads: "Dear Sister Ruta, they say mothers couldn't be everywhere everytime, so God made sisters. Ani" (col. 5), and "My Loving Sister, for me you're like both mother & father. You're next to God & your love is next to Divinity. Rays of your love & blessings enlivened me like Rays of the Ultimate. Symbol of love & sacrifice, I adore your feet today. Deeyech" (col. 7). But alongside the expression of these more conventional sentiments, one might consider the humor of the ad from one "Feh": "Dear Bro. Nirlek. You are the perfect Brother to have — good height, strong built, lots of money, and no brain" (col. 5), or the lampooning of India's family planning programs: "Adarniya, [Respected] Bachelor Padhanmantriji [Prime Minister] no solution for population control? Try popularising Raksha-Bandhan day all throughout India. Love. Joekar" (col. 7).

The delicate cord tied by the sister to the brother on this day pulsates with this sublime sentiment. History and legends of Bharat abound in touching episodes of ladies seeking protection from far-off, unacquainted heroes, though the Raakhi. A story is told of Alexander's wife approaching his mighty Hindu adversary Pururavas and tying Raakhi on his hand, seeking assurance from him for saving the life of her husband on the battlefield. And the great Hindu king, in the true traditional Kshatriya style, responded; and as the legend goes, just as he raised his hand to deliver a mortal blow to Alexander, he saw the Raakhi on his own hand and restrained from striking.

A more poignant instance is of the princess of a small Rajput principality. It speaks of the spell the Raakhi had cast even on those of alien faiths. The princess sent a Raakhi to the Moghal Emperor Humayun to save her honor from the onslaught of the Gujarat Sultan. The emperor who was engaged in an expedition against Bengal, turned back and hastened to the rescue of his Raakhi sister. But, alas, to his utmost sorrow, he found that the kingdom had already been overrun and the princess had committed Jauhaar, i.e., leaped into the flames to save her honor.

The sister-brother relationship highlighted by the Raakhi goes far beyond the mere personal protection of a female from a male. It also implies the basic element of an amicable and harmonious social life where all members of the society look upon themselves as brothers and sisters and as children of one common motherland.

The congregational Raakhi function carries this social content. Particularly, the tying of Raakhi to the sacred Bhagavaa Dhwaj at the start of the function signifies this social and cultural aspect. Not only do the participants in the function develop a sense of love and affection amongst themselves but they also affirm their loyalty and devotion to the society of which they are the children. Their commitment to protect each other and also the society as a whole is emphasized through this simple ceremony.

In the Hindu tradition the Rakshaa has indeed assumed all aspects of protection of the forces of righteousness from the forces of evil. Once, Yudhishthira asked Sri Krishna how best he could guard himself against impending evils and catastrophes in the coming year. Krishna advised him to observe the Rakshaa Ceremony. He also narrated an old incident to show how potent the Rakshaa is.

Once, Indra was confronted by the demon king—the Daitya-raaja—in a long-drawn battle. At one stage, the Daitya-raaja got better of Indra and drove him into wilderness. Indra, humbled and crest-fallen, sought the advice of Brihaspati, the Guru of Gods. The Guru told him to bide his time, prepare himself and then march against his adversary. He also indicated that the auspicious moment for sallying forth was the Shraavana Poornima. On that day, Shachee Devi, the wife of Indra, and Brihaspati tied Raakhis around Indra's right-wrist. Indra then advanced against the Daitya-raaja, vanquished him and reestablished his sovereignty

It is not merely that the spirit of Rakshaa manifests itself on occasions of mortal peril to the life and honor of the beloved ones or to the society. It is not like the Home Guards or the militia which are expected to come to the rescue of the people in times of war or natural calamities. No, it is far more deep and all-encompassing. It is like the flow of bloodstream through every limb and organ of the body, carrying strength and nourishment to every cell thereof. As a result, even a small wound anywhere in the body is promptly attended to by the entire body. Every other limb spontaneously scarifies a part of its blood and energy to heal that wound and keep that organ healthy and strong.

The chaste bond of love between a brother and a sister is one of the deepest and noblest of human emotions. 'Raksha Bandhan' or 'Rakhi' is a special occasion to celebrate this emotional bonding by tying a holy thread around the wrist. This thread, which pulsates with sisterly love and sublime sentiments, is rightly called the 'Rakhi'. It means 'a bond of protection', and Raksha Bandhan signifies that the strong must protect the weak from all that's evil.

This ritual not only strengthens the bond of love between brothers and sisters, but also transcends the confines of the family. When a Rakhi is tied on the wrists of close friends and neighbors, it underscores the need for a harmonious social life, where every individual co-exist peacefully as brothers and sisters. All members of the community commit to protect each other and the society in such congregational Rakhi Utsavs, popularized by the Nobel laureate Bengali poet Rabindranath Tagore.

It won't be wrong to say the fashionable friendship band in vogue today is an extension of the Rakhi custom. When a girl feels a friend of the opposite sex has developed a kind of love too strong for her to reciprocate, she sends the guy a Rakhi and turns the relationship into a sisterly one. This is one way of saying, "let's just be friends", without hurting the other person's soft feelings for her.

In Northern India, Rakhi Purnima is also called Kajri Purnima or Kajri Navami, when wheat or barley is sown, and goddess Bhagwati is worshipped. In Western states, the festival is called Nariyal Purnima or the Coconut Full Moon. In Southern India, Shravan Purnima is an important religious occasion, especially for the Brahmins.

23

Ram Navami

> The world expects results. Don't tell others about the labor pains. Show them the baby.
>
> —*Arnold Glasow*

Ramanavami celebrates the birth of Lord Rama or Ramachandra. On the ninth day of the first fortnight of Chaitra the birth of Rama is commemorated. The story of Rama was first written by Valmeeki in about the 4th century B.C. Rama is supposed to have lived during the 8th or 7th century B.C. In some parts of India, it is a nine-day festival, coinciding with the Vasanta Navaratri. Ayodhya is the focus of great celebrations. Devotees throng the temples of Ayodhya and Pondicherry, two places closely connected with the events of the Ramayana to participate in Ramnavami festivities.

The public worship starts with morning ablutions, chanting Vedic mantras dedicated to Vishnu, and offering flowers and fruit to the god. People keep a fast throughout the day, breaking it only at midnight with fruit. In some parts of India, especially Bihar and Uttar Pradesh, public gatherings called satsangs are organised to commemorate the birth of Rama. Excerpts from the Ramacharitamanas, extolling the glory of Rama, are recited. People of all castes and creeds participate in these gatherings to listen to the stories and their explanations offered by the learned.

The country of Kosal was situated on the banks of the

river Sarayu. Ayodhya was the capital founded by the king rishi Manu. During the reign of king Dasarath, Ayodhya reached a period of great prosperity. But Dasarath faced a big problem: he had no children. Therefore he decided to perform a sacrifice known as "ashvamedh", or horse-sacrifice. Elaborate and difficult rituals had to be observed. A very holy man, rishi Rishyashring, was chosen to conduct the sacrifice with the utmost accuracy. The performance of this sacrifice was a great event in Ayodhya. At the end Rishyashring recited a mantra and made an offering to the fire. Then the gods, gandharvas, siddhas, and rishis present and began to pray to Brahma.

At that time Ravana, king of Lanka, was terrorizing the people, and all were longing for liberation from his menace. Ravan had acquired great power because he had obtained from god Brahma the boon that he would never die at the hands of gods, or gandharvas, or yakshas (demigods) or demons. As he was not afraid of men he did not care to include men in the list of his potential slayers. So Brahmadev declared that Ravan would die at the hands of a man. Then the gods went to Vishnu with the request, "Dasarath is a glorious king. Please, take birth in the wombs of his three queens in four different degrees of your divinity."

When Dasarath's sacrifice came to an end a shining figure appeared over the sacrificial kund, and offered the king a divine beverage called "payasam" to be given to his queens Kausalya, Kaikayi, and Sumitra. In due time Kausalya gave birth to Rama, Kaikayi to Bharat and Sumitra to Laxman and Shatrugna. Rama was born at noon of the bright ninth day of Chaitra. He was believed to be the embodiment of half degree of Vishnu's divinity.

The effigy of the ten-headed Ravana swaggers through the town, wearing a gaudy crown and exaggerated moustache, with shouting hordes following. But once Ravana reaches the open ground that is his final destination, he is suddenly deserted by most of his "followers"—because the noble Rama has made his appearance.

In the end, righteousness does triumph, even in Kali Yuga. Rama engages him in battle, and finally pierces him with a potent arrow. And the huge effigy of Ravana, filled to bursting with firecrackers, is set alight, and explodes into a thousand bits amid loud cheers from the crowd and shouts of Jai Shri Ram. This ritual is an important part of the Rama Navami celebrations in most parts of North India.

Rama Navami falls on the ninth day of the shukla paksha, or bright phase of the moon, in the lunar month of Chaitra (April-May). The first day of Chaitra , or Ugadi, also marks the beginning of the Indian year.

Rama is one of the ten avatars of Lord Vishnu, and one of the two most popular, along with Krishna. Consequently, Rama Navami is widely celebrated, though not on the scale of festivals like Diwali or Dussehra.

Rama was the first of the four sons of King Dasharatha of Ayodhya. When it was time for Rama to be made crown-prince, his stepmother, Kaikeyi, got Dasharatha to send him to the forest for 14 years. His wife Sita and his brother Lakshmana also accompanied him. In the forest, Sita was kidnapped by Ravana, the demon king of Lanka. Rama, together with Hanuman and the monkey army, built a bridge to Lanka, killed Ravana, and brought Sita back.

It is believed that listening to the story of Rama cleanses the soul. Meditating on the noble Rama and chanting his name is believed to ease the pains of life and lead one to moksha, or liberation. It is also common practice to chant the name of Rama while rocking babies to sleep. Though Rama Navami is a major festival for Vaishnavites, it is widely celebrated by worshippers of Shiva, too. It is considered auspicious to undertake a fast on the day in the name of Rama. The more devout fast for nine days, from Ugadi to Rama Navami. The objective of the fast is not to ask for special favours of the deity but to seek perfection as a human being. Devotees perform elaborate pujas and chant the name of Rama. Temples of Rama have special services and bhajan sessions through the day.

One significant and popular element of the celebration is the Ramayana parayana, a discourse on the Ramayana, by a pundit or a professional story-teller. It usually lasts nine days, beginning on Ugadi and ending on Rama Navami. A skilled story-teller who can liven up the event by weaving in contemporary events attracts massive crowds.

Since Rama is also one of the most sung-about deities in Indian classical music and literature, week-long (and sometimes, month-long) musical programmes are organised.

Sacred places associated with Rama, like Ayodhya, Ujjain and Rameshwaram, draw tens of thousands of devotees. In Rameshwaram, thousands take a ritual bath in the sea before worshipping at the Ramanathaswamy temple.

Many places in North India host fairs in connection with the festival, culminating in spectacular fireworks on Rama Navami.

Again, Ramnavami is one of the most important festivals of the Vaishnava sect of the Hindus. However, even those who adore Lord Shiva celebrate the occasion. Some observe a strict fast on the day. Temples are decorated and the image of Lord Rama is richly adorned. The holy Ramayana is read in the temples. At Ayodhya, the birthplace of Sri Rama, a big fair is held on this day.

In South India the Sri Ramnavami Utsavam is celebrated for nine days with great fervour and devotion.

The Ramayana, the Rama story, teaches two lessons: the value of detachment and the need to become aware of the Divine in every being. Faith in God and detachment from objective pursuits are the keys for human liberation. Give up sense objects, and you gain Rama. Sita gave up the luxuries of Ayodhya so she could be with Rama during His exile. When she cast longing eyes on the golden deer and craved it, she lost Rama's presence. Renunciation leads to joy; attachment brings about grief. Be in the world, but not of it.

Rama's brothers, comrades, companions, and collaborators are all examples of people saturated with dharma. Dasaratha is the representative of the merely physical, with the ten senses. The three qualities (gunas) — serenity, passion, sloth (sathva, rajas, thamas)— are the three Queens. The four goals of life (purusharthas) are the four sons. Dharma (Rama), Artha (Lakshmana), Kama (Bharatha) and Moksha (Shatrughna). These four aims of man have to be systematically realised, always with the last one, Moksha, clearly before the eye. Sugriva is discrimination (viveka). Vali is despair. Hanuman is the embodiment of courage. The bridge is built over the ocean of delusion. The three demon (rakshasa) chiefs Ravana, Kumbhakarna, and Vibhishana are personifications of the passionate, slothful, and serene (raajasic, tamasic, and satvik) qualities. Sita is the awareness of the Universal Absolute (Brahmajnaana), which the individual must acquire and regain while undergoing travails in the crucible of life. With these to help him, Rama seeks the Truth and succeeds. That is the lesson of the Epic to every man.

The entire Ramaayana is like a game of chess. The scene, in the Ramaayana, is a kind of battlefield, where the forces of right and wrong are waging war. Rama represents righteousness and Ravana represents unrighteousness. The battle between the two is the war fought on the battlefield.

Ravana taught a great lesson to the world. He exclaimed: "Oh men! Do not live as I have lived and ruin your lives." What is the root cause of Ravana's ruin? Unable to conquer his desires, unwilling to get rid of his impulses, he ruined his entire clan. His sons were killed, his brother and other kinsmen were killed, and ultimately his country itself was reduced to ashes. Ravana confessed, "In the end I ruined myself." This was Ravana's message to his countrymen in his last moments. Only by suppressing desires does a man manifest his humanness. A man who is unable to put an end to his desires puts an end to himself. By his good conduct, a good man achieves greatness. Ravana sought to achieve greatness but did not strive to lead a good life.

Some observe a strict fast on this day. The diet of such a person would include potatoes made in any form without *haldi* (turmeric), garlic, ginger or onion. He can also eat fruit and root vegetables of any kind. Curd, tea, coffee, milk, and water are also permitted.

On the face of it Sri-Ramnavmi appears to be just a festival commemorating the reign of a king who was later deified. But even behind present-day traditions there are clues which unmistakably point to the origin of Ramnavmi as lying beyond the Ramayana story.

A huge fair is held in Ayodhya (*Ram Janam Bhumi*) on Ram Navami day, where thousands of devotees gather to celebrate this festival.

24

Teej

According to Hindu mythology, on the 3rd day (teej) after the new moon in the month of Shravan Goddess Parvati went to the house of lord Shiva, her husband and was united with him. This day is celebrated as Teej all over India and especially so in Rajasthan. Apart from its mythological origins this festival also heralds the arrival of the rainy season. In the month of Shravan the long awaited monsoon finally arrives in Rajasthan bringing relief to the parched land. Like a magic wand it transforms the hot, dusty and barren summer landscape of Rajasthan into the fertile green beehive of activity. The Teej festivities also celebrate this rejuvenation.

Teej is celebrated mainly by the women folk of Rajasthan. Married women who idolize Parvati for her devotion to her husband Shiva celebrate Teej. The festivity revolves around singing and dancing in praise of Parvati. The rituals allow the women to pamper and enjoy themselves, to feast, to dress in the best of cloths, finery and jewellery, in fact to look the stunning best.

Held during the monsoons, July-August Teej is also dedicated to Lord Shiva and Parvati and this time it is married women who pray for a happy and long married life. Though celebrations are held all over the state, it is particularly colorful in Jaipur where a procession winds its way for two days through the Old City. It is the festival of swings which are decorated with flowers and hung from trees. Young girls and women dressed in green clothes sing songs in celebration of the advent of the monsoon. The Teej idol is covered with a canopy whereas the Gangaur idol is open.

All over Rajasthan, even in remote villages, Jhoolas (swings) are hung from trees and decorated with leaves and flowers. Ladies and girls can be seen enjoying on these swings, playing games, singing folk songs and applying Mehandi (henna) on their palms. In Jaipur an idol of Goddess Parvati (Teej Mata) is taken out in a royal procession from the city palace so that the general public can have a chance to pay homage to the Goddess. Antique gilt palanquins, bullock carts pulling cannons, chariots, gaily decorated elephants with silver haodas, horses, camels, brass bands, and group of dances all form a part of this grand spectacle. The Pamaquin of Goddess Paravati is carried by 8 men dressed in red color. This kilometer long procession winds its way through the lanes of the old city. Local people come in huge numbers, dress in their best traditional clothes. Space is at a premium as people perch on top of building, windows even trees to catch a glimpse of Goddess. A huge band of urchins follows the Pamaquin to grab these offerings. A lot of merriment prevails during the Teej procession. Groups of men and women can be seen singing dancing and playing musical instruments. Men and women dressed as gods and Goddess also join in the procession.

25

Vasant Panchami

> If a man does' not keep pace with his companions, perhaps it is because he hears a different drummer. Let him step to the music which he hears, however measured or far away.
>
> —*Henry David Thoreau*

Vasant Panchami is the festival dedicated to Saraswati, the goddess of learning. Vasant Panchami is a festival full of religious, seasonal and social significance and is celebrated by Hindus all over the world with verve and new sense of optimism. Vasant means, "the spring season". This is the great spring festival, falling on the fifth day of the month of Magh, the first day of spring.

Magh Sud 5 (5th day of the bright fortnight of the lunar month of Magh) is the day of Vasant Panchami. Hindus all over the world celebrate this festival with great enthusiasm. This Panchami is also known as Saraswati Day. It is believed that this day is Saraswati's birthday. Hindu temples are full of activities on this day.

Yellow colour is given special importance on this day. On Vasant Panchami, Saraswati is dressed in yellow garments and worshipped (with Puja, Havan etc.). Men and women try to wear yellow clothes on this day. Sweetmeats of yellowish hues are exchanged with relations and friends.

Some people feed Brahmanas on this day. Pitri-Tarpan

(ancestor worship) is done on this day. The god of love (Kamdev) is also worshipped on this day.

On this day Goddess Saraswati is worshipped as the Goddess of Learning, the deity of Gayatri, the fountain of fine arts and science, and the symbol of supreme vedantic knowledge. Religious paintings depict each of these goddess alighted on a vehicle that symbolizes their special power. The white swan of Saraswati symbolizing Satwa Guna (purity and discrimination), the lotus of Lakshmi the Rajas Guna and the tiger of Durga the Tamas Guna. Saraswati is shown possessing four hands and plays "Veena", an Indian string musical instrument. Vasant Panchami is also known as Saraswati Day and commemorates the birth of goddess Saraswati. Hindu temples throng with people and are abuzz with prayers and rituals.

Children are taught their first words on this day (as an auspicious beginning to learning). Schools, colleges etc., (places of learning) organise special worship of Saraswati. Pandit Madan Mohan Malviya laid the foundations of Kashi Hindu Vishwa Vidyalaya on Vasant Panchami. This has become a world famous top class academic institution. Hinduism has taken into account special significance of seasons and interwoven that with religious festivals e.g., Makar Sankranti, Vasant Panchami. People generally feel inclined to worship the presiding deity of the family (Ishta Devata or Devi) according to the individual's faith and desires. Also, people generally tend to accumulate wealth and power. During the Kala Yuga (present age), the pursuit of money (wealth, power, name and fame) is everything to most people. Money is accorded god-like status.

But men of principle (men who can discriminate) worship goddess Saraswati for spiritual enlightenment. In their opinion, there can be no comparison between the king and the learned (spiritually advanced). The king is honoured within his kingdom, whereas the learned is respected (or worshipped) everywhere. Saintly people and people inclined towards spiritual progress attach great importance to the worship of goddess Saraswati.

The vehicle assigned to each of the three goddesses also symbolically represent their special powers. The white swan of Saraswati is symbolising Sattwa Guna (purity and discrimination). The owl of Lakshmi and the lion or tiger of Durga symbolise the other two gunas (Rajas and Tamas).

Saraswati literally means 'the flowing one'. In Rigveda it is said she represents a river and the deity presiding over it. In the later mythology, Saraswati was identified with Vach or Speech. The 'flowing one' in allegorical sense may mean speech also; perfect speech which denotes intelligence. On this Vasant Panchami day, Brahma is said to have created Saraswati and infused speech into her and bestowed the Vina in her hands. She was thus named as 'Veena Vandini (Vina player) and 'Vani Dayyani recipient of speech). As the spouse of Brahma and the goddess of wisdom and eloquence, She is known by various names such as Vinapani (due to holding the Vina), Sharada (giver of essence), Vagisvari (mistress of speech), Brahmi (wife of Brahma), Mahavidya (knowledge supreme) and so on.

In the Maratha countries, Goddess Saraswati is sometimes called the wife of Ganesh and sometimes his attendant. At the name-giving ceremony in marriage, if a man's name, for instance, is Ganesha, his wife is named Saraswati, just as a Ramachandra's wife is named Sita, or a Krishna's wife is named, after his spouse Rukmini.

Vasant Panchami is also known as Shri Panchami. As Saraswati Puja, it is observed religiously almost in all parts of India expecially in Bengal. Goddess Saraswati being pure and white and representing learning, no animal sacrifice is made to her. Idols of Saraswati are brought and worshipped.

Floral offerings are made in a big scale. Books, articles, instruments of music and arts are placed before her. In the evening after the Puja is over, the idol is immersed in the sea with serenity unlike other major festivals. In all educational institutions of music, arts and science, Saraswati Puja is observed with great reverence. Legend has it that on this day Lord Shiva burnt the God of Love, Cupid of Kamadev. Lord Shiva was lost in Samadhi and to break his Samadhi into impassion him to beget a son powerful enough to kill the demon Tarakasur, Gods send Cupid the God of Love. Cupid or Kamadev discharges an arrow at Lord Shiva from behind a tree. But, Shiva gets terribly angry and reduces Cupid or Kamadev to ashes with his third eye. The Festival of Vasant Panchami is observed on a grand scale in Punjab and the North when the mustard crop is ripe. They cook yellow rice and also wear yellow garments. Saraswati Puja is also performed during the Navaratri or Dussehra.

Hinduism is a way of life rather than a religion, demure to the special significance of seasons in our lives through religious festivals. Vasant Panchami is one of them. Vasant Panchami is referred to as the spring festival, and signifies the beginning of Vasant Ritu (spring season). Magh Sud 5 (5th day of the bright fortnight of the lunar month of Magh) is the day of Vasant Panchami. It is also called as Shree Panchami and Saraswati Puja is also celebrated on the same day.

The first faint signals of the forthcoming festival of Holi manifest at Vasant Panchami. Seasons undergo change. The coming of springtime is heralded. Trees are displaying new shoots. New life is evident in the woods and fields. Nature decorates Mango trees with new blossoms. Wheat and other crops enliven with evidence of new life.

On this day everyone wears a yellow cloth. It represents the ripening of the spring crops. Even the food is coloured yellow by using saffron. Spiritually, the yellow colour is a sign of prosperity; it is the colour of love.

On this day we offer special worship to the sun god, to Mother Ganga (the deity of the sacred river Ganges), and Mother Earth. They provide us the means of acquiring food and all that we need to keep alive. We express our gratitude to them by worshipping them. Hindus are ever mindful of the debt they owe to all nature. Worship of nature is extremely important to them.

Vasant Panchami heralds the beginning of spring. Cool lingering breeze replaces the cold harsh winter and there is a touch of rejuvenation and joy in the air. The buds of leaves and flowers come into full bloom. Girls in different shades of yellow dresses enhance the beauty of nature on the day of Basant Panchami. Kite flying, a popular sport in India, is associated with the Basant Panchami day. It is a day for the students – no studies, only merry making.

26

Prominent Cultural Festivals of India

> The most distinctive mark of a cultured mind is the ability to take another's point of view; to put one's self in another's place, and see life and its problems from a point of view different from one's own. To be willing to test a new idea; to be able to live on the edge of difference in all matters intellectually; to examine without heat the burning question of the day; to have imaginative sympathy, openness and flexibility of mind, steadiness and poise of feeling, cool calmness of judgment, is to have culture.
>
> —*A.H.R. Fairchild*

I

BIKANER FESTIVAL

The famous Bikaner festival is held in the month of July in Bikaner which is dedicated to the indispensable 'ship of the desert', camel. The desert town of Bikaner is located in the Northern part of Rajasthan. This festival starts off with a magnificent procession of elegantly bedecked camels against the red sandstone backdrop of the Junagarh Fort in the town. It is a colourful spectacle of beautifully decorated camels that fascinates the onlookers with their charm and grace. The festivity advances to the open sand-spreads of the Polo Grounds, followed by camel races, camel milking, fur cutting design, the best breed competition, camel acrobatics, camel bands and a host of other programmes.

The camels display amazing footwork, dancing gracefully to the slightest direction of their riders. Their displays and competitions accompany the colour, music and rhythm unique to a fair in Rajasthan. The jubilant skirt swirling dancers, the awe-inspiring fire dance and the dazzling fireworks light up the fortified City of Bikaner. The festivities reach to the peak with a different tenor as the renowned artists display a medley of folk dances and songs.

There is a unique camel-breeding farm just outside the town. Other interesting places in adjacent areas are the Junagarh Fort and Karni Matha Temple where thousands of rats are worshipped with deep veneration.

II

CHAPCHAR KUT

Etymologically, "Kut" means festival in Mizo language, and the state of Mizoram celebrates 3 of them: Chapchar Kut, Mim Kut and Pawl Kut. All are connected with agricultural activities, and all are celebrated with great gaity, feasts and dances.

Representing glorious tribal heritage, Chapchar Kut celebrates the arrival of spring. The festival begins with *Kut Puipate*, the inauguration ceremony, followed by the *Then Katna*, arranging of the dance groups in the stadium. Once the *Then Hnihna* begins, elders, dressed in traditional costumes to represent the various tribes of the region, take part in a fantastic procession called *Kut rore*. This is followed by various tribal dances, the most important being the *Cheraw* (bamboo dance). The function ends with the *Then Thumna,* an event where local singers present traditional popular songs, with the cheering crowd joining in.

III

CHENNAI DANCE AND MUSIC FESTIVAL

Chennai music and dance festival is a celebration of classical music and dance of South India (Carnatic Music) held during mid December to mid January in the capital city of Chennai. The festival is held at a number of venues around the city by various sabhas or organizations.

Chennai music and dance festival is a celebration of classical music and dance of South India held during mid December to mid January in the capital city of Chennai. The festival is held at a number of venues around the city by various 'sabhas' or organizations. Besides the auditoriums, well-known temple premises and heritage bungalows are being used as venues. The month long dance and music extravaganza will have performances of famous artistes from various parts of India.

The 'Margazhi festival of dance and music' started early back in 1927, to commemorate the anniversary of Madras Music Academy every December, was later adopted by various organizations which held art festivals in different parts of the city. The Tamil month of 'Margazhi' is a sacred month of the Hindus. South Indian classical music (Carnatic Music), which has its roots in devotion to the gods, has been a traditional form of worship from time immemorial.

The city comes alive with the festival, which has now developed, into a cultural extravaganza with more than 2000 participants in over 300 concerts. The festival also known as December Season also attracts expatriate Indians and scholars from around the world.

Performances include Vocal and Instrumental music, Dance - solo and group, both by junior and senior artistes. Even upcoming artists get a chance to perform along with well-established artists. The music includes songs in various South Indian languages like Tamil, Telugu and Kannada and instruments like Flute,'Veena' (a large string instrument) 'Goottuvadyam' (similar to Veena but without frets), 'Nagaswaram' (pipe), 'Thavil' (percussion instrument), 'Mridangam' (drum), and even 'Ghatam' (a mud pot). The season goes on till mid January when the scene shifts to Tiruvaiyaru to celebrate the birth of one of the greatest Carnatic composers and one of the trinity of music - Thyagaraja. Information about. The 'Margazhi festival of dance and music' started early back in 1927; to commemorate the anniversary of Madras Music Academy every December was later adopted by various organizations, which held art festivals in different parts of the city.

The city comes alive with the festival, which has now developed, into a cultural extravaganza with more than 2000 participants. Performances include Vocal and Instrumental music, Dance - solo and group, both by junior and senior artistes.Even upcoming artists get a chance to perform along with well-established artists. The music includes songs in various South Indian languages like Tamil, Telugu and Kannada and instruments like Flute, 'Veena' (a large string instrument) 'Goottuvadyam' (similar to Veena but without frets),'Nagaswaram' (pipe),'Thavil' (percussion instrument),'Mridangam' (drum), and even'Ghatam' (a mud pot). Information about the tickets and the venues can be had from the tourist office, Chennai.

IV

ELEPHANTA FESTIVAL

This festival is held across the Mumbai harbour, on the Elephanta Island, near the world-renowned Elephanta Caves (A World Heritage Site). This feast of music and dance, celebrated under the stars, transforms the entire island into a large auditorium.

Elephanta, a small island 10kms away from the Mumbai harbour, is a favoured destination for culture lovers during the festival held in February. The Elephanta Island is known for its great cave shrine, excavated in the 6th century.

Elephanta caves, earlier known as Gharapuri, are the tranquil abode of Lord Shiva. This land was renamed, Elephanta by the Portuguese, after the majestic carved elephant on this island.

The temple here has large pillars and nine marvelous sculptured panels, set on the wall, which are awe-inspiring. The sculptures display the changing moods of Lord Shiva, with the magical interplay of light and shade intensifying the overall effect.

The festival of Music and Dance is organised by the Maharashtra Tourism Development Corporation (MTDC). The main highlights of the festival are the illuminated Maheshmurti (Shiva-idol), in the main cave of the island. Folk dances by the local fisher folk, ethnic local food varieties add to the ambiance. Over the years, the festival has become a major tourist attraction for Mumbaites and for incoming domestic and foreign tourists.

V

ELLORA FESTIVAL

It is a festival of dance and music held every March in the splendid surroundings of the world-heritage listed cave temple of Ellora, about 30 km from Aurangabad, Maharashtra. There are 34 caves cut out of the sloping side of the Chamadri hills. Excavated between 600-1000 AD, the caves belong to Buddhists, Jain and Hindu faiths.

Ellora represents some 300 years of experiments carried out by different faiths with their very different iconography and structural compulsions.

The archaeological Survey of India has discovered another 28 caves later. The masterpiece of Ellora is the Kailash Temple. It is the world's largest monolithic sculpture, sculpted out of a rock by 7000 labourers over a 150-year period.

This festival showcases the best talents and is a unique and charming way to experience the magnificent caves, imbibing centuries of history and culture. This Festival is organised by Maharashtra Tourism Development Corporation (MTDC) where India's renowned artists perform their talents in music and dance with the caves forming a splendid backdrop.

It is a festival of dance and music held December in the splendid surroundings of the world-heritage listed cave temple of Ellora, about 30km from Aurangabad, Maharashtra. There are 34 caves cut out of the sloping side of the Chamadri hills. Excavated between 600-1000 AD, the caves belong to Buddhists, Jain and Hindu faiths. Ellora represents some 300 years of experiments carried out by different faiths with their very different iconography and structural compulsions. The archeological Survey of India has discovered another 28 caves later. The masterpiece of Ellora is the Kailash Temple. It is the world's largest monolithic sculpture, sculpted out of a rock by 7000 labourers over a 150-year period.

This festival showcases the best talents and is a unique and charming way to experience the magnificent caves, imbibing centuries of history and culture. This Festival is organised by Maharashtra Tourism Development Corporation (MTDC) where India's renowned artists perform their talents in music and dance.

VI

GOA CARNIVAL

February heralds the carnival at Goa. For three days and nights the streets come alive with colour. Held in mid February the weeklong event is a time for lively processions, floats, the strumming of guitars, graceful dances and of non-stop festivity. One of the more famous of the Indian Carnivals the Goa Festival is a complete sell out in terms of tourism capacities.

Among the many and various colourful feasts and festivals that are celebrated in Goa, the Goa Carnival is the most eagerly awaited event.

The 'Carnival' is exclusive and unique to Goa, and was introduced by the Portuguese who ruled over Goa for over five hundred years. Christians primarily celebrate the three-day festival, it has also absorbed Hindu tradition revelry, western dance forms, and turned into a pageantry of sorts. Though it started as a celebration enjoyed only by the local population, it has today crossed the state frontiers and attracts thousands of people from all over the country.

The carnival is meant to be a feasting-drinking-merrymaking orgy just before the austere 40 days of Lent. Huge parades are organized throughout the state with bands, dances and floats out all night on the streets, and grand balls held in the evenings. The carnival concludes with the famous red-and-black dance held by the Club National in Panajim on the final day.

Among the many and various colourful feasts and festivals that are celebrated in Goa, the Goa Carnival is the most eagerly awaited event. The carnival is held in February for three days and nights, when the legendary king Momo takes over the state and the streets come alive with music and colour. Then begins the weeklong event, which is a time of unbridled festivity and merry-making, which has been celebrated since the 18th Century.

The word Carnival (Carnival in Portuguese) is derived from a Latin word meaning 'to take away meat' and is an expression of the 40-day period of fasting of Lent, during which abstinence from meat is a rule. The carnival is not celebrated anywhere else in India and was in decline even in Goa in the last few years of Portuguese rule. Its revival with the Liberation of Goa, and a boost to its tourism was therefore welcome. From being almost on the brink of decline, this three day festival of gay abandon and riotous revelry now attracts thousands of tourists to Goa from all over India every year! The origins and nature of the carnival can be traced to the hedonistic feasts of ancient Rome and Greece. These carnivals started in the Spanish and Portuguese colonies, and gradually became known for their singing, dancing and drinking. The carnival is presided over by King Momo, who on the opening day orders his subjects to party. Hotel bookings must be done in advance for carnival as the festival attracts thousands of tourists.

VII

HAMPI FESTIVAL

The magnificent ruined city of Hampi, Karnataka once the capital of the Vijayanagar Empire (One of the greatest empires in the history of India), comes alive during the lively festival of dance and music, held in the first week of November.

Hampi holds many delightful surprises. The most famous is the King's Balance where kings were weighed against gold or money, which was then distributed to the poor.

Also worth a visit are the Queen's Bath with its arched corridors, projecting balconies and lotus shaped fountains, the two storeyed Lotus Mahal, the huge Elephant Stables, the splendid Vitthal Temple with its musical pillars and the Stone Chariot, the Virupaksha Temple, Ugra Narasimha, the 6.7 meters tall monolith, the Pushkarini Tank, the Mahanavami Dibba, etc. Virupaksha temple is still in use.

Vishu is one of the most popular festivals of Kerala. Vishu falls on the first of Medam (March-April), which is the Malayalam New Year's Day. Since it is considered propitious to view good things on this day for year round good fortune, Vishu morning is an important time. The heart of this festival of Kerala is the preparation of the kani (the lucky sight or gift).

Organized by the Government of Karnataka, the Hampi festival includes Dance, drama, music, fireworks; puppet shows and spectacular processions, all combine to recreate the grandeur of the bygone era.

The magnificent ruined city of Hampi, 353 kilometres from Bangalore, Karnataka once the capital of the Vijayanagar Empire (One of the greatest empires in the history of India), comes alive during the lively festival of dance and music, held in the first week of November.

The Vijaynagar city ruins near the village of Hampi are one of the most fascinating historical sites in South India. It has ruins of stone temples, elephant stables, barracks and palaces. Temples of this city are noted for their large dimensions, florid ornamentation, bold and delicate carvings, stately pillars, and magnificent pavilions. Most of the site is early 16th century, built during the 20-year reign of the great Vijayanagar ruler, Krishna Deva Raya (1509 -1529). Hampi holds many delightful surprises. The most famous is the King's Balance where kings were weighed against gold or money which was then distributed to the poor. Also worth a visit are the Queen's Bath with its arched corridors, projecting balconies and lotus shaped fountains, the two storied Lotus Mahal, the huge Elephant Stables, the splendid Vitthal Temple with its musical pillars and the Stone Chariot, the Virupaksha Temple, Ugra Narasimha, the 6.7 meters tall monolith, the Pushkarini Tank, the Mahanavami Dibba, etc. Virupaksha temple is still in use.

Organized by the Government of Karnataka, the Hampi festival includes Dance, drama, music, fireworks, puppet shows, spectacular processions, all combine to recreate the grandeur of the bygone era.

VIII

HEMIS FESTIVAL

The courtyard of Hemis Gompa (monastery), the biggest Buddhist monastery in Ladakh, in the state of Jammu & Kashmir, is the stage for this festival, which celebrates the birth anniversary of Guru Padmasambhava, revered as a reincarnation of Buddha. The colourful two-day pageant falls on the 10th day (Tse-Chu) of the Tibetan lunar month. A raised dais with a richly cushioned seat is erected in the courtyard, and a small, finely painted Tibetan table is placed here. Ceremonial items - cups full of holy water, uncooked rice, tormas made of dough and butter, incense sticks - are placed on the table. Traditional music is played, with four pairs of cymbals, pan drums, small trumpets and large wind instruments. Locals dress up in their finest traditional garb for the occasion. *Lamas* (monks) perform splendid masked dances and sacred plays to the accompaniment of cymbals, drums and long horns. The head lama presides over the function. Every 12 years, in the Tibetan Year of the Monkey, the two-storey high *Thanka* depicting Padmasambhava, richly embroidered with pearls and semi-precious stones, is displayed. The last display was in 2004. A colourful fair, displaying some beautiful handicrafts, is the special highlight of the festival.

IX

HOLLA MOHALLA

This Sikh festival begins the day after Holi, in March, and lasts for 3 days. It is celebrated at the sleepy town of Anandpur Sahib (close to Chandigarh) in Punjab. Sikhs from all over the state (and outside) congregate at the Gurdwara Keshgarh Sahib, the place where the Khalsa (Sikh brotherhood) was founded. Early morning prayers herald the event. A large number of community kitchens offer *langar* (free food) to those present. Dressed in traditional costumes, the Nihang Sikhs (traditional members of the Sikh army founded by Guru Gobind Singh) delight those present with a display of their skills in archery, fencing, tent pegging, bareback horse riding (standing erect on 2 speeding horses) and shooting.

Mock battles are enacted with enthusiasm and the area resounds to the sounds of the firing of ancient cannons. Of course, this IS Holi, so there's a lot of spraying each other with colour. A fair comes up around the Gurudwara. Evenings are for cultural events, including music and poetry competitions. The highlight of the last day is a long procession led by the Panj Piaras which makes a round of all the gurdwaras in the area.

X

HOYSALA MAHOTSAVA

The splendidly sculpted Hoysala temples of Belur and Halebid in Karnataka, a UNESCO World Heritage site, are the venue for this dance festival.

XI

INTERNATIONAL FLOWER FESTIVAL

Held every summer during the peak flowering season, this festival showcases the exotic flora of the tiny North Eastern state of Sikkim. On display are flowers, orchids, gladioli, roses, magnolia, cacti, alpine plants, creepers, climbers, ferns, and herbs. There are seminars and lectures by experts. And, of course, momos and other delectable Sikkimese delicacies. If you like what you see, why not plan a trip to Sikkim? The best time to go is from March to May, when the plants (including 600 species of orchids, 240 species of trees and ferns, 150 varieties of gladioli, 46 types of rhododendrons) are in full bloom. Bonus attractions are river rafting and the yak safari.

XII

INTERNATIONAL MANGO FESTIVAL

Mango lovers, like wine lovers, are passionate about their favourites, and at this festival, you can savour the many myriad varieties of the king of fruits and find out why. Cultural programmes liven up the event still further.

XIII

KONARK DANCE FESTIVAL

The sun temple in Konark is famed as a world heritage site. The exquisite 'Natyamandir' or the 'dancing hall' of this 700-year old shrine is an architectural wonder with well-adorned sculptures in Odissi dance poses.

Konark Dance Festival is held in December in the beautiful backdrop of the Sun temples in Konark, Orissa. This world heritage sight formed way back in the 13 th century on the beach of Chandrabagha. The exquisite 'Natamandir' or the 'dancing hall' of this shrine is an architectural wonder.

Every inch of its walls have been covered with fine artistic designs of the ancient times. Musicians playing drums, cymbals and other musical instruments adorn the sculptures in Odissi dance posses. It is blessed with changing intensity and a range of emotions.

This is the venue of a joyous festival of classical dance and music, which is held annually on December. A host of celebrated dancers from all over the country perform in the open-air auditorium. The festival is a celebration of the much appreciated Odissi, Bharathnatyam, Manipuri, Kathak and Chau Dance—a lavish feast for the eyes and ears. The sound of Ghungroo bells, flute and Pakhauj gives it a festive mood. There is also a crafts mela, with a variety of handicrafts and tasty cuisine during the festival. The festival is jointly organised by Orissa Tourism and Odissi Research Centre.

Konark Dance Festival takes place in an open-air auditorium against the backdrop of the floodlit temples that reverberates with the beats of 'Raga' and 'Tala' to fill the air with the sounds of classical music. The classical extravaganza is a journey through eternal ecstasy.

Konark Dance Festival takes place in an open-air auditorium against the backdrop of the floodlit temples that reverberates with the beats of 'Raga' and 'Tala' to fill the air with the sounds of classical music. The classical extravaganza is a journey through eternal ecstasy.

The festival provides a platform for both to the performing artiste and the dance connoisseurs in appreciating the essence of various classical dance forms of the country and also to the new artists who are yet to make their mark on the international scale.

XIV

KURUKSHETRA FESTIVAL

The festival in Kurushetra, Haryana coincides with the Gita Jayanti, signifying the birth of the Srimad Bhagavad Gita. A visit to Kurukshetra during the festival is an exhilarating and spiritual experience.

Bhagavat Gita, the holy book of the Hindus. Bhagavat Gita comprises the basic truths and declares that whatever way of life, whatever mode of worship man has and shall adopt, so long as it is guided by an earnest desire for betterment, they are to be deemed worthy of recognition and respect.It is the ancient holy land where the essence of Hinduism originated.

It is also the land where the sage Manu penned his 'Manusmriti' and where learned 'rishis' compiled the Rig Veda and Sama Veda. It has been graced with the visits of Lord Krishna, the Buddha and the Sikh gurus.

Pilgrims gather to take a dip in the sacred tanks of Brahma Sarovar and Sannehit Sarovar. Week -long Bhagwad katha (presenting stories in Bhagwad Gita, sacred book of the Hindus), Shloka recital, dance, dramas and 'deep daan' at Brahma Sarovar are part of the religious festivities. Free medical camps, book exhibitions and 'bhajan' recitals in classical tradition are organized.

XV

LUCKNOW FESTIVAL

This festival is celebrated between 25th November and 5th December in Lucknow, the capital city of U.P. It captures the undying elegance and splendours of ancient city Awadh, now known as Lucknow. This festival celebrates Lucknow's living culture, which provides an insight into the old, cultured, atmosphere of the city. Colourful processions, traditional dramas, Kathak dances in the style of the famous Lucknow Gharana, Sarangi and sitar recitals along with ghazals, qawalis and thumri create a festive atmosphere. Exciting events like ekka races, kite flying, cock fighting and other traditional village games recreate an atmosphere of bygone Nawabi days. There is a display of crafts and one can have a taste of the famous Nawabi cuisine. The annual Lucknow Festival showcasing Avadhi culture, tradition and cuisine started in Lucknow on the bank of River Gomti on November 25.

The 15-day festival, organised jointly by UP Tourism and Lucknow District Administration, will, this time, also have stalls by the craftsmen of other states presenting a composite culture of the entire country. Besides providing a platform for the local talents, the festival will also have programmes by well-known personalities including Shovana Narayan, the Vadali brothers, Shubha Mudgal, Hansraj Hans, Pandit Jasraj, Hema Sardesai and Sapna Awasthi.

The Lucknow Festival, held in the months of November-December every year, captures the undying elegance and splendour of Awadh, now Lucknow. A brilliant showcase of the arts, crafts, and above all the exotic cuisine of this land, the festival is a once-in-a-lifetime experience.

During the festival, the city of Lucknow is abuzz with excitement and activity. Colourful processions, traditional dramas, Kathak dances in the style of the famous Lucknow gharana,sarangi and sitar recitals along with ghazal; qawali and thumri sessions create a festive atmosphere. Exciting events such as ekka races, kite flying, cock fighting and other traditional village games recreate an atmosphere of Awadh's nawabi days.

And to top it all, one can taste the traditional delicacies of Lakhnawi cuisine, ranging from mouth-watering vegetarian cuisine to the lip-smacking non-vegetarian spread for which Lucknow is famous.

XVI

MARWAR FESTIVAL

Fairs in Rajasthan are mythological in nature relating to Gods and Goddesses. They are even celebrated to commemorate the brave deeds of medieval heroes. The Marwar Festival, held in memory of the heroes of Rajasthan is one such example.

It is a festival devoted to the music and dance of Marwar region. The festival was originally known as Maand Festival. Held for two days on full moon - sharad purnima, folk artists bring to life the myths, legend and folklore of the area.

The festival is celebrated in the Hindu month of Ashwin (Sept-Oct) in Jodhpur, the former capital of Marwar Province. The festival has on display the music and dance of the Marwar region. The spirited folk dancers assembled here, perform with gusto and entertain the audience with Rajasthani folklore.

These folk artists bring to life the myth and legends of the area and sing songs in memory of the brave heroes. Other attractions include of the festival include horse riding and horse polo. Various other competitions are also held during the festival.

The massive Mehangarh fort and the impresive Umaid Bhawan Palace which are symbols of might and valour of the Rajputs, make Jodhpur an ideal location for the festival. It was originally known as the 'Maand Festival', a classical style of folk music centred on the romantic lifestyle of Rajasthan's rulers. The festival is held for two days during the full moon of Sharad Purnima. The Marwar festival displays the music and dance of the Marwar region. The spirited folk dancers gathered here, perform with zest and entertain the audience with Rajasthani folklore.

XVII

SINDHU DARSHAN FESTIVAL

The Sindhu Darshan Festival is organised annually at Leh, the capital of Ladakh, in June. A s the name suggests, it is a celebration of the river Sindhu (also known as the Indus), which originates from Kailash Mansarovar in Tibet. As part of the celebrations, water is brought from other mighty rivers in the country, and merged with the Sindhu river, thereby establishing the Sindhu river as a symbol of multi-dimensional cultural identity, communal harmony and peaceful co-existence. The festival is the perfect time to visit the beautiful regions of Leh and Ladakh.

The Sindhu Darshan Festival, as the name suggests, a celebration of River Sindhu, also known as the Indus has come prominence only recently. The Festival was organised from 6-8 June 2000 at Shey livened up by the presence of a wide variety of cultural troupes from various corners of India. Troupes from States where the mighty Rivers of India run, brought with them water from those rivers in earthen pots and immersed the pots in the Indus, thereby mingling the waters from all over India with that of the mighty 'Indus', the river that gave India its name.

The Prime Minister laid the foundation stone of the Sindhu Cultural Center and also inaugurated the new office complex of Ladakh Autonomous Hill Development Council.This complex will be helpful in bringing out the unique culture of Ladakh region and its people. The facilities proposed at the complex include an auditorium for seating 500 people, an open air theatre, an exhibition gallery, a music room, a small library and a souvenir shop where Ladakh handicrafts could be available to visiting tourists.

The Sindhu Darshan Festival is organised annually at Leh. People travel for a Darshan and Puja of the River Sindhu (Indus), which originates from the Mansarovar in Tibet. The festival is a celebration of this river. The Festival aims at projecting the Sindhu River as a symbol of multi-dimensional cultural identity, communal harmony and peaceful co-existence in India. It is also an opportunity for people from around the country and overseas to visit the beautiful regions of Leh and Ladakh.As part of the celebrations, various groups from different states in India bring water from the other mighty rivers in the country in earthen pots and immerse these pots in the Sindhu River, thereby mingling the river water with other waters of the land.

The Sindhu Cultural Centre was inaugurated a few years back as well as the new office complex of Ladakh Autonomous Hill Development Council.This complex will be helpful in bringing out the unique culture of the Ladakh region and its people.The facilities proposed at the complex include an auditorium for seating 500 people, an open-air theatre, an exhibition gallery, a music room, a small library and a souvenir shop where Ladakh handicrafts could be available to visiting tourists.The Sindhu Darshan Festival aims at projecting the Sindhu as a symbol of multi-dimensional cultural identity, communal harmony and peaceful co-existence in India. Whilst promoting tourism to this area, this festival is also a symbolic salute to the brave soldiers of India who have bravely fought the odds at Siachin, Kargil & other places. The Sindhu Darshan Festival will help forge a bond of unity with those who live in far-flung corners of the country and provide an opportunity to visit the beautiful region of Ladakh.

As a National Integration Program, the festival was welcomed by the Ladakh Buddhist Association, Shia Majilis, Sunni Anjumam, Christian Moravian Church, Hindu Trust and Sikh Gurudwara Prabandhak Committee. The three day programme will be inaugurated on June 1, 2001 at Shey is being organized by the Government of Jammu and of Kashmir with the support of Ministry of Tourism and Culture, Govt. of India. The festival promises a kaleidoscope of Indian culture and an exciting array of performing arts being brought together at an exciting place. Indian Airlines is expected to operate special flights for the festival.The Sindhu Darshan Festival is organised annually at Leh. The first time when this Festival was organised in October 1997, over seventy people from all over India had travelled to Leh for a Darshan and Puja of the River Sindhu (Indus) which originates from the Mansarovar in Tibet.

XVIII

TAJ MAHOTSAV

The Taj Mahotsav is a non-stop 10 day carnival held annually at Shilpgram, near Tajmahal. The impressive festival commences with a spectacular procession inspired by Mughal splendor. Bedecked elephants and camels, drum beaters, folk artists and master craftsmen together recreate the glorious past of the Mughals.

The Taj Mahal Mahotsav area becomes a live culture, crafts and traditions. It is a great opportunity for legendary artisans to display their exquisite works of art. Marble of course rules the festivities each year for obvious reasons.

Besides these, crafts include wood carvings from Saharanpur, brass and other metal ware from Moradabad, handmade carpets of Badohi, the pottery of Khurja, chickan-work of Lucknow, the silk of Banaras and much more.Indian festivities can never be complete without the preparation of exotic cuisine. Some of the best and richest foods are available during this time.

Add to this the soul-stirring performances from folk artists of various states casting a spell on the visitors. Throughout the Taj Mahotsav, one can experience a profusion of folk music and dances of Dundelkhand, 'Nautanki' (Drama), 'Sapera' dance of Rajasthan, Lavani of Maharashtra... performed just the way they used to be centuries ago. Visitors join in with the folk dancers enjoying swinging to a different tune and dance style.

The Taj Mahotsav is truly India at her best with a glimpse of her rich heritage and extraordinary legacies.

27

Prominent Fairs of India

I

BANESHWAR FAIR

Baneswar Fair is celebrated in Durgapur, Rajasthan, situated 13 kms. from Udaipur in the month of February every year. Mahadev Temple is the main venue of the fair. The name 'Baneshwar' is derived from the Shivlinga, which is kept in the Mahadev Temple in Dungarpur. 'Baneshwar' means the 'Master of the Delta' in the local Vagdi language which name was ascribed to the Shivlinga. The Baneshwar fair is held at a small delta formed by the river Som and Mahi, from Magh Shukla Ekadashi to Magh Shukla Purnima every year.

Baneshwar fair in its present form is actually one of two fairs: one which used to be held in of Baneshwar Mahadev and another fair, which started after the construction of the Vishnu Temple by Jankunwari, daughter-in-law of Mavji, a highly revered saint. Two disciples of Mavji named Aje and Vaje built the Lakshmi Narain Temple near the confluence of rivers Som and Mahi. The 'pran-pratishtha' ceremony of the idols was performed on Magh Shukla Ekadashi and since then, the fair is held on this day. The large congregation that gathers here at the time of the fair pays homage to all the deities with equal reverence and faith.

On Magh Shukla Ekadashi, Mathadhish (the head priest), arrives at the fair site from Sabla, in a huge procession. A 16 cms silver image of Mavji on horseback is also brought here. The river water supposedly becomes holier when the Mathadhish takes a bath. Hence, people bathe along with him in the river. The Bhils consign the ashes of their dead at the confluence of the rivers.

In fact, Baneshwar fair is a tribal fair with more than half of the congregation consisting of local Bhils. They revere Baneshwar Mahadev as well as Mavji. The majority of the gathering is from the Districts of Dungarpur, Udaipur, Banswara beside other far-flimged places.

The temple of Baneshwar Mahadev remains open from 5.00 a.m. to 11.00 p.m. during the fair. In the morning, saffron (Kesar) is applied to the Shivlinga after it is bathed and an 'aarti' takes place. In the evening, 'bhabhut' (ash) is applied to the Linga and an 'aarti' with a fine-wick lamp is performed. Devotees offer wheat flour, pulses, rice, jaggery, ghee, salt, chillies, coconut etc.

Simultaneously, prayers are offered five times a day in the temples of Lakshmi -Narayan and Brahma. Big brass gongs are struck at the time of 'aarti'. During the fair, 'aarti' of Mathadhish is also performed and Raslila takes place at night in the Lakshmi Narayan Temple.

The Bhils attending Baneshwar Fair sing traditional folk songs in high pitched voices sitting around a bonfire every night. Cultural shows are arranged by youngsters of the clan. Groups of villagers are also invited to participate in the programme.

Added features of the fair are the gaiety of songs, folk dances, magic shows, animal shows and acrobatic feats. Adding to the excitement are the joy rides on merry-go-rounds and swings. Many shops in the fair provide services for marketing to local paople.

II

GANGA SAGAR FAIR

Gangasagar Fair is the largest fair celebrated in West Bengal. This fair is held where the Ganga and the Bay of Bengal form a nexus. Hence the name Gangasagar Mela.

The river Ganga which originates in the Gangotri glacier in the snow clad Himalayas, descends down the mountains, reaches the plains at Haridwar, flows through ancient pilgrimage sites such as Benares and Prayag, and drains into the Bay of Bengal. Sagar Island, at the mouth of the river Hooghly in Bengal (accessed from Diamond Harbor), where the Ganga breaks up into hundreds of streams, and drains into the sea, is revered as a pilgrimage centre.

A dip in the ocean, where the Ganga drains into the sea is considered to be of great religious significance particularly on the Makara Sankranti day when the sun makes a transition to Capricorn from Sagittarius and this town becomes home to vast fairs, drawing visitors and recluses from all over the state. There is a common belief among the locals that the girls who take the holy dip get handsome grooms and the boys get beautiful brides. When they are done with the ritual obligations, they head towards the Kapilmuni Temple situated nearby, to worship the deity as a mark of respect.

The village priest leading his horde of devotees chants *sab teerth baar baar, Gangasagar ek bar*. You can go to all the holy places, but a pilgrimage to Ganga Sagar equals them all. A dip means redemption for all wrong done. This place is Sagar Island, on the confluence of the Ganga with the Bay of Bengal. The day "Makar Sankranti" or the last day of the month of *Paus* (December).

Legend goes thus, before joining the sea, the Ganga

watered the mortal remains of King Sagar's 60000 sons liberating their souls once and forever. It was standing on the Sagar Island that the mythical Kapil Muni condoned the sins of the sons of King Sagar who had dared to stop the horse blessed at Lord Indra's Aswamedha Yajna and tied it to a post near his temple. It is this legend that attracts people to this little island in a remote southern corner of West Bengal.

The Ganga Sagar *mela* (fair) is the largest annual assemblage of devotees in India. The greatness of the mela can be assessed from the fact that over a million pilgrims come from far-flung corners of India and beyond, speaking different languages and belonging to diverse castes and creeds, for a sacred dip at this holy confluence. For this, no invitation is given. No propaganda is carried out and overall no authority exists for carrying out the mela.

It is indeed a tough journey. A few days in packed buses and trains bring the pilgrims to Kolkata. From there, again a long bus journey to ferry *ghats* or jetty in Sunderbans area, followed by crossing the tidal river stretching for miles across. The last leg involves either walking or traveling by a local bus upto 30 kilometres depending on the location of embarkation point.

The journey can be tiring but religious fervour of the pilgrims overcomes all hardships. *Kapil Muni ki jai, Kapil Muni ki jai*, (Hail Kapil Muni), the din rises above the grinding motors of the launches ferrying the pilgrims across the Ganga and the countless buses plying between Kolkata and Namkhana. The problem of traveling doesn't deter even the weak and vulnerable. Old people in their eighties, and village women carrying babies and little children in tow are a common sight. The large stream of pilgrims keeps pouring in throughout the day and night before the auspicious day and occupies any available space on the sandy beach. They move about the place in groups, many displaying saffron and red flags, identifying the religious *Akhara* (group) they belong to as well as acting as beacon to the members who stray out of the group. People walks to the sound of the bells, blowing conch shells and chanting prayers. Strains of devotional songs can be heard from far and near. And, the ceaseless din of loudspeakers. An array of shops, stacked with heaps of vermilion, rudraksha, colourful beads, conch shells line the pathways.

Many a visitor stands wide-eyed before the shops selling everything from food stuff, household utensils to remote controlled toys. People crowd around the *naga sadhus* (naked ascetics) without whom the Ganga Sagar mela is incomplete. Sitting naked in little huts near the temple and enjoying a *chillum of ganja*, they are also the target of tourists' camera. While devotees jostle in front of numerous temporary shrines of Hindu deities to pay homage, Kapil Muni's temple remains the chief attraction.

The temple of Kapil Muni, as we see it today, is by no means the spot where the sage meditated. It went under the sea millennium ago followed by the many others built in its place, which subsequently was also swallowed, by the advancing sea. The present one was built only some decades ago, quite a bit away from the sea. The tall dome of the temple is visible from a distance. In the temple, three images engraved in stone are displayed, the one in the middle is that of Kapil Muni. The sage is seen in a *jogasana*; his eyes wide open, looking towards the sea with millions of devotees before him. The idols of Ganga and King Sagar flank Kapil Muni and the horse of the sacrificial yagna stands at a distance.

Notably, the typical Ganga Sagar pilgrim is a country rustic, generally elderly, hardy, remarkably disciplined and fervent in his devotion. His dhoti seldom going below his knees, a cloth bound packet, containing everything needed for survival, on his head. And, of course, his women – heavily tattooed and clad in colourful saris.

At the early dawn sandy track to the water's edge is crowded with people who sit around fires before proceeding for the bath, chanting devotional songs and prayers. The seaside presents a spectacle in the darkness before dawn with the large bonfire lit by the bathers to keep off the cold.

At midnight, the high tide drives the pilgrims back. The biting cold wind of mid – January from across the sea lashes the bare body. But there is a confidence on their faces and a kind of fire in their eyes. The confidence in God and the fire of earnest faith makes them brave the chill. The stars in the sky have quite a long time to fade when the moment of truth comes. As soon as the priest announces, the auspicious pre-dawn hour, the crowds surge forward to meet the tide with a loud chorus *Kapil Muni ki jai* and plunge into the sea.

After taking their holy dips, the shivering devotees trudge the one kilometre expanse leading to the brightly lit temple of Kapil Muni, where prayers were performed. Coconuts, flowers, vermilion, sweets, and money are offered to the image of the ancient sage. The bustle of activity continues for quite sometime in the morning as the pilgrims perform a series of rituals including the symbolic *godan* to Brahmins. A calf is symbolically handed over to the Brahmin priest by the devotee.

Many perform the symbolic crossing of the river of blood, *baitarani* to attain moksha or transcendation. It is interesting to observe the people, clutching the tail of a cow and wading through a puddle a few paces. Many people shave their heads and perform the last rites of departed relatives. A number of marriages are solemnized on the beach during the day. Also, many local girls get married to the sea. This will ensure that theoretically they never become widows, even if their menfolk, braving the rough sea and tiger infested jungle for a living, die.

But the majority of the pilgrims take it easy. After the rituals are complete, they dry their clothes and hair, cook their food on open fires, eat and rest. Happy, contented and smiling, having made the pilgrimage.

The Ganga Sagar fair continues to throb with life, with the energy of millions of pilgrims. The pilgrimage may be extremely tough, but the pilgrims know that the visit will purify their souls. The visit fulfils their lifelong desire and often one can see tears of joy rolling down their cheeks. That is the magic of religion.

Remarkably, arrival of the English New Year in the eastern part of India coincides with Gangasagar pilgrimage and fair, the second largest congregation of mankind known to the religious and domestic tourism history of the country after the holy Kumbha Mela. That Kumbha is observed once in four years at alternate location in north, central and central-west parts of the country makes Gangasagar all the more unique. Because, Gangasagar fair and pilgrimage is held annually on the Sagar Island's southern tip in the Ganges delta atop the Bay of Bengal, attracting flocks of the faithful from all parts of India and even from neighbouring countries, like Nepal, Bhutan and Bangladesh. Pilgrims from all walks of life have been visiting this holy place—famous for the mythical shrine of Sage Kapil—to offer prayers at his temple, after taking once-in-a-life-time dip in the confluence of River Ganges and the Sea.

Makar Sankranti—call it Lohri, Pongal or Sankranti; the festival conveys the bond of brotherhood and the spirit of oneness despite all odds—is celebrated throughout India as the festival of new harvest. It has been a traditional way of giving thanks to Mother Nature for her bounty. This is the period when the winter starts receding, paving way for the summer and the time when farmers bring home their harvest.

In the coastal regions of south, it is a festival dedicated to Indra. In North India, a ritual bath in the river is important on this day. Khichri is eaten and given away as charity, and people also distribute rice and lentils to the poor and needy. In Maharashtra and north India, a special dish called tilgul/ tilua, or laddoos made of jaggery and sesame seed, the chief crop of the season, is popular. In Gujarat and Rajasthan it is celebrated as the Kite flying day. Traditionally, this period is considered the most auspicious time of the Hindu calendar. As per Mahabharata, the dying Bhishma waited—for this Solar transition—on a bed of arrows for his last breath, after felling to the arrows of Arjuna. According to other religious scriptures the Sun on this day visits the house of his son Shani, who is said to be the lord of Makar Rashi. Ordinarily, the father-son duo does not get along nicely but for this day when Sun makes it a point to visit his son. From Uttarayana starts the time of the Gods, while Dakshinayana is said to be their 'night', giving upper hand to the evil. The auspicious things are done during this time. It was on this day when Lord Vishnu ended the rein of terror of the demon Asuras by finishing them off and burying them under the Mandar Mountain. It is also believed that Bhagirath—mythically credited with bringing down the purest of all river, mother Ganges to this planet—finally led Ganga near the Kapil Muni Ashram, at the present day Ganga Sagar, and performed 'tarpan' with her holy waters for the salvation of his unfortunate ancestors (60,000 descendants of King Sagar of Lord Rama's clan). He thus liberated their souls from the old curse of Sage Kapil, the presiding deity at the Gangasagar temple. Mythical belief goes that those who die in this period have no rebirth. The beginning of January has therefore been the most favoured time of annual domestis tourism since time immemorial attracting thousands of worshippers—against all odds invloved in reaching the far flung remote island of Sagar in the bygone era—from down south, west and north alike. Times now have changed to the maximum positive levels with direct ferry services, all motorised and well-monitored against the overloading mishaps. Special bus and train services are available from Kolkata during January 12 to 15 to mark the Makar Sankranti Mela on the Sagar Island. Large vessels of Kolkata Port Trust and other public organisations are available from Kolkata and about 110 KMs downstream, besides the Ganges at Kashinagar Point (Lot 08) and Namkhana, to ferry the pilgrims across the river to the island for an onward 45 minute bus journey to the fair grounds. Direct buses are posted to pick up and drop mela bound or returning pilgrims at Howrah and Kolkata Bus Stands, which run between these points and Namkhana and back.

The traditional fair still serves as the most attractive cause for domestic travel of the rural tourists to the east as it did in the ancient past. The myth that the Kapil Muni Temple only emerges out of water on the Makar Sankranti day to receive prayers of the devotees, remains the catch-point to bring herds of natives from interiors of Gujarat, Kerala, Tamil Nadu, Maharashtra, Andhra Pradesh and Karnataka. Haryana, Rajasthan, Madhya Pradesh, Uttaranchal, Uttar Pradesh, Bihar, Himachal Pradesh, Punjab and Jammu & Kashmir. Nobody knows how and when the notion spread across the span of India! The Gangasagar fair on its peak day on January 14th attracts no less than a mini India in all its hues and traditions, serving as the time-tested bond of oneness of the nation enriched with unique range of cultural and linguistic variety.

The Gangasagar fair attracts almost half a million people every year who take a holy dip at the confluence of the holy Ganga—some in the hope of washing away their sins, others expecting to win spouses of their dreams.

The fair is held on Sagar island, 156 km south of here, for several days, but Wednesday is the most auspicious occasion when the holy bath takes place. The day marks the Hindu auspicious day of Makar Sankranti that falls on the last day of the Bengali month of Poush. It also marks the winter solstice.

Legend has it that on Makar Sankranti, when the sun begins its northward journey, the doors of heaven are kept open. A bath at the auspicious hour promises deliverance.

A special prayer is performed for the sun god as a thanksgiving for a good harvest. During evening prayers, worshippers set leaf baskets filled with flowers and lighted earthen lamps filled with camphor adrift in the Ganges.

There is a common belief among locals that girls who take the holy dip get handsome grooms and the boys get beautiful brides.

Groups of pilgrims huddled in front of the sages as they deliver their discourses on spirituality on the sandy beaches of the island are a common sight. Many of the sadhus are seen wearing costly goggles, yet others can be spotted with mobile phones- all objects they describe as gifts from disciples.

Hundreds of such interesting mendicants and sages are passing through Kolkata on their way to Sagar island. Several NGOs have set up resting camps and are even serving sumptuous vegetarian meals for free for them.

Makar Sankranti also entails preparing traditional rice-sweets called pithey in Bengali households.

The Eastern Railway has this year completed its remaining construction of broadguage tracks on the Diamond Harbour section from Laxmikantapur to Namkhana and the officials are trying their best to provide direct access to incoming trains from upland to this nearest railhead on way to Sagar. Beyond this point travellers to Sagar have to cross the Ganges—from two points—on vessels. Fair

Administration the Namkhana—Chemaguri water route has traditionally been less secure for boat journeys due to silting of the river. The Fair administration prefers Lot Number Eight—Kachuberia route for allowing round-the-clock plying of passenger vessels during the annual fair. The pilgrims, therefore, are advised to reach for the second route to avoid unavoidable delays during low tides and the resultant rush of waiting passengers, most of whom are taken to the fair and back by tour arrangers of hinterland states who usually are themselves unfamiliar to this problem. The next caution is to avoid package tours by vessel from Kolkata (Babughat) to Sagar.

III

KUMBHA MELA

The pilgrimage to Kumbh occurs four times every twelve years, once at each of the four locations. Each twelve-year cycle includes the Maha (great) Kumbha Mela at Prayag, (Allahabad) attended by millions of people, making it the largest pilgrimage gathering around the world. The observance of Kumbha Mela is believed to have originated as follows: thousands of years ago, perhaps in the Vedic period, gods and demons made a temporary agreement to work together in obtaining *amrita* (the nectar of immortality) from the Milky Ocean, and to share this equally. However, when the Kumbha (pot) containing the amrita appeared, the demons ran away with the pot and were chased by the gods. For twelve days and twelve nights (equivalent to twelve human years) the gods and demons fought in the sky for the possession of this pot of amrita. It is said that during the battle, drops of amrita fell on to four places : Prayag, Haridwar, Ujjain and Nasik. Thus, Kumbha mela is observed at these four locations where the nectar fell.Kumbha Mela is attended by millions of people on a single day. A ritual bath at a predetermined time and place is the major event of this festival. Other activities include religious discussions, devotional singing, mass feeding of holy men/women and the poor, and religious assemblies where doctrines are debated and standardized. Kumbha Mela is the most sacred of all the Hindu pilgrimages. Thousands of holy men/women (monks, saints, sadhus) grace the occasion by their presence. The suspiciousness of Kumbha Mela is in part attributed to the gathering of thousands of holy men/women at one place on earthAccording to astrologers, the 'Kumbh Fair' takes place when the planet Jupiter enters Aquarius and the Sun enters Aries. On Mahavir Jayanti, much emphasis is also placed on self control. Thus, the controlling of the senses and emotions takes precedence. Evening meals are eaten before sunset and Jains are enjoined not to lose control of their emotions. On this day, typically four kinds of donations are made. These donations are intended to instil a sense of generosity and compassion for the less fortunate. It is also intended to remind Jains to not be too attached to material possessions. The four kinds of donations recommended for every Jain include:

— *Abhay daan:* protecting people from bad actions
— *Gyan daan:* sharing of knowledge
— *Aushad daan:* donating medicines
— *Ahaar daan:* giving food

The *Maha Kumbh Mela* ("great festival of the pot of nectar of immortality") is held every three years in each of four different locations, returning to each of four places every twelve years. An Ardh (half) Mela (festival) takes place six years after the Maha Kumbh in each location. Kumbh Mela is a sacred Hindu pilgrimage and bathing festival that takes place at the following 4 locations of India:

1. Prayag (near the city of Allahabad, in the state of Uttar Pradesh) at the confluence of three rivers Ganga, Yamuna and Saraswati.

2. Hardwar (in the state of Uttaranchal) where the river Ganga enters the plains from Himalayas.
3. Ujjain (in Madhya Pradesh), on the banks of holy Ksipra river.
4. Nasik (in Maharashtra) on the banks of pious Godavari river.

The precise dates of the *Kumbh Mela* are astrologically determined, based upon the positions of the Sun, the Moon and Jupiter. At Prayag, the *Maha Kumbh Mela* is held in the month of Magh (January/February in the Gregorian calendar). The highest spiritual merit is attached to bathing on the new moon day, when Jupiter is in Taurus and both the Sun and Moon are in Capricorn. At Haridwar, the Kumbh Mela is held in the months of Phalgun and Chaitra (February/ March/April), when the Sun passes to Aries, the Moon is in Sagittarius and Jupiter is in Aquarius. In Ujjain, the festival is held in the month of Vaishakha (May), when other planets are in Libra, the Sun and Moon are in Aries and Jupiter is in Leo. At Nashik, the Kumbh Mela takes place in the month of Shravana (July), when the Sun and Moon are in Cancer and Jupiter is in Scorpio.

It is also said that the elixir of life is filled in a Kumbh (Pot) in Swarg (heaven) so with certain combination of Sun—Moon—Jupiter combination, the elixir falls from heaven to earth, and kumbh mela is held on that locations.

The Triveni Sangam, or the intersection of Yamuna and Ganga River is the venue where devotees perform rituals. Kumbh Mela is attended by millions of people on a single day. The major event of this festival is a ritual bath at the banks of the rivers in each town. Other activities include religious discussions, devotional singing, mass feeding of holy men and women and the poor, and religious assemblies where doctrines are debated and standardized. Kumbh Mela is the most sacred of all the Hindu pilgrimages. Thousands of holy men and women (monks, saints and sadhus) attend, and the auspiciousness of the festival is in part attributable to this.

Once every 12 years, millions of the world's most zealous Hindu pilgrims gather at the confluence of the Ganga and Yamuna rivers near the city of Allahabad for the greatest of India's immersion rituals, the Maha Kumbh Mela. Maha Kumbh Mela (2001) was particularly auspicious, being the first of the new millennium and coinciding with an astrological planetary alignment occurring only once every 144 years. By the time the 2001 Kumbh Mela ends on February 21st, approximately 70 million saints, sinners, Sadhus, faith healers, preachers, gurus, charlatans and devotees from across India and the world will have participated in perhaps the single most colossal gathering of humanity since the dawn of time.

The Maha Kumbh Mela is truly a microcosm of Indian society at its most spectacular. The six-week spectacle is a passion filled festival, which transcends creed, caste and religion. For the throngs of Hindu devotees who will travel here it is a chance at salvation.

Of the 70 million or so attendees at the Kumbh, most are rural villagers and commoners who have traveled for days, weeks or even months by any means possible on a personal search for the divine. Carrying bundles of provisions on their heads, unprepared for the low temperatures, they will sleep on the open ground; eat whatever is available and brave conditions that most westerners would find unimaginable. They have come for the opportunity of a lifetime, the opportunity for a miraculous dip into the cleansingly frigid waters of the Ganges on this sacred occasion.

Apart from the Sadhu ashrams, the entire Mela grounds were a riot of sights, sounds, smells, colors and movement. Among the crowd were some 5000 barbers, on site to service the millions who elected to have their heads shaved before bathing in the Sangam. A shaved head costs around 10 Rupees (25 cents)—a small price to pay for a spiritual advantage (Hindu's believe that each strand of hair is the equivalent of buying a cow for the God of your fancy). Shaving one's head therefore speeds up one's journey to heaven. Intermingled with the barbers were legions of beggars who offered yet another way to create good Karma for one's self. We witnessed even the poorest of pilgrims filling a beggar's extended hand with anything from a rupee to a cup of rice. Beggars in India provide a unique type of symbiotic relationship with those who are more fortunate. Begging allows those who are able to give, the opportunity to do a good deed. Beggars come in all types, but none were more heart wrenching than the hundreds of lepers at the Kumbh. Many were wheeled in on makeshift wooden carts or carried on the backs of family members. Almost all the lepers were covered with wool blankets, their effected limbs bandaged with hopelessly soiled rags. Partial limbs protruded from beneath blankets for all to see, many lacked fingers, toes, or entire hands and feet. The most unfortunate lepers, with advanced disease, quivered and shook uncontrollably, as if shivering, despite the stifling mid day heat. Meanwhile, just steps away, processions of gilded coaches draped in silk, announced the arrival of important religious leaders. Competing for attention in this already deafening cacophony, were the chants of passing processions, intermingled with loudspeakers that blasted anything from religious mantras, to announcements in Hindi about cattle insurance and cigarettes. The decibel level seemed to deafen all but the most calloused Indian ears.

Kumbh Mela (the Urn Festival) is a Hindu pilgrimage that occurs four times every twelve years and rotates between four locations: Prayag, Haridwar, Ujjain and Nashik. Each twelve-year cycle includes one *Maha Kumbh Mela* (*Great* Kumbh Mela) at Prayag, which is attended by millions of people, making it the largest gathering anywhere in the world.

According to Hindu creation myths, the gods once fought a great battle over the *kumbh* (pitcher) containing the nectar of immortality. In the scuffle, four drops of the nectar spilled onto the earth, splashing on the ground of Allahabad, Nasik, Ujjain and Haridwar. A huge *mela* (fair) is held at each of the cities, attracting vast numbers of Hindu holy men, especially the naked *saddhus* and *nagas*, or militant Hindu monks. For India's 670 million plus Hindus, the four cities involved in the Kumbh Mela cycle are among the seven most sacred cities on the pilgrimage circuit.

The triennial pilgrimage attracts millions from all over the country. In Haridwar ('Gateway to the Gods') in 1998, more than 10 million Hindus came and washed in the Ganges in the sacred area where the river leaves the mountains and enters the plains. The Allahabad Kumbh Mela is the largest and holiest of all melas. Two of Hinduism's most important rivers, the Ganges and the Yamuna (as well as the mythical River of Enlightenment), converge here and Hindus consider that the confluence, known as the *sangam*, has great soul-cleansing properties. All pious Hindus hope to bathe here at least once in their lives. In 2001 around 70,000,000 people visited Allahabad during the Mela, with more than 15,000,000 pilgrims bathing on one day alone!

The once-in-a-144-years mega event, the Maha Kumbha Mela, is here. We dig out some legends associated with the Kumbha Mela and its esoteric meaning The Mahakumbha. This is your chance to attain *moksha*. It's now or never, because only once in 144 years do you get to see this unique combination of the spiritual energies. The much awaited and hyped *Mahakumbha mela* will be held at the holy land of Allahabad, India, through January till Mahashivratri in February. According to astrologers, the Kumbha mela takes place when the planet Jupiter enters the sign of Aquarius and the Sun enters into Aries.A ritual bath at Sangam, where the three rivers—Ganga, Yamuna and Saraswati—meet, at a predetermined time and place is the major part of this mela. Other activities include religious discussions, *yajnas* or sacrificial fire ceremony, devotional singing, mass feeding of holy men and women and the poor, and religious assemblies where doctrines are debated. The *Kumbha mela* is periodically celebrated every 12 years at one of the four holy places of Hardwar, Nasik, Ujjain and Allahabad. But a culmination of 12 times 12 will be in this year and as it coincides with a step into the new millennium, it is expected to increase spiritual vibrations globally. In 1989, over 15 million people attended the Kumbha mela at Allahabad and the *Guinnies Book of World Records* noted it as the greatest number of people assembling for a common purpose. Many foreign visitors aim to make it to the mela including New Agers Richard Bach, Billy Graham and Paulo Coelho. Writes Pandit Rajmani Tigunait, spiritual head of the Himalayan Institute in their website: "Many visitors will be traveling from the United States; others will be joining from 20 other countries." For this special occasion, many saints and sages, totally engrossed in their sadhana in the Himalayas will emerge for a bath at Sangam.The political parties also have an ace up their sleeves. The Week reports that the Vishwa Hindu Parishad (VHP) plans to unveil a model of the Ram Temple, to be built at Ayodhya, which is nearly complete, at a secret location in Jaipur. Designed by Gujarat-based architect Chandrakant Sompura, it is crafted by Chandresh Pandey from Jaipur. Kumbha literally means a pitcher. Astrological representation of Aquarius denotes a man holding a pitcher. The reference is to the pot filled with the nectar of immortality that emerged after the gods and demons churned the milky ocean. However, the symbolism inherent when we speak of Kumbha far transcends the literal translation.

Hindu scriptures tell us that the trinity of gods—Brahma (creator), Vishnu (whose name literally means the divine light that pervades everything, protector) and Shiva (destroyer), and all goddesses, including Mother Earth with her seven islands, and all knowledge in the form of the four Vedas—Rig, Yajur, Sama, Atharva—are present in the Kumbha. So Kumbha is symbolic of all that is and all that exists. In essence, the Kumbha mela is a celebration of all knowledge and all life. Though *kumbha* refers to an overflowing pot, it also refers to a body filled with knowledge. The nectar, or divine knowledge, lies within this kumbha, which is nothing but our body and we simply have to churn it to bring this knowledge out. If we look into the origins of the Kumbha mela, we find that this pitcher symbolises sharing and not hoarding. In *Vishnu Purana* a beautiful story is told of the war between the *rakshasas* (demons) and the *devatas* (gods). According to this, the demons were always fighting with their peace-loving brothers, the *devatas*. One day, the gods went to Brahma and asked for help: "If we continuously lose our brothers and sisters in the never-ending war with the demons, we will all perish." Brahma advised them to ask Vishnu for help. Vishnu responded: "If you churn the great milky ocean, you will find a golden pot of nectar. And a drop of nectar will make you immortal. Since you are not strong enough to churn the ocean yourselves, you must take the demons' help." Now, the gods were more distressed. They voiced their fear: "If the demons know that the reward is immortality, they will forcibly take the nectar and create more trouble. And if we don't tell them the reason, they will not agree to the churning." But Vishnu assuaged them and the perplexed gods convinced the demons to help them. It was no mean task to churn the vast milky ocean. Serpent Vasuki, Vishnu's seat, offered to be the rope and Vishnu incarnated as a turtle on whose back rested the mountain Meru. And so began the fantastic churning. After much hard work, a vicious smoke emerged, which filled the skies. This was not nectar, but deadly poison!

With people choking to death, this poison could not be ignored. Who would save them? Then the lord of the netherworld, Shiva, came forward and drank the poison. Today, after this sacrifice, Shiva is worshipped as the savior from death.

The churning resumed and shortly came out the golden pot of nectar. As soon as the pot came out, Indra, the lord of heavens, signaled Dhanwantari, the primordial physician, who leapt forward, grabbed the pot of nectar and ran away. The demons, quicker than him, pursued him relentlessly. Indra sought aid from Jupiter (the *dev* guru), Surya (the sun), Moon and Saturn to protect Dhanwantari and preserve the Kumbha. This long chase lasted 12 days, which was the equivalent of 12 years on earth. During this chase, which traversed all realms of the universe, Dhanwantari rested only four times, placing the Kumbha on the ground. And each time a few drops of the holy nectar spilled onto the earth in that place. These four places—Nasik, Ujjain, Hardwar and Allahabad in India—are today the centers of the Kumbha mela. In another legend, a demon named Shankhasura (*shankha*: conch, *asura*: demon) sent forth legions of creatures from the bottom of the sea to capture the sacred Vedas. And as the dark waters swallowed the knowledge of the mantras in the Vedas, the higher values of life also sank into the depths. Slowly, acts of charity and other forms of selfless service vanished. Fear, hunger, sleep and sex became the motivating forces for all human activities. Striving to appease their insatiable desires, humans plundered all. Scared, the gods sought refuge in the caves of Mount Kailash. Now, the conch demon demolished natural law and ushered in his reign with calamities—earthquakes, volcanoes, droughts. Chaos stalked the earth, and with the gods in hiding, the sages intervened. They meditated on Vishnu, the protector and nourisher, asking him for aid. In response to their plight, Vishnu advised them: "With a singular aim and disciplined mind, join forces to gather the knowledge of the Vedas once again. While you fulfill this task we will bring the benevolent forces of nature from their hiding place and dwell with them at Prayaga Raja (now Allahabad, India)." After the sages' departure, Vishnu assumed the form of an enormous fish, and vanquished Shankhasura. He then summoned the gods from their hiding place and brought them to Prayaga Raja, where they were joined by the other two of the trinity, Brahma and Shiva. Meanwhile the sages, through dhyana, discovered where the Vedas were hidden, fished them out of the mud, and joined the assembly at Prayaga Raja. There they asked Vishnu's permission to bring the knowledge of the Vedas into practice for the benefit of all creation. Granting their request, Vishnu said: "The secret of success lies in sacrifice, and the Vedas tell us how to walk this path. In every aspect of creation there is a continuous ceremony of sacrifice. Leaves decompose and nourish other organisms...."

The greatest among all sacrifices is the *ashwamedha* (the horse sacrifice) performed for the larger welfare. They train and tame their "horses", the mind and senses, and finally they share this harnessed energy with all living beings. This form of sacrifice nourishes humankind and every other form of life." So all present performed the *ashwamedha yajna*. The ritual lasted 12 years, and when it was completed the ecosystem was back into balance. Even the creatures from the netherworld were transformed. And with the natural world once again bursting with vitality, peace and prosperity reigned. The sages and gods requested Vishnu to bless the sacred Prayaga Raja: "May the energy emitting from Prayaga Raja guide humanity through all eternity." Hence, today this place is known as *brahma kshetra* (the field of pure consciousness) and *tirtha raja* (the lord of all holy places).

According to the *Padma Purana* these events took place when the Himalayas were still in their infancy and the area around Badrinath, now well above the timberline, was covered by a lush forest. From that time on Prayaga Raja has been regarded as a spiritual center. Great sages—Markandeya, Chyavana, Pulastya, Bharadvaja—guided their students through prolonged, intense practices here. Noble kings—Pururava and Bharata—whose dedication to spiritual practices and acts of charity earned them the status of *raja rishi* (royal seers), instituted a series of group practices here that went on, uninterrupted, for decades. These stories remind us that a materially successful society eventually ends up with a Shankhasura, a demon who systematically drowns the higher values of life. "Whether myth or fiction, for centuries these legends have inspired people to find the sacred in the mundane," writes Tigunait. "Most religions teach us that the spiritual and the worldly cannot coexist. What solace! These stories imply that there is no mediator between the aspirant and God, no rigid rules or laws. Simply listen to the voice of your heart, they say, and surrender the fruits of your deeds to the Almighty, who dwells in this sacred land." In this one national event the nectar of love, satsang, knowledge and grace is distributed to all without any discrimination.

During the Hindu festival, Kumbh Mela, millions of people congregate to bathe in the waters of certain rivers on auspicious days to cleanse their souls. Depending on the year of the 12-year cycle, sages, yogis, and devotees gather in temporary cities for a month of music, dancing, prayers, and ceremonies. Based on the ancient doings of gods who consecrated four sites along the banks of rivers with the honey of immortality, Kumbh Mela is the Hindu equivalent of a holy pilgrimage.

As the story goes, there was a pot, the kumbh, full of the elixir or nectar of immortality. Yet the gods fought over who got to carry the pot, and in the process, four drops fell at four different places. These came to be known as Prayag, Hardiwar, Ujjain, and Nasik, and they correspond to the four Kumbh Melas that take place every three years. On astrologically propitious days, determined by the paths of planets, the nectar is said to return to these rivers so that bathing in them will bring peace and purification.

Prayag occurs at the point where the Ganges and Yamuna Rivers meet the fabled Saraswati River. Haridwar brings people to the Ganges, where it flows from the Himalaya Mountains onto the wide valley. Ujjain occurs at the Ksipra River, while the Godavari River is the site of the Kumbh Mela called Nasik. The exact dates of each pilgrimage vary from year to year, depending on when the Sun enters Aries and Jupiter enters Aquarius.

Some days are more holy for bathing than others, according to the stars, and on these days non-Hindus are asked to respectfully stay out of the water. Otherwise, the banks are crowded with throngs of tourists and Hindus alike, praying, playing music on drums, burning incense, saying prayers, and reciting mantras. It is a remarkable ceremony that blends mythology, culture, and deep, spiritual beliefs.

Disregarding the heavy expenses and the long tiring journey people come from all parts of the country and band together to form the world's and most colourful religious concourse—the Kumbh Mela which comes after twelve long years of waiting. Hindus regard that a dip in the holy Ganga specially at Haridwar which is believed to be the gangadwar of ancient mythology. As in ages gone by, the powerful call of Kumbh Mela still draws millions of people from all over India. It is indeed fantastic to behold the ancient past blending so naturally with the reality of the present world. The large gatherings of millions are seen once every six years in Ardha-Kumbh Mela and once in twelve years in the Kumbh melas. In these Kumbh Melas there are hermits and sages from the higher reaches of the Himalayas, Pilgrims, Swamis and missionaries from South of India and from far away lands like America. The faces of unlead ash-smeared sadhus, known as "Digambars", add to the mystic atmosphere. Bringing all of these together to the same place and at the same time certainly speaks of the overpowering strength of religious traditions in India and also of their staunch faith in their own religious precepts.

As the auspicious Kumbh Mela at Haridwar draws near thousands of emergency shelters spring up-modern tents, old style bamboo cottages like those used long ago by ancient sages. Atop of these flutter thousands of coloured flags of various religious sects. A common feature of this mela is fakirs sitting with their twisted limbs on their sharp spikes and ascetics standing on their heads. As the auspicious hour for the dip draws near some 100,000 Sadhu take out a procession, which is led by a Sadhu, riding an unsadled horse, followed by caprisoned elephant behind which the holy men march in long files. The whole corsage proceeds in regal splendour down to the water's edge with some of the Sadhus reclining under gorgeous parasols in decorated palanquins. The route of the procession is lined with crowds of pilgrims. A ripple runs through the crowd as the first sect of Sadhus steps into the water to be followed by wave after wave of Sadhus dip in the holy river. Then excited people enter the water to have their holy bath. In the ancient literary works the importance of Haridwar as one of the seven holy cities of the Hindus is highly emphasised. It is at Haridwar, rightly known as the "gateway to reach the gods" that the great holy Ganga enters the plain after a journey of two hundred miles through the rugged mountains. Thus beauty and sanctity are seen together at Haridwar. Wooded hills, cradle the youthful Ganga not yet defiled by city wastes, as she emerges from the protective girdle of the majestic Himalayas, holding forth a promise of a million years in heaven no deities need to be propitiated , no temple bells are required to be rung! Just a bath in the magic waters of the Sacred Ganga at Haridwar and you reach nearer to heaven. As evening falls at Haridwar and hundreds of lighted floats go bobbing down in the waters of Ganga, pilgrims sitting around the fire narrate the mythical episode of the churning of the sea by the gods and the demons for a continuous thousand years to finally bring out from the sea the Kumbh containing the elixir of immortality. The crowds listen to the legend of the fight between the gods and the demons to take possession of that Kumbh and also to the many stories that have sprung from that one episode. Apart from the Hindu devotees, there are a great many who came with truly pious sentiments. It is to such people that the Kumbh and Ardh-Kumbh melas owe their tremendous impact and popularity.

IV

NAUCHANDI MELA

The Nauchandi mela is held on the second Sunday after Holi every year in Meerut in the northern state of Uttar Pradesh. For a month, the city hums with activity as people from far and near coming to participate in the fair. Initially, the management of the mela was in the hands of the landlords but now it is organised by the local municipal corporation. The management of the mela is striking. It has over a thousand stalls, and plays host to over 50,000 people every day.

The fair has its own history and numerous legends and stories are woven around it. It started in AD 1672 as a one-day affair mainly for cattle traders but has since undergone many changes. Cattle trading has been replaced by a multitude of activities-religious rituals, commercial activity, artistic creativity and rustic merriment.

The mela also figured during the First War of Indian Independence in 1857 when one of the prominent figures of the revolt, Nana Saheb, came here to motivate the locals to raise arms against the British. When the British regained control, they put up posters of Nana Saheb and his warriors at the Nauchandi mela to gain favor of the local populace.

According to another story, the East India Company used to put up the fair as a revenue collection center around 1800. And in 1884, F.N.Wright, the then collector of Meerut district started a horse exhibition where thoroughbred stallions were sold. Of course, other activities commensurate with the mela used to be organized to attract prospective buyers.

The period of the mela stretches for over a month now. Except in 1858, a year after the revolt against the East India Company rule started from Meerut, the fair has been held here regularly.

Significantly, the mela is a rare symbol of communal harmony with both Hindu and Muslim shrines-the Nauchandi temple and the dargah (mausoleum) of Bala Mian, a Muslim saint-situated close by. Visitors pay obeisance at both the shrines irrespective of the religion they belong to.

The sprawling four-and-a-half square kilometer area where the fair is held is strewn with red sand, which brightens up the place. The neat pathways are interspersed with flowerbeds and fountains.

Thousands of bulbs and tube-lights illuminate the premises and the four main gates are lavishly decorated. The stalls and shops are also decorated with spotless white cloth known as chandhnis in local parlance. The mela, which originally brought sellers and buyers of utensils and domestic animals together, has increased its repertoire to include various kinds of goods, entertainment, and food. Shopkeepers from all over Uttar Pradesh and Delhi put up stalls here. A fascinating variety of things can be found at the mela.

Chikan work from Luckhnow, brassware from Moradabad, carpets and rugs from Varanasi, footwear from Agra, leather items from Kanpur, kohl from Bareilly, perfumes from Kannauj, bangles from Ferozabad, china clay items from Khurja, costume jewellery from Jaipur, bed sheets from Panipat, cane furniture from Assam and a lot more are up for grabs for the visitor to the mela. Meerut's own products like sports goods, scissors, and gajak (a sweetmeat) are also available at reasonable prices.

One of the special charms of this fair is the happy blend of urban and rural flavors seen here. There are swings, merry-go-rounds, circus shows, toys, boating and various fun competitions to keep children and even the elders pleased.

The mela is a feast not only for the eyes but for the palate too as there are stalls selling a wide variety of food- the famous giant size halwa-paratha, a special flavored jalebi, mouth watering chole bhature and makki ki roti with sarson ka saag, golgoppas and even idli, dosa and vada can be had. Then, there are various kinds of flavored mild, jal-jeera, soft drinks, ice creams and kulfis to keep the palate cool.

Stalls selling churan, pachak-ki-goli (digestive pills) and paan are some other attractions. A fruit one could be seeing for the first time at this mela is the yellow kesar fruit.

Legend has it that Mandodari, the wife of Ravan (the demon king of Lanka in the epic Ramayana), was born in a devil's house in Meerut. She was, however, a great devotee of goddess Chandi and had a temple constructed in honor of the goddess. A religious festival was held to celebrate this occasion. Since then the fair has been held every year. As the legend of the dargah goes, Syed Salar Masood Ghazi was a commander in the army of Mahmood of Ghazni who invaded India in AD 1017 and proved his mettle in the fight against the local king. During the course of a battle, he lost one of his fingers. Syed Salar subsequently denounced violence, became an ascetic, and took the name Bala Mian. The present dargah was built in his memory in AD 1194 by Qutub-ud-din Aibak, at the spot where his cut finger had fallen during the battle.

The cultural aspect of the Nauchandi Mela is also as important. Every evening some cultural programme or the other is held, which goes on till the early hours of the morning. The mela has had the honor of playing host to artistes like the internationally renowned Pandit Ravi Shankar. Besides, the mela committee has started a few new events like beauty contests, honoring the aged, organizing women's conferences, fireworks and music competitions. Plans are also afoot to set up an art gallery and museum to preserve the historic, cultural and artistic aspects of the mela.

While nautankis (melodramas performed by professional theatre companies) are still staged, the real crowd puller are the musical programmes with modern orchestra.

V

PUSHKAR FAIR

Rajasthan is at its colorful best during fairs and festivals. There are numerous fairs throughout the year in the state, which brighten the otherwise hard and dreary lives of the villagers of the deserts.

One of the most popular and colorful fairs of the Thar desert is the Pushkar fair, which begins on Kartik Shukla Ekadashi & goes on for five days till Kartik Purnima. The time of the fair coincides with the bright half of the moon during the months of October-November. The lake at Pushkar is one of the most sacred in India. From time immemorial, people have been gathering here annually during the month of Kartik to pay obeisance to Lord Brahma.

The picturesque lake of Pushkar is set in a valley just about 11 kilometres northwest of Ajmer, surrounded by hills on three sides and sand dunes on the fourth. Pushkar forms a fascinating location and a befitting backdrop for the annual religious and cattle fair. Turbaned heads of men, and colorful veils and skirts of the women, bring alive the arid desertscape. The village women dress in their best clothes and finery for the five-day mela.

Like Varanasi, Pushkar is one of the sacred places for the Hindus, with 400 temples of which the most important is dedicated to Lord Brahma - the creator of the universe. Fifty-two ghats bind the lake. During the days of the mela, the otherwise tranquil lake is engulfed with religious fervor. Thousands of devotees congregate to take a dip, sadhus descend from the Himalayas and people pray for salvation to the sound of verses from the Holy Scriptures, which fill the air.

In the afternoons, people crowd the stadium where camels, horses, and cows are paraded and raced. Camels are bought and sold during the Pushkar fair.

On the roadside, stalls of all kinds are set up to sell a cornucopia of items. Almost every household is engaged in setting them up as the locals try to capitalize on the massive influx of people. It is impossible to drive around because of the large crowds. Either you hire a camel or you walk. In this aspect, it is truly a rural bazaar.

An interesting part of the Pushkar Fair is the mass trading of camels. Of course, cattle and other livestock are also traded, but it's camels that hold center stage at Pushkar. Camel-traders and villagers from miles away converge to Pushkar with their humped beasts. Over 25,000 camels (and that's on the conservative side) are traded; making this world's largest camel fair.

Since Pushkar is a religious place alcohol and non-vegetarian food is prohibited. Magha Saptami (January-

February) heralds the occasion for performance of the Pushkar rituals at a beach three kilometers from Konark. The roots of this festival are traced to a mythical tale wherein Shambhu, the son of Lord Krishna, trespassed into the chamber of his parents when they were in a state of private bliss. Upon this, Krishna cursed his son with leprosy. Since the punishment was too acute for such an inadvertent act by Shambhu, Narad took pity on him and instructed him to seek a cure at the Pushkar River. The place where Shambhu is said to have meditated and worshipped the sun God after ablutions in the river for twelve years has become a sacred spot possessing curative properties.

Today, the river is not visible. What is left could be described either as a large pond or a very small lake. Yet, the faith in the cleansing powers of its waters is unquestionable. For, on this day of Magha Saptami, hundreds of thousands of people go through the bathing rituals. Those who do not find space, do so in the sea, which is just 100 m away. The ritual bathing takes place from 3 am onwards, commencing with the thakurs (priests) and followed by the rest. After purification, by dawn, a sea of humanity expectantly faces the Bay of Bengal with their eyes focused on a brighter section of the horizon.

After darshan (worship), nearly 80 per cent of the people begin the journey back home, stopping on their way for offerings at the local shrines on the beach and the thakurbari (home of the local priest) where ceremonies still continue. The scenario along the beach gradually changes at this stage. Small groups, mostly family members, can be seen gathered around pandas (priests) who perform pujas. After etching the outline of the Jagannath temple in the sand, small mounds of wet sand representing each family member are placed within, along with earthen lamps and flowers. This, accompanied by the panda's chanting, which is repeated by family members, is intended to usher prosperity. These rites last from fifteen to thirty minutes.

As the morning stretches, the sands and the fisher folk, with their catamarans, regain authority on Pushkar. While the wind and the caves will erase, all traces of this mammoth congregation, the celestial drama, though repeated daily shall remain an ordinary event until the next Magha Saptami.

Pushkar is the only place in India where there is a temple dedicated to Lord Brahma. A legend recounts how Brahma sought abode on earth. He sat on his hansa (his vehicle, the swan) and flew over the earth. He dropped petals of a lotus as he flew and lakes sprung up where they landed. He descended upon this site to perform a yajna, which however could not be performed, as his wife was not present. Narada was dispatched to fetch Savitri. She made preparations to arrive ceremoniously. Brahma, afraid that the auspicious moment would pass, asked Indra to "bring a wife from wherever you can". A young milkmaid, Gayatri was brought to the yajna and the puja performed. When Savitri appeared, she was so enraged that she put a curse upon Brahma-that he would not be worshipped anywhere except in Pushkar and that too only once a year. She then left for the Ratnagiri Hill and immolated herself. There is a temple atop this hill dedicated to Savitri. Another legend has it that the Mughal ruler Aurangzeb, who was a devout Muslim but intolerant other religions, once went to Pushkar to get the temples there demolished. On reaching there, the King went to wash his face in the Pushkar lake but recoiled on seeing that the reflection in the lake was that of an old man with gray hair et al. Taking this as a bad omen, Aurangzeb decided against having the temples demolished and went back to his capital Delhi. Pushkar is 11 kilometres northwest of Ajmer, which is located on National Highway No, 132 kilometres west of Jaipur.. Ajmer is well connected with Jaipur and Delhi by road and rail. One can fly to Jaipur and then easily drive down to Pushkar, the site of the fair.

VI

SURAJKUND CRAFTS MELA

Surajkund is a historic site, eight km from the southern border of Delhi. The Sun temple stood here during AD 1000, the remains of which can still be seen here. The temple and the enchanting surroundings of this place won the heart of a Tomar chieftain Surajpal, who belonged to a clan of sun worshippers. Raja Surajpal had a sun pool and amphitheatre built in this area with the sun temple at its periphery. After the chieftain Surajpal, who built the complex, the place was named Surajkund. It was around this temple and sun pool that a resort property came up in Surajkund. What began as simple tourist center in 1987 flowered into a center of pilgrimage and a haloed piece of land that celebrates centuries old crafts and traditions of our colorful country at the annual Surajkund Crafts Mela.

As spring glides in, full of warmth and vibrancy leaving the gray winter behind, Surajkund adorns itself with colorful traditional crafts of India. Craftsmen from all over the country assemble at Surajkund during the first fortnight of February to participate in the annual celebration known as the Surajkund Crafts Mela. This Mela (fair) is a meeting ground for talented artists, painters, weavers, sculptors and craftsmen form all over India who exhibit their creations for the arts and crafts lovers who come from the world over to admire and acquire these creations. Surajkund (literally, 'Lake of the Sun') is a dusty little town in Haryana, on the outskirts of Delhi. For two weeks every year, on February 1-15, it gets transformed into a sprawling and comprehensive craftsmen's village. The Surajkund Mela is not just the biggest artisans' fair in the country; it is also unique in that every year there is a different theme to the fair. So, nobody can say, "I've been to it," and ignore this celebration of the essence of Indian culture and traditional crafts.

This delightful handloom and handicrafts fair is held annually at Surajkund. Skilled Artisans from all over the country display the rich crafts tradition of India in the typical setting of a rural Indian marketplace. Cultural programmes and rural cuisine are also a part of this colorful fair. The theme that changes every year, works on two levels. First, it has a state theme, which dictates the look of the entrance, the fair grounds, and the setting. One can get the specific ambience of the particular state-the characteristic colors, materials, architecture, furniture and decorations. The other is less cosmetic and more purposeful-each year highlights one craft, and about half the stalls are dedicated to that craft. And there are a total of about 400 stalls.

So, if the theme is pottery/terracotta, it has stalls that display the various kinds of pottery and clay craft available in the country. The stalls also function as workshops, where artisans from all over the country make their wares: pots, vases, urns, molded images, trinkets.

Apart from this, there are stalls that cater to the other crafts, where again one gets first-hand experience of how the artisans work and how things are made. Woodwork, metalwork, papier-mache, weaving, embroidery, sculpture, and bamboo and cane craft are all featured at the Mela.

A fair of this magnitude would naturally have supplementary interests. So, one has an equally interesting food section that serves a variety of Indian cuisines, which is traditional although there are several stalls selling fast food like burgers and chow mien too. Apart from that, there is the usual gamut of entertainment-rides and shows for kids, and daylong cultural events, including folk dance and music recitals, with stress on the state theme. The potter's wheel always holds a special enchantment for visitors as the artisans mould pots and pans with their deft fingers.

The crafts in the Surajkund Mela are the creation of people coming from the remotest parts of the country. The craftwork of the people rain forest area of Assam and Manipur, the deserts of Rajasthan, the Nilgiri hills of south, the tribal lands of Bastar and from all the other areas come here to display their aesthetic pieces of work.

The story of how the sun pool came into existence is an interesting tale. Over a thousand years ago, the clan of Tomar chieftains began establishing their supremacy near Delhi. They built their domain here, calling it 'Dellikha'. The Tomars were sun worshippers. One chieftain Raja Surajpal worked to build a sun temple at this site. Legend has it, that it was after this Raja that the place came to be known as Surajkund. But the Tomar kings could not stay here for long. Mauraders vanquished the Tomar clan and desecrated the temple. But the amphitheatre sun pool built adjacent withstood the onslaught of time to become the celebrated fair ground that it is today.

Glossary

Aaru Padai Veedu: The six permanent abodes of Lord Muruga before He vanquished Surapadman as the generalissimo of the divine forces

Abhayam: Refuge

Abishekam: A holy ritual ablution given to the Deity with oil, milk, scented powder, honey, rose water, ghee, sugar-cane juice etc.

Adi Sesha: Divine serpent said to have one thousand heads and represented as forming the couch of Lord Vishnu.

Agamas: Traditional principles governing worship, construction, festivals in temples.The word Agama means tradition

Ahura Mazda: God (or more accurately the embodiment of good) in the dualist Zoroastrian faith

Aiavatham: The legendary white elephant of Indra, the King of the Devas

Alwars: Vaishnavite saints whose hymns in praise of Vishnu constitute the tamil canon - considered to be on par with the Vedas.

Amirtham (Amrit): Nectar of immortality

Amman, Ambal: Goddess

Angootiyan: Rings (in reference to Tolkein's 'The lord of the Rings')

Angra Mainyu: The devil (or more accurately the embodiment of evil) in the Zoroastrian faith

Appar: Tirunavukkarasar, one of the foremost of the 63 Saivite Nayanmar saints; associated closely with Tiruvatikai, Paatirippuliyur, Tiruvaiyaru and Tiruppugalur

Arattu: A kind of holy bath given to the festival images of the deities, when they are immersed in water on the final day of the annual festival in Kerala and in Kanyakumari district of Tamilnadu

Archana: Devotional worship offered to the deity by the priest with flowers or saffron

Artha Mandapam: An intermediary space between the Sanctum Sanctorum and the exterior of the temple

Arthajamam: The last of the daily poojas performed at night

Ashram: A hermitage or abode of ascetics

Ashtothram: A form of Archana worship usually offered to the deity with a recital of 108 names of a deity

Asthana Mandapam: Assembly Hall

Asura: Demon

Avataram, Avtar: An Incarnation of God

Bali Peetham: Altar or the sacrificial stone

Bhajanai, Bhajan: Group singing of divine songs

Bhaktha, Bhakth: Devotee (The word Bhakti means devotion)

Bhattachariar: A Brahmin priest belonging to the Vaishnavite sect who offers poojas in a Vishnu temple

Chakram: Discus of Lord Vishnu

Chapparam: Chariot

Dakshinayanam: The sun's progress south of Equator(July-December)

Darshan, Darisanam: Sight of God or of holy men

Dasavatharam: The ten incarnations of Vishnu to punish the wicked

Deepa Aradhanai: A ceremonial waving of lamps - Illuminating the image of a deity with camphor or with a deepam (oil, clarified butter lamps)

Devasthanam: A body administering the affairs of the temple

Devaswom: The Keralite name for temples

Dwajasthambam: The flag-mast, usually a pillar fixed outside the main shrine in line with the Sanctum Sanctorum

Dwapara Yugam: The third among the four Yugas or aeons of time, the current aeon being Kaliyugam

Dwara Palakas: Figures of guards of the deities found on either side of the entrance to the Sanctum Sanctorum

Garbagriham: The interior of Sanctum Sanctorum

Garuda: A mythological bird, the vehicle of Lord Vishnu

Ghats: Slope, hills, the adjective is ghati (also used as a perjorative reference to people from the hills, sort of like hill-billy). There are two mountain ranges (on either side of the Deccan plateau) called the Western and Eastern ghats. When Rushdie uses it, it would generally refer to the Western Ghats, which are the first thing one encounters on moving from Bombay to the mainland. shamshan ghat is the equivalent of 'boot hill', a place where the dead are cremated (a reference to the steps leading to the Ganga at Varanasi)

Gopuram: Temple Tower crowning entrances; the foremost of these towes crowning the main entrance is the Raja Gopuram.

Guru: Preceptor, Teacher

Gurukkal: A priest belonging to the Saivite sect who offers pooja in aSiva temple; a gurukkal is also known by the name Sivachariar.

Holi: A North Indian festival celebrated in spring, where people douse each other in water, and colour each others faces.

Homam: Sacrificial ritual conducted with an altar of fire, as a part of daily worship, festivals and special occasions.

Hundi: A sealed receptacle with a slit at the top in which devotees make offerings to a temple

Jeer: A spiritual head of Vaishnavites

Wadi Sue: Nickname for Premlata, Maharaji's oldest daughter (born 1975). Also the name of Maharaji's previous yacht.

Bibliography

Agarwal, Anil. "Human-Nature Interactions in a Third World Country." In *Ethical Perspectives on Environmental Issues in India,* ed. George James, 31–72. New Delhi: A. P. H. Publishing Corporation, 1999.

Akula, Vikram K. "Grassroots Environmental Resistance in India." In *Ecological Resistance Movements: The Global Emergence of Radical and Popular Environmentalism,* ed. Bron Raymond Taylor, 127–45. Albany, N.Y.: State University of New York Press, 1995.

Alagh, Yoginder K., and Dhananjay Trambaklal Buch. "The Sardar Sarovar Project and Sustainable Development." In *Toward Sustainable Development: Struggling over India's Narmada River,* ed. William F. Fisher, 291–318. Armonk, N.Y. and London: M. E. Sharpe, 1995.

Alagh, Yoginder K., R. D. Desai, G. S. Guha, and S. P. Kashyap. *Economic Dimensions of the Sardar Sarovar Project.* New Delhi: Har-anand Publications, 1995.

Allchin, Bridget. "Early Man and Environment in South Asia 10,000 BC-500 AD." In *Nature and the Orient: The Environmental History of South and Southeast Asia,* eds. Richard H. Grove, Vinita Damodaran, Satpal Sangwan, 29–50. Delhi: Oxford University Press, 1998.

Alley, Kelly D. *On the Banks of the Ganga: When Wastewater Meets a Sacred River.* Ann Arbor: University of Michigan Press, 2002.

Alter, Stephen. *Sacred Waters: A Pilgrimage up the Ganges Rivers to the Source of Hindu Culture.* New York: Harcourt, Inc., 2001.

Altvater, Ilmar. "Ecological and Economic Modalities of Time and Space." In *Is Capitalism Sustainable?: Political Economy and the Politics of Ecology,* ed. Martin O'Conner, 76–90. New York: Guilford Press, 1994.

Amanullah, Md.1988, *Dashera of Bastar,* Bhopal, MP: Tribal Research & Development Institute, Banya Prakashan.

Anderson, Mary, 1998. *The Festivals of Nepal*, Calcutta, Allahabad, Bombay, Delhi: Rupa & Co.

Ambasta, S. P., ed. *The Useful Plants of India.* New Delhi: Publications and Information Directorate, CSIR, 1986.

Apffel-Marglin, Frédérique with Purna Chandra Mishra. "'Sacred Groves' Regenerating the Body, the Land, the Community." In *Global Ecology: A New Area of Political Conflict,* ed. Wolfgang Sachs, 197–207. Atlantic Highlands, N.J.: Zed, 1993.

Apffel-Marglin, Frédérique. "Introduction: Rationality and the World." In *Decolonizing Knowledge: From Development to Dialogue,* eds. Frédérique Apffel-Marglin and Stephen A. Marglin, 1–39. Oxford: Clarendon Press, 1996.

Appadurai, Arjun. "Comments on The Jungle and the Aroma of Meats: An Ecological Theme in Hindu Medicine." *Social Science and Medicine* 27, no. 3 (1988): 206–207.

Appadurai, Arjun. "How Moral is South Asia's Economy?—A Review Article." *Journal of Asian Studies* 43, no. 3 (1984): 481–97.

Appadurai, Arjun. "Introduction: Commodities and the Politics of Value." In *The Social Life of Things: Commodities in Cultural Perspective,* ed. Arjun Appadurai, 3–63. Cambridge: Cambridge University Press, 1986.

Ardener, Shirley, ed. *Women and Space: Ground Rules and Social Maps*. Oxford: Berg Publishers, 1993.

Arnold, David, and Ramachandra Guha, eds. *Nature, Culture, and Imperialism: Essays on the Environmental History of South Asia*. Delhi: Oxford University Press, 1995.

Balapure, K. N., J. K. Maheshware, and R. K. Tandon. "Plants of the Ramayana." *Ancient Science of Life* 7 (1987): 76–84.

Banerjee, Sures Chandra. *Flora and Fauna in Sanskrit Literature*. Calcutta: Naya Prokash, 1980.

Banuri, Tariq, and Frédérique Apffel-Marglin, eds. *Who Will Save the Forests?: Knowledge, Power, and Environmental Destruction*. London: Zed, 1993.

Banwari. *Pancavati: Indian Approaches to Environment*. Translated by Asha Vohra. Delhi: Shri Vinayak Publications, 1992.

Bartolomé, Leopoldo J. "Forced Resettlement and the Survival Systems of the Urban Poor." *Ethnology* 23, no. 3 (1984): 177–92.

Basu, Helene. *Habshi-Sklaven, Sidi-Fakire: Muslimische Heiligenverehrung im westlichen Indien*. Berlin: Das Arabische buch Verlag, 1995.

Bauer, Stefan. "Bambus: AngepaBte Anwendungen in der Architektur tropischer und subtropischer Länder." *Archiv für Völkerkunde* 47 (1993): 171–89.

Bauer, Stefan. *Angepasste Technologie: Augewählte ethnologische Fall-beispiele aus Indien unter besonderer Berücksichtigung der Abfallverwertung*. Magistergrades der Philosophie: Universität Wien, 1994.

Baviskar, Amita. *In the Belly of the River: Tribal Conflicts over Development in the Narmada Valley*. Delhi: Oxford University Press, 1995.

Beck, Brenda E. F. "The Symbolic Merger of Body, Space

and Cosmos in Hindu Tamil Nadu." *Contributions to Indian Sociology* 10, no. 2 (1976): 213-43.

Benthall, Jonathan. "The Greening of the Purple." *Anthropology Today* 11 (June 1995): 18–20.

Benveniste, Emile. *Indo-European Language and Society.* Coral Gables, Fla.: University of Miami Press, 1973.

Berleant, Arnold. *The Aesthetics of Environment.* Philadelphia, Pa.: Temple Univerity Press, 1992.

Berman, Morris. *The Reenchantment of the World.* Ithaca, N.Y.: Cornell University Press, 1981.

Bhabha, Homi K. *The Location of Culture.* New York: Routledge, 1994.

Bharara, L. P. "Notes on the Experience of Drought: Perception, Recollection, and Prediction." In *Desertification and Development: Dryland Ecology in Social Perspective,* eds. Brian Spooner and H. S. Mann, 351–61. London: Academic Press, 1982.

Bhattacharji, Sukumari. *Fatalism in Ancient India.* Calcutta: Baulmon Prakashan, 1995.

Bhide, A. D., and B. B. Sundaresan. "Street Cleansing and Waste Storage and Collection in India." In *Managing Solid Wastes in Developing Countries,* ed. John R. Holmes, 139–49. New York: John Wiley and Sons, Ltd., 1984.

Biardeau, Madeleine. *Hinduism: The Anthropology of a Civilization.* Delhi: Oxford University Press, 1989.

Bishnoi, Shri Krishna. *Bishnoi Dharm-Sanskar.* Bikaner: Dhok Dhora Prakashan, 1991.

Blincow, Malcolm. "Scavengers and Recycling: A Neglected Domain of Production." *Labour, Capital, and Society* 19, no. 1 (1986): 94–115.

Blinkhorn, Thomas A., and William T. Smith. "India's Narmada: River of Hope." In *Toward Sustainable*

Development?: Struggling over India's Narmada River, ed. William F. Fisher, 89–112. Armonk, N.Y.: M. E. Sharpe, 1995.

Braidotti, Rosa, Ewa Charkiewicz, Sabine Hausler, and Sakia Wiernga. *Women, the Environment, and Sustainable Development: Toward a Theoretical Synthesis.* London: Zed, 1994.

Breman, Jan. "Labor Relations in the 'Formal' and 'Informal' Sectors: Report of a Case Study in South Gujarat, India." *Journal of Peasant Studies* 4, nos. 3–4 (1977): 171–205; 337–59.

Broder, Jonathan. "Pollution Threatens the Ancient Purity of the Ganges." *San Francisco Examiner* 31, 8–9 March 1997, Travel Section.

Brooks, Charles R. "A Unique Conjuncture: The Incorporation of ISKON in Vrindaban." In *Krishna Consciousness in the West,* ed. David G. Bromley and Larry D. Shinn, 165–87. Lewisburg, Pa.: Bucknell University Press, 1989.

Brooks, Charles R. *The Hare Krishnas in India.* Princeton, N.J.: Princeton University Press, 1989.

Buckley, Thomas, and Alma Gottlieb, eds. *Blood Magic: The Anthropology of Menstruation.* Berkeley, Calif.: University of California Press, 1988.

Burgat, Florence. "Non-violence towards Animals in the Thinking of Gandhi: The Problem of Animal Husbandry." *Journal of Agricultural and Environmental Ethics* 17 (2004): 223-248.

Buttel, Frederick H. "Environmentalization: Origins, Processes, and Implications for Rural Social Change." *Rural Sociology* 57, no. 1 (spring 1992): 1–27.

Buttel, Frederick H., and Peter Taylor. "Environmental Sociology and Global Environmental Change: A Critical

Assessment." *Society and Natural Resources* 5, no. 3 (July-September, 1992): 211–30.

Callicott, J. Baird and Roger T. Ames, eds. *Nature in Asian Traditions of Thought: Essays in Environmental Philosophy*. Albany, N.Y.: State University of New York Press, 1989.

Callicott, J. Baird. *Earth's Insights: A Multicultural Survey of Ecological Ethics from the Mediterranean Basin to the Australian Outback*. Berkeley, Calif.: University of California Press, 1994.

Capra, Fritjof. *Belonging to the Universe: Explorations on the Frontiers of Science and Spirituality*. San Francisco, Calif.: Harper San Francisco, 1991.

Carman, John Braisted, and Frédérique Apffel-Marglin. *Purity and Auspiciousness in Indian Society*. Leiden: E. J. Brill, 1985.

Cenkner, William. *A Tradition of Teachers: Sankara and the Jagadurus Today*. Delhi: Motilal Banarsidass, 1983.

Chaitanya, Krishna. "Man, Nature and Cosmos in Vedic India." *The Ecologist* 30, no. 1 (2000): 21-24.

Chakrabarty, Dipesh. "Open Space/Public Place: Garbage, Modernity and India." *South Asia* 14, no. 1 (1991): 15–31.

Champion, Sir Harry George, and S. K. Seth. *A Revised Survey of the Forest Types of India*. Delhi: Manager of Publications, 1968.

Chandrasekhar, Sripati. "The Hindu Understanding of Population and Population Control." In *Ethical Perspectives on Environmental Issues in India,* ed. George A. James, 189–216. New Delhi: A. P. H. Publishing Corporation, 1999.

Chapple, Christopher Key, and Mary Evelyn Tucker, eds.

Hinduism and Ecology: The Intersection of Earth, Sky, and Water. Cambridge, Mass.: Harvard Divinity School, Center for the Study of World Religions, 2000. Distributed by Harvard University Press.

Chapple, Christopher Key. "Religions of India and Ecology." In *Religion and Ecology: Toward a More Creative Interaction,* ed. Joseph Bracken, 71-83. Cincinnati, Ohio: The Brueggeman Center for Interreligious Dialogue, 2001.

________. "Religion, Economics, and Ecology: A Hindu Response." In *Ethics and World Religions: Cross-Cultural Case Studies*, eds. Regina Wentzel Wolfe and Christine Gudorf, 252-259. Maryknoll, New York: Orbis Books, 1999.

________. "Toward an Indigenous Indian Environmentalism." In *Purifying the Earthly Body of God: Religion and Ecology in Hindu India,* ed. Lance Nelson, 13–37. Albany, N.Y.: State University of New York Press, 1998.

________. "Hindu Environmentalism." In *Worldviews and Ecology: Religion, Philosophy, and the Environment,* eds. Mary Evelyn Tucker and John A. Grim, 113–23. Maryknoll, N.Y.: Orbis, 1994.

________. "India's Earth Consciousness." In *The Soul of Nature: Celebrating the Spirit of the Earth,* eds. Michael Tobias and Georgianne Cowan, 145–51. New York: Plume, 1994.

________.ed. *Ecological Prospects: Scientific, Religious, and Aesthetic Perspectives.* Albany, N.Y.: State University of New York Press, 1994.

________. *Nonviolence to Animals, Earth, and Self in Asian Traditions.* Albany, N.Y.: State University of New York Press, 1993.

_______. "Ecological Nonviolence and the Hindu Tradition." In *Perspectives on Nonviolence*, ed. V.K. Kool, 168-177. New York: Springer-Verlag, 1990.

Chattopadhyaya, D. P. "Indian Perspectives on Naturalism." In *Nature Across Cultures: Views of Nature and the Environment in Non-Western Cultures*, ed. Helaine Selin, 147-159. Boston: Kluwer Academic Press, 2003.

Childs, John Brown. "Rooted Cosmopolitanism: The Transnational Character of Indigenous Particularity." Stevenson Programme on Global Security Colloquium, University of Santa Cruz, 1992.

Chopra, Ram Nath, I. C. Chopra, K. L. Handa, and L. D. Kapur. *Indigenous Drugs of India*. 2d ed. Calcutta: Academic Publishers, 1958.

Claiborne, William. "Devout Hindus Resist Efforts to Clean Up the Sacred Ganges." *The Washington Post,* 8 May 1983, 18–19 (A).

Clarke, John James. *Oriental Enlightenment: The Encounter between Asian and Western Thought.* London: Routledge, 1997.

Cobb, John B., Jr. *Sustainability: Economics, Ecology, and Justice.* Maryknoll, N.Y.: Orbis, 1992.

Cooper, David E. and Joy A. Palmer, eds. *Spirit of the Environment: Religion, Value and Environmental Concern*. New York: Routledge, 1998.

Cornell, Laura. "What can Yoga contribute to the environmental movement?" *Yoga Chicago* 12, no. 5 (2005): 6-7. (http://www.yogachicago.com/sep05/greenyoga.shtml)

Corocoran, Maura. *Vrndavana in Vaisnava Literature: History, Mythology, Symbolism.* New Delhi: D. K. Printworld and Vrindaban Research Institute, 1995.

Covarrubias, Miguel. *Island of Bali.* Kuala Lumpur: Oxford University Press, 1974.

Coward, Harold, ed. "Hindu Views of Nature and the Environment." In *Nature Across Cultures: Views of Nature and the Environment in Non-Western Cultures,* ed. Helaine Selin, 411-419. Boston: Kluwer Academic Press, 2003.

Crawford, S. Cromwell, ed. "Hindu Ethics for Modern Life." In *World Religions and Global Ethics,* 5–35. New York: Paragon, 1989.

Crawford, S. Cromwell. *The Evolution of Hindu Ethical Ideals.* Delhi: Arnold-Heinemann, 1974.

Cremo, Michael A., and Mukunda Goswami. *Divine Nature: A Spiritual Perspective on the Environmental Crisis.* Los Angeles, Calif.: Bhaktivedanta Institute, 1995.

Croll, Elisabeth, and David Parkin, eds. *Bush Base, Forest Farm: Culture, Environment, and Development.* London: Routledge, 1992.

Cutler, Norman, Joanne Punzo Waghorne, and Vasudha Narayanan, eds. *Gods of Flesh, Gods of Stone: The Embodiment of Divinity in India*. Chambersburg, PA: Anima Publications, 1985.

Darian, Steven G. *The Ganges in Myth and History.* Honolulu, Hawaii: University Press of Hawaii, 1978.

Das Gupta, S. *Alpana.* Delhi: Ministry of Information, 1960.

Das Gupta, Shashi Bushan. "Evolution of Mother Worship in India." In *Great Women of India,* eds. Swami Madhavananda and Ramesh Chandra Majumdar, 49–86. Mayavati Pithoragarh, Himalayas: Advaita Ashrama, 1982.

Das, Veena. *Structure and Cognition: Aspects of Hindu Caste and Ritual.* 2d ed. Delhi: Oxford University Press, 1982.

Dasa, Ranchor. "Reviving the Forests of Vrndavana." *Back to Godhead: The Magazine of the Hare Krishna Movement* 26, no. 5 (September-October 1992): 24–39.

Deegan, Chris. "The Narmada in Myth and History." In *Toward Sustainable Development?: Struggling over India's Narmada River,* ed. William F. Fisher, 47–68. Armonk, N.Y.: M. E. Sharpe, 1995.

Denslow, Julie Sloan, and Christine Paoch, eds. *People of the Tropical Rain Forest.* Berkeley, Calif.: University of California Press, 1988.

Department of Public Relations, 1991. *Fairs and Festivals of Kerala,* Kerala: Govt. of Kerala, Department of Public Relations.

Deutsch, Eliot. "A Metaphysical Grounding for Natural Reverence: East-West." In *Nature in Asian Traditions of Thought: Essays in Environmental Philosophy,* eds. J. Baird Callicott and Roger T. Ames, 259–65. Albany, N.Y.: State University of New York Press, 1989.

Deutsch, Eliot. "Vedanta and Ecology." *Indian Philosophical Annual* 7 (1970): 79–88. Madras: The Center for Advanced Study in Philosophy, 1970.

Dharmadhikary, Shripad. "Hydropower at Sardar Sarovar: Is It Necessary, Justified, and Affordable." In *Toward Sustainable Development?: Struggling over India's Narmada River,* ed. William F. Fisher, 135–53. Armonk, N.Y.: M. E. Sharpe, 1995.

Douglas, Mary, and Baron Isherwood. *The World of Goods: Towards an Anthropology of Consumption.* London: Allen Lane, 1979.

Dove, Michael. "The Dialectical History of 'Jungle' in Pakistan: An Examination of the Relationship between Nature and Culture." *Journal of Anthropological Research* 48, no. 3 (1992): 231–53.

Drèze, Jean, Meera Samson, and Satyajit Singh, eds. *The Dam and the Nation: Displacement and Resettlement in the Narmada Valley*. Delhi: Oxford University Press, 1997.

Dua, Kamal Kumar. *Bhagavad Gita and Environment*. Delhi, India: Koshal Book Depot, 1999.

Dumble, Lynette J. "Vandana Shiva, 1952 —." In *Fifty Key Thinkers on the Environment*, ed Joy A. Palmer, 313-321. New York: Routledge, 2001.

Dumont, L., and D. Pocock. "Pure and Impure." *Contributions to Indian Sociology* no. 3 (1959): 9–34.

Dwivedi, O. P. "Environmental Protection in the Hindu Tradition." In *Ethical Perspectives on Environmental Issues in India,* ed. George A. James, 161–88. New Delhi: A. P. H. Publishing Corporation, 1999.

Dwivedi, O. P. and B. N. Tiwari. *Environmental Crisis and Hindu Religion.* New Delhi: Gitanjali Publishing House, 1987.

Eliade, Mircea, ed., 1987. *The Encyclopedia of Religion,* New York: MacMillan Publishing Company.

Emett, Carolyn. "The Tree Man." *Resurgence: An International Forum for Ecological and Spiritual Thinking,* no. 183 (July-August 1997): 42.

Erdosy, George. "Deforestation in Pre- and Proto-Historic South Asia." In *Nature and the Orient: The Environmental History of South and Southeast Asia,* eds. Richard H. Grove, Vinita Damodaran, and Satpal Sangwan, 51–69. Delhi: Oxford University Press, 1998.

Erndl, Kathleen M. *Victory to the Mother: The Hindu Goddess of Northwest India in Myth, Ritual, and Symbol.* New York: Oxford University Press, 1993.

Eschmann, Anncharlott, Hermann Kulke, and Gaya Charan Tripathi., eds. *The Cult of Jagannath and the Regional*

Tradition of Orissa. South Asian Studies Series, no. 8. New Delhi: Manohar, 1978.

Eschmann, Anncharlott. "Prototypes of the Navekelevara Ritual and their Relation to the Jagannath Cult." In *The Cult of Jagannath and the Regional Tradition of Orissa,* eds. Anncharlott Eschmann, Hermann Kulke, and Gaya Charan Tripathi, 265–83. New Delhi: Manohar, 1978.

Feldhaus, Anne. *Connected Places: Region, Pilgrimage, and Geographical Imagination in India.* New York: Palgrave Macmillan, 2003.

Feuerstein, Georg. "The Practice of Eco-Yoga." In *The Deeper Dimensions of Yoga*, 210-214. Boston: Shambhala Publications, 2003.

Fields, Rick. "The Time is Now: A Spiritual Response to the Ecological Devastation of our Planet." *Yoga Journal* 138 (1998): 67-68.

Findly, Ellison Banks. Review of *Hinduism and Ecology: The Intersection of Earth, Sky, and Water*, eds. Christopher Key Chapple and Mary Evelyn Tucker. *Journal of the American Oriental Society* 122, no. 4 (2002): 925-927.

First International Meeting of People Affected by Large Dams. Declaration of Curitiba, Brazil, 14 March 1997.

Fisher, William F. "Doing Good? The Politics and Anti-Politics of NGO Practices." *Annual Review of Anthropology* 26 (October 1997): 439–64.

Fleet, John Faithful. *Inscriptions of the Early Gupta Kings and Their Successors.* Varanasi: Indological Book House, 1997.

Flinders, Carol Lee. *At the Root of This Longing: Reconciling a Spiritual Hunger and a Feminist Thirst.* San Francisco, Calif.: Harper San Francisco, 1998.

Frater, Alexander. *Chasing the Monsoon.* Calcutta: Penguin Books, 1991.

Freeman, J.R. "Gods, Groves and the Culture of Nature in Kerala." *Modern Asian Studies* 33, no. 2 (1999): 257-302.

Friends of Vrindavan. "Protecting Sacred Forests: Linking Leicester's Community with the Sacred Forests of India." Friends of Vrindavan, 1993.

Fuller, C. J. "Gods, Priests and Purity: On the Relation Between Hinduism and the Caste System." *Man* n.s., 14, no. 3 (September 1979): 459–76.

Furedy, Christine. "Survival Strategies of the Urban Poor-Scavenging and Recuperation in Calcutta." *Geo-Journal* 8, no. 2 (1984): 129–36.

Fürer-Haimendorf, Christoph von. *Tribes of India: The Struggle for Survival.* Berkeley, Calif.: University of California Press, 1982.

Fürer-Haimendorf, Christoph von. *Tribal Populations and Cultures of the Indian Subcontinent.* Leiden-Köln: E. J. Brill, 1985.

Gaard, Greta, ed. *Ecofeminism: Women, Animals, Nature.* Philadelphia, Pa.: Temple University Press, 1993.

Gadgil, Madhav and Ramachandra Guha. *Ecology and Equity: The Use and Abuse of Nature in Contemporary India.* London: Routledge, 1995.

Gadgil, Madhav and Ramachandra Guha. *This Fissured Land: An Ecological History of India.* Delhi: Oxford University Press, 1992.

Gadgil, Madhav and Subash Chandran. "Sacred Groves." *Indian International Center Quarterly* 19, nos. 1–2 (1992): 183–88.

Gadgil, Madhav. "The Indian Heritage of a Conservation Ethic." In *Ethical Perspectives on Environmental Issues in India,* ed. George A. James, 141–60. New Delhi: A. P. H. Publishing Corporation, 1999.

Gallagher, Robert. *The Rickshaws of Bangladesh.* Dhaka: The University Press, Ltd., 1992.

Gandhi, Mohandas. *Collected Works of Mahatma Gandhi.* Vol. 38. Delhi: Publications Division, Ministry of Information and Broadcasting, Government of India, 1946.

Ghosh, Arun. "Ecology and Environment." In *Nature, Man, and the Indian Economy,* ed. Tapas Majumdar, 64–80. New Delhi, India: Oxford University Press, 1993.

Giddens, Anthony. *The Consequences of Modernity.* Princeton, N.J.: Princeton University Press, 1990.

Gilmore, Rachna. Illustrated by Alice Priestly. Lights for Gita. Tilbury House, Pub., 1994.

Gold, Ann Grodzins, and Bhoju Ram Gujar. "Of Gods, Trees, and Boundaries: Divine Conservation in Rajasthan." In *Folk, Faith, and Feudalism: Rajasthan Studies,* ed. Narendra Kumar Singhi and Rajendra Joshi, 33–54. Jaipur: Rawat Publications, 1995.

Gold, Ann Grodzins. "Story, Ritual, and Environment in Rajasthan." In *Sacred Landscapes and Cultural Politics-Planting a Tree*, eds. Philip P. Arnold and Ann Grodzins Gold, 115-137. Aldershot: Ashgate Publishing, Limited, 2001.

Goldsmith, Edward, and Nicholas Hildyard. *The Social and Environmental Effects of Large Dams.* Camelford, U.K.: Wadebridge Ecological Centre, 1984.

Gosling, David L. *Religion and Ecology in India and Southeast Asia*. London: Routledge, 2001.

Government of Gujarat. "Comment on the Report of the Independent Review Mission on Sardar Sarovar Project." Unpublished draft report. Government of Gujarat. Gandinagar, 1992.

Green Yoga Times 1, no. 1 (2004): 1-12. (http://www.greenyoga.org/newsletter1.pdf)

Greenberg, Brian, "Sustainable Futures and Romantic Pasts: Political Ecology and Environmental History in North India." Unpublished paper presented in SAME Workshop, University of Chicago.

Grothues, Horstmar von Jürgen. *Aladins Neue Lampe: recycling in der Dritten Welt.* München: Trickster Verlag, 1988.

Grove, Richard H., Vinita Damodaran, and Satpal Sangwan, eds. *Nature and the Orient: The Environmental History of South and Southeast Asia.* Delhi: Oxford University Press, 1998.

Grove, Richard. *Green Imperialism: Colonial Expansion, Tropical Island Edens, and the Origins of Environmentalism, 1600–1860.* Cambridge: Cambridge University Press, 1995.

Gruzalski, Bart. "Gandhi's Contributions to Environmental Thought and Action." *Environmental Ethics* 24 (2002): 227-242.

Guha, Ramachandra. *Environmentalism: A Global History.* New York: Addison-Wesley, 1999.

Guibbert, Jean-Jacques. "Ecologie populaire urbaine et assainissement environnemental dans le Tiers Monde." *Environnement Africain* 8, nos. 1–2 (1990): 21–50.

Gupta, Lina. "Ganga: Purity, Pollution, and Hinduism." In *Ecofeminism and the Sacred,* ed. Carol J. Adams, 99–116. New York: Continuum, 1994.

Haberman, David. *Journey Through the Twelve Forests: An Encounter with Krishna.* New York: Oxford University Press, 1994.

Harman, William P. *The Sacred Marriage of a Hindu Goddess.* Bloomington, Ind.: Indiana University Press, 1989.

Havell, Ernst Binfield. *Benares: The Sacred City*. Varanasi: Vishwavidyalaya Prakashan, 1990, c1905.

Hawley, John Stratton, and Donna M. Wulff, eds. *The Divine Consort: Radha and the Goddesses of India*. Berkeley, Calif.: Graduate Theological Union; Delhi: Motilal Banarsidass, 1982. Reprinted. Boston: Beacon Press, 1986.

Haynes, Edward. "Land Use and Land-Use Ethic in Rjasthan, 1850–1980." Paper presented at Conference on South Asia, Madison, Wisconsin.

Herring, Ronald J. "Rethinking the Commons." *Agriculture and Human Values* 7, no. 2 (1990): 88–104.

Hiltebeitel, Alf. "Draupadi's Garment." *Indo-Iranian Journal* 22, no. 2 (April 1980): 98–112.

Hopkins, E. Washburn. "Mythological Aspects of Trees and Mountains in the Great Epic." *Journal of the American Oriental Society* 30, no. 4 (1910): 347–74.

Hull, R. B. and G. R. G. Revell. "Cross-cultural Comparison of Landscape Scenic Beauty Evaluations: A Case Study of Bali." *Journal of Environmental Psychology* 9 (1989): 177–91.

Illich, Ivan. *H2O and the Waters of Forgetfulness: Reflections on the Historicity of "Stuff."* Dallas, Tex.: Dallas Institute of Humanities and Culture, 1985.

Inden, Ronald. "World's Toxic Trash Bin: India Accepting Toxic Products from Industrialized Nations." *India Currents Magazine,* 13 July 1995.

Independent Commission on International Humanitarian Issues. *Indigenous Peoples: A Global Quest for Justice: A Report for the Independent Commission on International Humatarian Issues.* Atlantic Highlands, N.J.: Zed, 1987.

Indian National Trust for Art and Cultural Heritage (INTACH). Bhagirathi Ki Pukar 4 (1993).

International Commission on International Humanitarian Issues. *Indigenous Peoples: A Global Quest for Justice.* Atlantic Highlands, N.J.: Zed, 1987.

Jacobsen, Knut A. Review of *Hinduism and Ecology: The Intersection of Earth, Sky, and Water*, eds. Christopher Key Chapple and Mary Evelyn Tucker. *Environmental Ethics* 25 (2003):333-336.

Jaini, Padmanabh S. "Indian Perspectives on the Spirituality of Animals." In *Buddhist Philosophy and Culture: Essays in Honour of N. A. Jayawickrema,* eds. David J. Kalupahana and W. G. Weeraratne. Colombo, Sri Lanka: N. A. Jayawickrema Felicitation Volume Committee, 1987.

James, George A., ed. *Ethical Perspectives on Environmental Issues in India.* New Delhi: A. P. H. Publishing Corporation, 1999.

Jha, Dwijendra Narayan. *The Myth of the Holy Cow*. London: Verso, 2002.

Jodha, N. S. "Rural Common Property Resources: Contributions and Crisis." *Economic and Political Weekly,* 30 June 1990, A65–A78.

Joshi, Vidyut. *Rehabilitation, A Promise to Keep: A Case of the SSP.* Ahmedabad: The Tax Publications, 1991.

Kacker, Anisha. Illustrated by Kushum Ohri. *Ravi's Diwali Surprise.* Modern Curriculum Press, 1994.

Kalpagam, U. "Coping with Urban Poverty in India." *Bulletin of Concerned Asian Scholars* 17, no. 1 (1985): 2–18.

Kalpavriksh. *Narmada: A Campaign Newsletter* (New Delhi), nos. 5–14 (1990–1994).

Kane, Pandurang Vaman, 1974. *History of Dharmastra,* Vol.V Part 1, Poona: Bhandarkar Oriental Research Institute.

Khanna, Madhu. "Nature as Feminine: Ancient Vision of

Geopiety and Goddess Ecology." In *Man in Nature*, ed. Baidyanath Saraswati. Volume 5. New Delhi: Indira Gandhi National Centre for the Arts, 1995.

Khilnani, Sunil. *The Idea of India.* New York: Farrar, Straus Giroux, 1991.

Khoshoo, T. N. "Gandhian Environmentalism." In *Ethical Perspectives on Environmental Issues in India,* ed. George A. James, 241–82. New Delhi: A. P. H. Publishing Corporation, 1999.

Kilambi, Jyotsna. "Muggu: Threshold Art in South India." *Res: The Journal of Aesthetics and Anthropology* 10 (1985): 71–102.

Kinsley, David. "Learning the Story of the Land: Reflections on the Liberating Power of Geography and Pilgrimage in the Hindu Tradition." In *Purifying the Earthly Body of God: Religion and Ecology in Hindu Tradition,* ed. Lance E. Nelson, 225–46. Albany, N.Y.: State University of New York Press, 1998.

Kipling, John Lockwood. *Beast and Man in India: A Popular Sketch of Indian Animals in their Relations with the People.* London: MacMillan, 1904.

Klostermaier, Klaus. "Bhakti, Ahimsa, and Ecology." *Journal of Dharma* 16 (July-September 1991): 246–54.

Korom, Frank J. "On the Ethics and Aesthetics of Recycling in India." In *Purifying the Earthly Body of God: Religion and Ecology in Hindu India,* ed. Lance E. Nelson, 197–224. Albany, N.Y.: State University of New York Press, 1998.

Kothari, Smitu, and Pramod Parajuli. "Nature without Social Justice: A Plea for Cultural and Ecological Pluralism in India." In *Global Ecology: A New Arena of Political Conflict,* ed. Wolfgang Sachs, 224–41. London: Zed, 1993.

Krishnan, M. *The Handbook of India's Wildlife.* Madras: Travelaid, 1982.

Kulke, Hermann. "Tribal Deities at Princely Courts: The Feudatory Rajas of Central Orissa and Their Tutelary Deities [ishtadevatas]." In *The Realm of the Sacred: Verbal Symbolism and Ritual Structures,* ed. Sitakant Mahapatra, 56–78. Bombay: Oxford University Press, 1992.

Kurin, Richard. "Cultural Conservation through Representation: Festival of India Folklife Exhibitions at the Smithsonian Institution." In *Exhibiting Cultures: The Poetics and Politics of Museum Display,* eds. Ivan Karp and Steven D. Lovine, 315–43. Washington, D.C.: Smithsonian Institution Press, 1991.

Lal, Basant K. "Hindu Perspectives on the Use of Animals in Science." In *Animal Sacrifices: Religious Perspectives on the Use of Animals in Science*, ed. Tom Regan, 199-212. Philadelphia: Temple University Press, 1986.

Lalas, Sitaram. *Rajasthani Sabad Kos.* 9 vols. Jodhpur: Rajasthani Sodh Sansthan, 1962–1978.

Lansing, J. Stephen. *Priests and Programmers: Technologies of Power in the Engineered Landscape of Bali.* Princeton, N.J.: Princeton University Press, 1991.

Larson, Gerald. "'Conceptual Resources' in South Asia for 'Environmental Ethics.'" in *Nature in Asian Traditions of Thought: Essays in Environmental Philosophy,* eds. J. Baird Callicott and Roger T. Ames, 267–77. Albany, N.Y.: State University of New York Press, 1989.

Lawyers Committee for Human Rights. "Unaceptable Means: India's Sardar Sarovar Project and Violations of Human Rights." Lawyers Committee for Human Rights. October 1992 through February 1993.

Leopold, Aldo. *A Sand County Almanac.* London: Oxford University Press, 1949.

Leslie, Julie, ed. *Sri and Jyestha: Ambivalent Role Models for Women.* New Delhi: Motilal Banarsidass, 1992.

Ludden, David. "Productive Power in Agriculture: A Survey of Work on the Local History of British India." In *Agrarian Power and Agricultural Productivity in South Asia,* eds. Meghnad Desai, Susanne Hoeber Rudolph, and Ashok Rudra, 51–99. Delhi: Oxford University Press, 1984.

Lynch, Owen. "Pilgrimage with Krishna, Sovereign of Emotions." *Contributions to Indian Sociology* 22, no. 2 (1988): 171–94.

Madan, T. N. "Concerning the Categories *subha* and *suddha* in Hindu Culture: An Exploratory Essay." In *Purity and Auspiciousness in Indian Society,* eds. John Braisted Carman and Frédérique Apffel Marglin, 11–29. Leiden: Brill, 1985.

Madan, T. N. *Non-Renunciation: Themes and Interpretations of Hindu Culture.* Delhi: Oxford University Press, 1987.

Majumdar, Ramesh Chandra., ed. *The History and Culture of the Indian People: The Classical Age.* Delhi: Bharatiya Vidya Bhavan, 1988.

Mathur, Jivanlal. *Braj-Bhavani.* Sawar: Mani Raj Singh, 1977.

Mathur, Sri Rakesh. "Can India's Timeworn *Dharma* Help Renew a Careworn World?" *Hinduism Today* 17 (July 1995): 1, 9.

Maw, Geoffrey Waring, and Marjorie Sykes, eds. *Narmada: The Life of a River.* Hoshangabad, Madhya Pradesh, India: Distributed by Friends Rural Centre, 1991.

Mawdsley, Emma. "The Abuse of Religion and Ecology: The Vishva Hindu Parishad and Tehri Dam." *Worldviews: Environment, Culture, Religion* 9, no. 1 (2005): 1-24.

McKibben, Bill. *Hope, Human, and Wild: True Stories of Living Lightly on the Earth.* St. Paul, Minn.: Hungry Mind Press, 1995.

Mies, Maria, and Vandana Shiva. *Ecofeminism.* London: Zed, 1994.

Motichandra, D. *Kashi Ka Itihas.* 2d ed. Varanasi: Vishwavidyalaya Prakashan, 1985.

Mumme, Patricia Y. "Models and Images for a Vaisnava Environmental Theology: The Potential Contribution of Srivaisnavism." In *Purifying the Earthly Body of God: Religion and Ecology in Hindu India,* ed. Lance E. Nelson, 133–62. Albany, N.Y.: State University of New York Press, 1999.

Murti, C. R. K., K. S. Bilgrami, T. M. Das, and R. P. Mathur, eds. *The Ganga: A Scientific Study.* New Delhi: Ganga Project Directorate, 1991.

Naess, Arne. "*Self*-Realization: An Ecological Approach to Being in the World." In *Thinking Like a Mountain: Toward a Council of All Beings,* ed. John Seed, Joanna Macy, and Arne Naess, 19–30. Philadelphia, Pa.: New Society Publishers, 1988.

Nag, Sunil Kumar, 1983. *Popular Festivals of India,* Golden Books of India: Calcutta: Golden Books of India.

Nagar, Shanti Lal. *Varaha in Indian Art, Culture, and Literature.* New Delhi: Aryan Books International, 1993.

Nagarajan, Viyaya Rettakudi. "The Earth Goddess as Bhu Devi: Toward a Theory of 'Embedded Ecologies' in Folk Hinduism." In *Purifying the Earthly Body of God: Religion and Ecology in Hindu India,* ed. Lance E. Nelson, 269–96. Albany, N.Y.: State University of New York Press, 1998.

Nanavati, R. I., ed. *Purana-Itihasa-Vimarsah.* Delhi: Bharatiya Vidya Prakashan, 1998.

Narayan, Vasudha. "Water, Wood, and Wisdom: Ecological Perspectives from the Hindu Traditions." *Daedalus* 130, no. 4 (2001): 179-206. (*http://www.amacad.org/publications/fall2001/narayanan.aspx#*)

Nath, K. J. "Metropolitan Solid Waste Management in India." In *Managing Solid Wastes in Developing Countries,* ed. John R. Holmes, 47–69. New York: John Wiley and Sons Ltd., 1984.

Nelson, Lance, ed. *Purifying the Earthly Body of God: Religion and Ecology in Hindu India.* Albany, N.Y.: State University of New York Press, 1998.

Nelson, Lance. "The Dualism of Nondualism: Advaita Vedanta and the Irrelevance of Nature." In *Purifying the Earthly Body of God: Religion and Ecology in Hindu India,* ed. Lance E. Nelson, 61–88. Albany, N.Y.: State University of New York Press, 1998.

Omvedt, Gail. *Reinventing Revolution: New Social Movements and the Socialist Tradition in India.* Armonk, N.Y.: M. E. Sharpe, 1993.

Orenstein, Henry. "The Structure of Hindu Caste Values: A Preliminary Study of Hierarchy and Ritual Defilement." *Ethnology* 4, no. 1 (1995): 1–15.

Panwalkar, Pratima. "Processus de Recyclage du Plastique à Bombay." *Environment Africain* 8, nos. 1–2 (1990): 153–57.

Paranjpye, Vijay. *High Dams on the Narmada.* Studies in Ecology and Sustainable Development Series, no. 3. New Delhi: Indian National Trust for Art and Cultural Heritage, 1990.

Parisura, Manimekalai. *Vagai Vagaiyana Kolangal.* Madras: Manimekalai Pirusuram, 1980.

Parkhill, Thomas. *The Forest Setting in Hindu Epics: Princes, Sages, Demons.* Lewiston, N.Y.: Mellen University Press, 1995.

Patel, Anil. "What Do the Narmada Valley Tribals Want?" in *Toward Sustainable Development?: Struggling Over India's Narmada River,* ed. William F. Fisher, 179–200. Armonk, N.Y.: M. E. Sharpe, 1995.

Patel, Chandrakant C. "The Sardar Sarovar Project: A Victim of Time." In *Toward Sustainable Development?: Struggling Over India's Narmada River,* ed. William F. Fisher, 71–88. Armonk, N.Y.: M. E. Sharpe, 1995.

Patkar, Medha (in conversation with Smitu Kothari). "The Struggle for Participation and Justice: A Historical Narrative." In *Toward Sustainable Development?: Struggling Over India's Narmada River,* ed. William F. Fisher, 157–78. Armonk, N.Y.: M. E. Sharpe, 1995.

Peritore, N. Patrick. "Environmental Attitudes of Indian Elites: Challenging Western Postmodernist Models." *Asian Survey* 33 (1993): 804–18.

Peterson, Indira. "Singing of a Place: Pilgrimage as Metaphor and Motif in the *Tevaram* Hymns of the Tamil *Saivite* Saints." *Journal of the American Oriental Society* 102 (1982): 69-90.

Pillai, Moozhikkulam Chandrasekharam. *Mannarassala: The Serpent Temple.* Translated by Ayyappa Panikker. Harippad: Manasa Publications, 1991.

Pintchman, Tracy. "The Ambiguous Female: The Conception of Female Gender in the Brahmanical Tradition and the Roles of Women in India." In *Ethical and Political Dimensions of Modern India*, eds. Ninian Smart and Shivesh Thakur, 144-159. London: St. Martin's Press, 1993.

Powell, Robert, ed. *The Ultimate Medicine: As Prescribed by Sri Nisargadatta Maharaj.* San Diego, Calif.: Blue Dove Press, 1994.

Prajuli, Pramod. *Tortured Bodies and Altered Earth:*

Ecological Ethnicities in the Regime of Globalization. Unpublished manuscript, 1997.

Prime, Ranchor. *Hinduism and Ecology: Seeds of Truth.* London: Cassell, 1992.

Prime, Ranchor. *Vedic Ecology: Practical Wisdom for Surviving the 21st Century.* Novato, CA: Mandala Publishing, 2002.

Puri, Gophal Singh, V. M. Meher-Homji, R. K. Gupta, and S. Puri. *Forest Ecology. Phytogeography and Forest Conservation,* vol. 1. New Delhi: Oxford and IBH Publishing Company, 1983.

Raheja, Gloria Goodwin. *The Poison in the Gift: Ritual, Prestation, and the Dominant Caste in a North Indian Village.* Chicago: University of Chicago Press, 1988.

Raj, A. R. Victor. *The Hindu Connection: Roots of the New Age.* Saint Louis, Mo.: Concordia Publishing House, 1995.

Ram, Rahul N. "Benefits of the Sardar Sarovar Project: Are the Claims Reliable?" in *Toward Sustainable Development?: Struggling over India's Narmada River,* ed. William F. Fisher, 113–34. Armonk, N.Y.: M. E. Sharpe, 1995.

Ramanujan, A. K. "Is There an Indian Way of Thinking? An Informal Essay." *India through Hindu Categories,* ed. Mckim Marriott, 41–58. New Delhi: Sage Publications, 1990.

Rambachan, Anatanand. "The Value of the World as the Mystery of God in Advaita Vedanta." *Journal of Dharma* 14, no. 3 (July-September 1989): 287–97.

Rangarajan, Mahesh. *Fencing the Forest: Conservation and Ecological Change in India's Central Provinces 1860–1914.* Delhi: Oxford University Press, 1991.

Ray, Amit. "Rabindranath Tagore's Vision of Ecological

Harmony." In *Ethical Perspectives on Environmental Issues in India,* ed. George A. James, 217–40. New Delhi: A. P. H. Publishing Corporation, 1999.

Reddy, D. Narasimha, 1983. *A Study of Some Minor Temple Festivals according to p (n~)car_tra and vaikh nasa gamas,* Tirupati: Padmasri Publications.

Redford, Kent. "The Ecologically Noble Savage." *Orion Nature Quarterly* 9, no. 3 (1990): 24–29.

Richards, John F., Edward S. Haynes, and James R. Hagen. "Changes in the Land and Human Productivity in Northern India, 1870–1970." *Agricultural History* 59, no. 4 (1985): 523–48.

Rieger, Hans Christoph. "Whose Himalaya? A Study in Geopiety." In *Studies in Himalayan Ecology and Development Strategies*, ed. Tejvir Singh, 1-9. New Delhi: The English Book Store, 1980.

Robbins, Paul. "Shrines and Butchers: Animals as Deities, Capital, and Meat in Contemporary North India." In *Animal Geographies: Place, Politics, and Identity in the Nature-Culture Borderlands*, eds. Jennifer Wolch and Jody Emel, 218-240. New York: Verso, 1998.

Rolston, Holmes, III. "Can the East Help the West to Value Nature?" *Philosophy East and West* 37, no. 2 (April 1987): 172–90.

Rukmani, T. S. "Environmental Ethics as Enshrined in Sanskrit Sources." *Nidan.* Journal of the Department of Hindu Studies and Indian Philosophy. vol. 7, Durban, Westville, South Africa, 1995.

Sachs, Wolfgang. *Global Ecology: A New Arena of Political Conflict.* London: Zed, 1993.

Sampat, Payal. "What Does India Want?" *World Watch* 11, no. 4 (1998): 30–38.

Sankat Mochan Foundation. *Proposal for GAP Phase II at Varanasi.* Varanasi: Swatcha Ganga Campaign, 1994.

Saraswathi, R., and L. Vijayalakshmi. *Kothaiyar idum kolaangal.* Madras: Lakkumi Nilayam, 1991.

Savyasaachi. "An Alternative System of Knowledge: Fields and Forests in Abujhmarh." In *Who Will Save the Forests? Knowledge, Power and Environmental Destruction,* eds. Tariq Banuri and Frédérique Apffel-Marglin, 53–79. London: Zed, 1993.

Sax, William S. *Mountain Goddess: Gender and Politics in a Himalayan Pilgrimage.* New York: Oxford University Press, 1991.

Schiff, Bennett. "A Fantasy Garden by Nek Chand Flourishes in India." *Smithsonian* 15, no. 3 (1984): 126–36.

Schmidt-Raghavan, Maithili. "Animal Liberation and *Ahimsa.*" In *Ethical and Political Dimensions of Modern India,* eds. Ninian Smart and Shivesh Thakur, 60-81. London: St. Martin's Press, 1993.

Seed, John. "Spirit of the Earth: A Battle-Weary Rainforest Activist Journeys to India to Renew His Soul." *Yoga Journal* 138 (January-February 1998): 69–71, 132–36.

Sen, Geeti, ed. *Indigenous Vision: Peoples of India Attitudes to the Environment.* New Delhi: Sage, 1992.

Seshadri, Balakrishna. *India's Wildlife and Wildlife Reserves.* New Delhi: Sterling, 1986.

Shah, Ashivin A. "A Technical Overview of the Flawed Sardar Sarovar Project and a Proposal for a Sustainable Alternative." In *Toward Sustainable Development?: Struggling over India's Narmada River,* ed. William F. Fisher, 319–67. Armonk, N.Y.: M. E. Sharpe, 1995.

Sharma, Arvind. "Attitudes to Nature in the Early Upanisads." In *Purifying the Earthly Body of God: Religion and Ecology in Hindu India,* ed. Lance E. Nelson, 51–60. Albany, N.Y.: State University of New York Press, 1998.

Sharma, B. D. *Globalization: The Tribal Encounter*. New Delhi: Arand Publications, 1996.

Sharma, B. K. "No Bhagirath Came" (Koi Bhagirath Nahi Aya). *India Today,* 15 July 1987, 80.

Sharma, Brijenddra Nath, 1978. *Festivals of India,* New Dehli: Abinav Publications.

Sharma, R. K., ed. *Jnanabhaissjyamanjari*. Delhi: Nag Publishers, 1998.

Sherma, Rita DasGupta. "Sacred Immanence: Reflections of Ecofeminism in Hindu Tantra." In *Purifying the Earthly Body of God: Religion and Ecology in Hindu India,* ed. Lance E. Nelson, 89–132. Albany, N.Y.: State University of New York Press, 1998.

Sheth, D. L. "Politics and Social Transformation: Grassroots Movements in India." In *The Constitutional Foundations of World Peace,* eds. Richard A. Falk, Robert C. Johasen, and Samuel S. Kim, 275–87. Albany, N.Y.: State University of New York Press, 1993.

Shiva, Vandana and J. Bandyopadhyay. "The Chipko Movement." In *Deforestation: Social Dynamics in Watersheds and Mountain Ecosystems,* eds. J. Ives and D. Pitt, 224–41. London: Routledge, 1988.

Shiva, Vandana. *Water Wars: Privatization, Pollution, and Profit*. Cambridge: South End Press, 2002.

Sicular, Daniel T. *Scavengers, Recyclers, and Solutions for Solid Waste Management in Indonesia*. Berkeley, Calif.: Center for Southeast Asian Studies, University of California, 1992.

Singh, Mian Goverdhan, 1992. *Festival, fairs and customs of Himachal Pradesh,* New Delhi: Indus Publishing Co.

Singh, Rana P. B., ed. *Banaras (Varanasi): Cosmic Order, Sacred City, Hindu Traditions*. Varanasi: Tara Book Agency, 1993.

Singh, Shekar. "Sovereignty, Equality, and the Global Environment." In *Ethical Perspectives on Environmental Issues in India,* ed. George A. James, 131–40. New Delhi: A. P. H. Publishing Corporation, 1999.

Sivaramakrishnan. "Colonialism and Forestry in India: Imagining the Past in Present Politics." *Comparative Study of Society and History* 37, no. 1 (1995): 3–40.

Sivaramamurti, C. *Ganga.* Delhi: Orient Longman, 1976.

Skolimowsky, Henryk. *EcoYoga: Practice & Meditations for Walking in beauty on the Earth.* London, England: Gaia Books Limited, 2003.

Sochaczewski, Paul Spencer. "The Saga of Krishna's Gardens: Can Love and Faith Heal Environmental Sacrilege?" *International Herald Tribune,* 18 October 1994.

Sohoni, S. Shrinivas, trans. *Prthvisukta.* Sterling Publishers Pvt. Ltd., 1991.

Spanel, Ann. "Interview with Vandana Shiva." *Women of Power* 9 (1988): 27–31.

Sullivan, Bruce. "Theology and Ecology at the Birthplace of Krsna." In *Purifying the Earthly Body of God: Religion and Ecology in Hindu India,* ed. Lance E. Nelson, 247–68. Albany, N.Y.: State University of New York Press, 1998.

Swami, Praveen. "Narmada Home-Truths: A Movement Makes Some Headway." Electronic release to Narmada Action Committee, 16 February 1995.

The Hindu Survey of the Environment. Madras: Kasturi & Sons Ltd., 1991.

Thukral, Gurmeet, 1987. *Festive India,* New Delhi: Frank Bros. & Co.

Index